1983

KIERKEGAARD'S
EXISTENTIAL
ETHICS

KIERKEGAARD'S EXISTENTIAL ETHICS

GEORGE J. STACK

Studies in the Humanities No. 16
Philosophy

THE UNIVERSITY OF ALABAMA PRESS
University, Alabama

Library of Congress Cataloging in Publication Data

Stack, George J
  Kierkegaard's Existential Ethics.

  Includes bibiographical references.
  1. Kierkegaard, Søren Aabye, 1813-1855—Ethics.
2. Existentialism.   3. Nihilism (Philosophy)
4. Self (Philosophy) I. Title.
B4378.E8S8 1976   171   75-16344
ISBN 0-8173-6624-5 (Cloth)
ISBN 0-8173-6626-1 (Paper)

This book is affectionately dedicated to

my wife, Claire,

and to

my children, Christopher and Diane

Contents

Preface

The attempt to discover the fundamental meaning of the central themes of Kierkegaard's thought is fraught with difficulties, for he assumes almost as many forms as Proteus. What is required in attempting to provide an interpretation of Kierkegaard's writings in general, or his description of the ethical sphere of existence in particular, is a kind of sympathetic-imaginative understanding of his underlying intentions, a reconstruction of the thread of continuity that runs through the pseudonymous works.

Too often, it seems to me, many who have attempted to understand Kierkegaard have been intimidated by his proclamations of an antisystematic approach to the questions he dealt with or have been inhibited by the warning that his "aesthetic" works were written under pseudonyms that obscure what Kierkegaard himself said. While I cannot claim to have discerned Kierkegaard's *vrai visage,* I believe that I have discovered a continuity in his various representations of, or descriptions of, the ethical sphere of existence. Kierkegaard conceived of his task, in general, to be that of describing the various general modes of being (life or world orientations) that are open to man and, by indirection, suggesting what an authentic human existence would be like or, as he expresses it in *The Concept of Irony,* he intended to translate "the results of philosophy into the personal life" so as to engender the appropriation of these results. Obviously, if one merely has an abstract understanding of Kierkegaard—if nothing he writes impinges upon one's personal existence—then one has not understood him as he wanted to be understood.

In this hermeneutic enterprise I have attempted to relate the possibility of ethical existence to the conception of the "nihilistic standpoint" presented in Kierkegaard's phenomenology of Socrates' existence in *The Concept of Irony, with Constant References to Socrates*. I have done so, because I believe that his dithyrambic, dramatic portrayal of human existence owes as much to his own 'encounter' with nihilism as it does to the spirit of romanticism. As a thinker, Kierkegaard was polemical and skeptical, the kind of individual who was suspicious of every metaphysical system or theory that seemed to proffer objective certainty. It is Kierkegaard's proclivity towards skepticism, not to say nihilism, that intensifies his concern with the affirmation of subjectivity in ethical and religious existence. Like Socrates, as he understood him, Kierkegaard was turned "inward" by his doubts, by the vortex of dialectical reflection that seemed always to lead to yet another hypothetical possibility, another postulate that would fall before the negation of critical analysis. If there is objective certainty nowhere (except in the empty tautology), then perhaps, Kierkegaard seems to say, we must look for the only possible certainty in subjectivity. To lose sight of what I have called the nihilistic possibility that is always on the periphery of Kierkegaard's thought is to misunderstand the dialectical tension in his thought and his existence—it is to fail to see that his thought and his life were pervaded by a passionate search for meaningfulness.

It is the *existential category* of possibility that is central to what I have called the ethical "turn" or movement, a category that is intimately related to Kierkegaard's understanding of the self and its becoming. In the analysis of possibility I have tried to show, in some detail, how Kierkegaard's concept of possibility was apparently derived from Aristotle's notion of potentiality. While the relationship between Aristotle's thought and that of Kierkegaard has been mentioned in other studies of Kierkegaard, I believe that I have shown that the influence of Aristotle on Kierkegaard's formulation of a philosophical anthropology is much more pervasive than has previously been indicated. In this regard, I have argued that Kierkegaard's concept of choice is not a defense of irrational choice and that it is consistent, in signficant respects, with a rationalistic account of the process of choice. Since Kierkegaard's concept of choice has tended to be either praised or condemned without sufficient analysis of the concept, I have focused a good deal of my attention upon what he called the "dialectic of choice." Specifically, I have endeavored to determine the nature and meaning of "absolute" choice.

Since so much emphasis has already been placed upon Kierkegaard's description of the religious sphere of existence, I have attempted to deal with his existential ethics, or his ethics of subjectivity, without placing it in a theological context. In this regard, I believe that I am faithful to Kierkegaard's intention to present the ethical possibility as a possibility for any self-reflective individual. Since Socrates is a paradigm of the ethical individual, it is clear that, as Kierkegaard expresses it, "it is possible to exist with inwardness outside Christianity." Socrates is described in *The Concept of Irony* as one who "stands poised ready to leap into something, yet at every moment instead of leaping into this 'other,' he leaps aside and back into himself." It is not the case, then, that the "leap of faith" is absolutely necessary for an authentic ethical existence. This is made clear when one realizes how much Heidegger's existential analytic of "authentic existence" (*eigentlich Existenz*) owes to Kierkegaard's description of ethical existence. Heidegger managed to translate effectively the details of Kierkegaard's prescription for an ethical existence into the language of the ostensibly nonethical, nonprescriptive fundamental ontology of *Sein und Zeit*. While the relationship between Kierkegaard's existential ethics and Heidegger's phenomenology of *eigentlich Existenz* is not an explicit theme of my analysis, it is implicitly alluded to in my interpretation of Kierkegaard's description of an ethical mode of existence.

While Kierkegaard was obviously concerned, as he put it, with intensifying the subjective, he did not prescribe an epicurean withdrawal from the world or society. A life characterized by the various forms of inwardness (*Inderligheden*) is one that is necessarily lived in what he calls, in his journals, "the medium of our existence," that is, the world. He was not inclined to a philosophical idealism, but repeatedly emphasized the reality of empirical actuality. For Kierkegaard, one endeavors to live an individuated authentic existence while performing one's role or function in society. In *Either/Or* it is said explicitly that one must develop a "social, a civic self" and that one ought to "work in order to live." As Kierkegaard expresses it in *Concluding Unscientific Postscript,* "all honor to the pursuits of science, but the ethical [*ethisk*] is and remains the highest task for every human being. One may ask even of the devotee of science [although Kierkegaard refers here to *Videnskab,* there is an ironical significance in the English translation of this word] that he should acquire an ethical understanding of himself before he devotes himself to [his work], and that he should continue to understand himself ethically while immersed in his labors." Ethical self-existence, as a goal for one's life, should add a dimension of depth to human existence and entail that activity be conceived of as an intensification of self-being, a persistent, self-critical endeavor to attain authentic selfhood. For Kierkegard, "existence" is not a predicate; rather, it is an individuated way of being, an activity which is the ethical *telos* that gives meaning and purpose to human life.

Kierkegaard's radical emphasis upon the subjective perspective of human life was considered by himself as a corrective to the all-encompassing rationalism of Hegel, which tended to convert the individual into an insignificant fragment of a developing totality. Today, Kierkegaard may once more serve as a needed corrective to collectivistic ideologies that conceive of the individual as a relatively unimportant fragment of ostensibly significant groups. In addition, his emphasis upon the subjective core of lived experience is a corrective to behavioristic theories of the "self," which tend to ignore the personal, private dimension of human life. The predominance of mechanomorphic, technomorphic, and collectivistic conceptions of the human self are understandable in terms of the historical conditions that have generated them, but they are distortions of human experience and personal existence insofar as they apotheosize only one dimension of the human self. Kierkegaard is right, I believe, in insisting upon the preservation of each individual's "primitive impression of existence" in the face of wholesale attacks upon the subjective perspective. Of course, man—as a physical being subject to the laws of nature—can be understood in one dimension of his being from the physicalist perspective. Obviously, man can also be understood as an energy-system constituting a unit in a system of technological relations of which he is benefactor or victim. Of course, the individual emerges as an individual within a social framework of which he is a part, is born into this or that social group, is conditioned by his "station" and his "duties" as well as by "social forces" that impinge upon his life. Kierkegaard himself admits that each individual is conditioned by sociocultural causal factors over which he may have little or no control. But he adds a footnote to such conceptions of man, a footnote that refers to the importance of the individual's conception of himself, to his purposes or intentions, to his aspirations and projects, and to the search for a personal meaning for one's life.

Kierkegaard was concerned with calling attention to what may be called the spiritual world that underlies all human activities. The spiritual dimension of human existence is a legitimate and real aspect of human life—the dramatic tension of self-being that has so significant a place in our understanding of man. That this dimension of human life cannot be quantified or objectified does not mean that it does not exist. The spiritual aspect of human life is not ghostly; it is not an ethereal realm sheltered from actuality—indeed, it can only be expressed or realized in actuality. It is the motivating basis of the actuality of the self, the underlying subjective teleology that informs human existence, the conative aspect of the self that is the basis of aspiration, the search for meaning, and the will to exist. The subjective perspective emphasized by Kierkegaard is not, to be sure, the only legitimate perspective from which man can be understood; but it is an important key to the understanding of the human world, and it ought not to be casually dismissed.

In this analysis of Kierkegaard's existential ethics it will be shown, I believe, that his description of ethical existence is, in many respects, an original conception of practical ethics, notwithstanding its having been influenced by aspects of Socratic ethics (as Kierkegaard understood it) and by features of Aristotle's ethics and metaphysics.

Another, more general aim of this interpretation of Kierkegaard's conception of the ethical mode of being has been to focus upon philosophical bases of his thought, something that has often been neglected in interpretations of Kierkegaard. What Kierkegaard attempted to do, I believe, was to create a philosophical anthropology that would be the basis of a prescription of the best way by which man could realize his potentialities for becoming an authentic self. While a concept of man lies at the basis of all ethical theories, this is even more obviously the case in an existential ethics.

Because I believe that the problem of nihilism is central to an understanding of Kierkegaard's thought, I have tried to deal in the first chapter with the various facets of what he called the "ironic" or "nihilistic standpoint." In the second chapter I concern myself with the nature and meaning of existential possibility, relating it to its philosophical roots in the thought of Aristotle. In the penultimate chapter I attempt to provide an analysis of Kierkegaard's phenomenology of choice. And in the last chapter I try to indicate the relationship between his conception of the self and his description of ethical existence, and, finally, to suggest (in terms of my prior discussions) the inapplicability of the model of Kantian ethics for an understanding of Kierkegaard's existential, or subjective, ethics. While it is true that Kierkegaard thought that the religious sphere of existence was the highest possibility for man, he also maintained in his journals that "no authentic human life is possible without [one's] having lived through the ethical." And it is with interpreting and explicating the meaning of "the ethical" (*ethisk*) in relation to irony, human possibility, absolute choice, consciousness, and subjectivity that I will primarily be concerned.

Den enest Virkelighed der er for

en Existerende er hans egen ethiske.

The highest actuality there is for an existing individual
is his own ethical existence

S.K., *Concluding Unscientific Postscript*

KIERKEGAARD'S
EXISTENTIAL
ETHICS

1

Irony and Existence:
The Nihilistic Possibility

"... there can be no schoolmaster ... in the
art of existing. .... In relation to existing there
is for all existing persons one schoolmaster
—existence itself."—S. K., *Journals*

In one of the many *obiter dicta* in his journals Kierkegaard once
remarked that he began with 'the Socratic'. This comment may
seem to be quite clear, not needing further elaboration. It is,
however, like so many of his asides, somewhat ambiguous. Did
he mean that he began with a Socratic approach to human existence, with the subjectivity that he later stresses so much? Did
he mean that he began with Socratic inquiry? Or did he mean,
perhaps, that he began with a skepticism reminiscent of that of
Socrates? One could find evidence in Kierkegaard's writings to
support a positive answer to each of these questions—unless that
is, we did not have *The Concept of Irony*. For, what he means
by 'the Socratic' is unveiled in this remarkable phenomenological
analysis of the being of a man who represented for Kierkegaard
the paradigmatic individual. It is Socrates who represents the
individual who shows the intimate relationship between thought
and life—the dialectical, existential thinker par excellence. Basically, what Kierkegaard called 'the Socratic' referred to a
polemical attitude towards conventional 'knowledge' or opinion,
the undermining of confidence in "objective" certainties and the
correlative search for self-knowledge as well as a subjective
basis for ethical self-being. From the point of view of objective
knowledge, or the pretension of reason to comprehend the totality
of reality, the Socratic standpoint is described by Kierkegaard as
nihilistic. In this regard, he was in agreement with Nietzsche's
judgment of Socrates, even though his understanding of the

meaning of Socrates' existence was far more profound than that of Nietzsche. *The Concept of Irony* is a phenomenological (in the Hegelian sense of the term) analysis and interpretation of the being of Socrates. That a work with such deep personal meaning for Kierkegaard should be presented in the form of something so pedestrian as a master's thesis is merely testimony to Kierkegaard's remarkable sense of irony.

The being of Socrates fascinated Kierkegaard from his early work on *The Concept of Irony* to some of the last entries in his journals, Kierkegaard's understanding of the Socratic 'standpoint' must be seen in the light of his own personal attempt to come to grips with his polemical tendencies, with a skepticism that brought him to the brink of a nihilism—a theoretical nihilism —that he never could accept. Although, with his usual irony, he retained the Hegelian language in his *The Concept of Irony,* Kierkegaard already repudiated what he called the "new wisdom," denying that "the Idea's own movements" should ever come to expression in himself.[1] He was, in fact, more offended by Danish Hegelians than by Hegel himself.[2] However, he had turned away from the hypnotic attraction of a speculative dialectic that resolves all oppositions in an ultimate, rational reconciliation, a dialectic that could appropriate Socratic subjectivism as well as the paradox of Christianity.

It was Socrates' irony that could be forged into an instrument to be used in an attack upon the pretensions of a speculative philosophy that could "abrogate" everything and convert every personal or intellectual phenomenon into a *moment* in a progressive, immanent teleology. The significance of Socrates' subjective "turn" was annulled by Hegel and was relegated to a mere "negative moment." Of course, some of the elements of Kierkegaard's existentialism are either implicitly or explicitly present in Hegel's *Phänomenologie des Geistes* (this is especially the case in regard to Kierkegaard's concept of 'spirit' in relation to concrete ethical actuality). But this does not mean that Kierkegaard did not use some of Hegel's philosophical terminology and some of his basic concepts in an original and creative way. In addition, it is false to suggest, as Walter Kaufmann does in his recent book on Hegel, that Kierkegaard was merely parasitic on

Hegelian 'wisdom'.[3] For Kierkegaard suggests that if Hegel had fully understood the meaning of Socratic subjectivity, or the dialectic of life, it would have been a stumbling block in the development of his universal, rationalistic system, a tempting foolishness that would have to be mysteriously annulled and preserved (*aufgeheben*). To make the existing individual the starting point of reflection, to concern oneself exclusively with the contingent dialectic of individual life, to hold that the existing authentic individual is the only reality we can truly *know*, would have been a scandal to Hegel. If the individual's purely contingent being were to have meaning, the cunning of reason (*der List der Vernunft*) would see to it that the individual would have unconsciously served a higher goal, a higher purpose, a supraindividual rational *telos*! Hegel was able to abrogate the Socratic ironic standpoint precisely because he did not fully appreciate what it meant. Certainly, Kierkegaard refused to allow the ironic or nihilistic standpoint to be "absorbed" into a holistic system that sees in irony only what is negativistic and discounts its significance for the personal and intellectual development of the individual thinker. Since Kierkegaard himself (as his journals indicate) lived through the nihilistic standpoint that he attributes to Socrates, and since he believed that it marked a turning point in his own philosophical and personal development, he is unwilling to have it treated casually as a mere negative phase or moment (*Momente*) in the process of the dialectic of spirit.

Obviously, Kierkegaard believed that the ironic standpoint of Socrates (in its purely negative form) must be transcended. But it must also be analyzed, described, and understood in order to see why it must be overcome and how it can be overcome. One does not overcome what I shall call the 'nihilism of reflection' by the accumulation of new knowledge, by the formulation of yet another possible interpretation of the nature of "reality" or "the world," by a new theory of the place of man in the *kosmos*. Any "new" metaphysics that claims to have discovered the ultimate, objective nature of reality will turn out to be yet another theoretical *possibility*, a possibility that negates the truth-claim of other metaphysical possibilities and that, perhaps, contains within itself the seeds of its own negation. The ironic standpoint can only be overcome by resolute choice, by decisiveness. This is an urgent matter for Kierkegaard since the overcoming of the "infinite negativity" of the ironic standpoint meant for him the "overcoming of nihilism" (*überwindung des Nihilismus*). It was Kierkegaard (and not Nietzsche) who first discerned the problem of nihilism as the underlying 'presence' in the world of his own time.[4] The nihilism he discusses in *The Concept of Irony* is the projected analysis of what was for him not only a theoretical standpoint but also an existential condition that he himself had lived through—a profound sense of the meaninglessness of existence that is the background against which we must view the intensity of his concern with the ethical and religious spheres of existence. A polemical use of irony was the outward expression of a nihilistic standpoint. In *The Concept of Irony* the ironic standpoint (because of the purely nihilating effects for which irony is used) is simply identified as a nihilistic standpoint.

Existential Irony

While it appears that Kierkegaard is primarily concerned with the "concept" of irony in his seminal work, it soon becomes clear that he is not concerned with this concept alone. In an implicit reversal of Hegel's procedure (i.e., to argue from the abstract, universal Idea to its manifestation in particularity), the "concept" of irony is analyzed by presenting a phenomenology of irony as it is revealed in the *existence* of Socrates. In order to understand the meaning of irony one does not begin with an a priori conception of irony; rather, one seeks to discern the nature of irony in its concrete expression in the being of an individual. In his hermeneutic analysis of Socrates' being he tries to show that Socrates displays the meaning of irony in his ironic standpoint —in his use of irony in his personal and philosophical relationships with others. For Kierkegaard, Socratic irony is a symbol or sign of the cultural emergence of the recognition of personal existence, of subjectivity. This is, indeed, a Hegelian view, insofar as Hegel maintained that irony is a manifestation of the most extreme form of subjectivity. Hegel thought that Socratic irony indicated that Socrates had formed some "Idea of the good," but that he had (mistakenly, Hegel thought) related it to the individual in an arbitrary manner. Irony, in Socrates' hands, is only a negative moment insofar as the subject is taken to be the determining "principle" of what is good. Since Hegel believed that the individual becomes a moral being by submitting his personal subjectivity to an objective "ethical order," it is not surprising that he tended to denigrate a positive individual morality, proclaiming it impossible of attainment.[5] Of course, Socrates (and any serious moralist) usually does not accept all aspects of the conventional morality of his time and place. In point of fact, moralists usually introduce a morality far more demanding than a legalistic morality determined in terms of conformity to civil law.

What was for Hegel only a "negative moment" in the development of the "Idea" of the good, or of moral consciousness, was for Kierkegaard the signification of the subjective concern characteristic of individuality. By undermining confidence in what Hegel described as the "universal ethos" Socrates seemed to be dangerous and subversive. By means of a combination of *elenchus* and irony Socrates showed that many individuals were not only ignorant about what they claimed to know (e.g., what piety is) but, worse than that, they were willing to act in accord with this ignorance. Irony was used by Socrates to negate claims to knowledge not only because error offended him but because he knew that what one thinks he knows will determine his actions. In the process of negation Socrates often seemed to leave no objective foundation for human knowledge standing.

Unlike a recent writer on "the philosophy of Socrates" who barely mentions irony (and, in this single reference, relates it to Socrates' "slyness"!),[6] Kierkegaard maintained that the fundamental characteristic of Socrates' existence is irony. He attributes many of the negative results of the Platonic dialogues to the annihilating effect of Socratic irony. Socrates undermines claims to knowledge and leads his opponents to hold positions that contradict their original assertions or that lead to conclusions that were implicit in their original stance, but which they sedulously wish to avoid. Irony, as Socrates uses it, is not merely a supplement to his method of *elenchus*. Rather, it is a corrosive cutting away of pretension, confortable certainty, and what might be called sophistic extremism (e.g., in the cases of Thrasymachus and Callicles). There is a marked tendency in Socrates' analyses to negate every objective theoretical possibility, to undermine conventional 'social' knowledge as well as the more sophisticated views of the Sophists. Is Socrates simply an archskeptic, a denier who can accept no holding-for-true? Is he the adept at critical reasoning who turns reason against itself? And, perhaps more importantly, why the irony?

The notion that Socratic irony is merely the nescience and self-disparagement that plays upon the surface of the Platonic dialogues is simplistic. For, irony is not merely a rhetorical device for Socrates, but it is a means by which others may be awakened to a moral self-consciousness, to a recognition of their own state of being, their own possibilities, their own capacity for an ethical existence. Socrates seems not only to be concerned that others think for themselves or with the correction of cognitive error; rather, he seems also to be concerned that others become self-reflcetive by leading an "examined life" in pursuit of self-knowledge. We may be sardonic toward those whom we despise and sarcastic towards those whom we wish to offend. But we are ironic toward those whom we wish to chatise or reform. We are ironic toward others when we wish them to change their thinking or their mode of life. And, finally, we are ironic toward ourselves when we realize that we are false to others or ourselves—when we know that we are not what we ought to be. For Socrates, irony is a fire that is used to burn away what is false in the thought or life of those he encounters. But it is not used to injure others or to do them an injustice; it reflects a concern for what the other is, albeit, by virtue of indirection. Kierkegaard is surely right in suspecting that there is a deeper meaning to Socratic irony than that preserved in the official view.

Irony has the capacity to induce self-consciousness in the individual to whom it is directed. It brings an apparently abstract discussion to a personal level and it suggests the faint possibility that there is a 'truth' that is other than what is conventionally accepted or other than a fashionable sophistic conceit. Surely, one can see that one of Socrates' central concerns in his use of irony was to awaken the individual from the sleep of complacency, to generate an interrogative mode of reflection. This is not surprising, since interrogation and wonder are the beginning of philosophical self-consciousness. In raising fundamental questions about language, Being, the world, or ourselves, the process of questioning is, as Heidegger puts it in *Sein und Zeit,* a mode of being of the questioner, a reflection of a need for interrogative inquiry.[7] At any rate, Socratic questioning is deemed necessary since the conventional, social 'knowledge' (despite some of its real practical value) that is possessed by individuals existing in a historical-cultural milieu has become solidified, crystallized into a system of interrelated notions that are ordinarily not subject to question or criticism. The conventional notions that are accepted as true in our sociocultural matrix do not comprise our own knowledge since they have not been self-consciously appropriated by ourselves. Socratic irony sought to free men from the dominance of such general, conventional notions in order that they would begin a personal search for truth. He desired to instill in others a subjective concern for philosophical questions, especially the ones that are related to the actual existence of the individual. In this regard, Kierkegaard later characterizes him as *the* existential thinker.

The destructive phase of irony is radical since its negation of every absolute seems to leave the individual with nothing. The phenomenal, conventional, socially determined world of actuality (which is usually the socially accepted world of overt behavior and ordinary language use) seems to be negated *in toto.* The philosophical opinions of the fashionable, dominant school of 'philosophy' (e.g., the Sophists), as well as the views of public common sense, are swept away and apparently nothing is left. The negation of objective certainties, Socrates seemed to believe, would lead individuals to self-conscious reflection, to an awareness of what they do not know, and to a knowledge of what they are not. In this regard, Kierkegard believed that Socrates concerned himself with the problem of what it means to be a man. To put it in other terms, the underlying Socratic question (which Kant will later call *the* philoosphical question) was: What is Man?[8]

Irony, then, was ultimately in the service of the question that

Kant had said encompassed the questions: What can I know? What ought I to do? What may I hope? For Kierkegaard, the answer to the question "What is Man?" is related to the only two meaningful modes of existence, namely, being an ethical individual or becoming a Christian. The Socratic questioning of oneself lies at the heart of Kierkegaard's concept of a mastered irony that contributes to the development of an ethical existence. Though an official encyclopedia of philosophy assures us that Socratic irony "contributed nothing to later [philosophical] developments,"[9] it is clear that Kierkegaard outdid Socrates in his mastery of irony. A philosophical use of irony is the most pervasive characteristic of all of Kierkegaard's writings . . . except, of course, his edifying discourses. This is true even of his *Concluding Unscientific Postscript*, an intricate analysis of the movements of faith that is a dialectical defense of the possibility of faith (*Troen*). Kierkegaard without his irony may be mistaken for a dogmatist, which is precisely what he was not.

In the *Concept of Irony* Kierkegaard emphasizes the fundamental negativity (*Negativitet*) of irony and refers repeatedly to its "infinite nothingness." Irony is the antithesis of conventional actuality; it is, by implication, a condemnation of actuality and is oriented in the direction of the ideal infinity of the possible. To be ironic in relation toward what is conventionally praised as virtue, for example, is to suggest that there is a higher mode of virtue that has not yet been recognized. To be ironic in relation to a metaphysical theory (as Kierkegaard was towards Hegel's metaphysics) is to suggest that something essential has been left out of the theory and that the claim to absolute truth in such a *Weltanschauung* is illicit.

In general, ironic expressions reveal contrasts, contradictions, paradoxes, or oppositions. The basic contrast is between what is and what could be, between conventional actuality and possibility, between a more or less universally accepted metaphysics (e.g., a metaphysics of language) and alternative "idealities." From the finite perspective of man—a man who adopts the ironic standpoint—there is only a multiplicity of possibilities. Thus, for Socrates, it is possible that it is better to be dead than alive; it is possible that after death we may continue to exist as we did on earth or it is possible that, as Schopenhauer put it, "before us there is certainly only nothingness." It is possible (i.e., it is a "likely story," or *mythus*) that the soul preexisted its present embodiment. It is possible, as the ancients held, that the injust will be punished for their misdeeds. As he is represented in the dialogues, the dominant modality of Socrates' thought is that of possibility. There is, Kierkegaard suggests, an intimate relationship among irony, possibility, and authentic existence.

Ordinarily, irony is conceived of as a method of dissimulating, of hiding one's true motives or feelings; in effect, it is a critical standpoint that conveys the possibility of the recognition of a truth that is, perhaps, inexpressible or is of such a nature that it cannot be apodictically demonstrated, but that is "seen" in evidential intuition or is directly encountered in lived experience. In addition, of course, irony also involves the recognition of the multiplicity of possibilities that confront one in finite experience and that is accompanied by the multiplicity of theoretical explanations of various phenomena that are themselves possibilities. The radical contrast between the ideal (e.g., conceived of as a hypothetical possibility) and the actual creates the conceptual and psychological *tension* of irony. The philosophical ironist, by juxtaposing the contradictory, makes the paradoxical manifest. In *Concluding Unscientific Postscript* Kierkegaard remarks that the ironist places himself as a "vanishing particularity" in relation to the "absolute requirement" of the ethical or the religious mode of being.[10] In this process is revealed the fundamental difficulty in human existence: the synthesizing of differences. The skeptical nature of irony (which, in a dialectical manner, always seems to suggest an alternative possibility in the face of any given possibility, practical or theoretical), the conceptual recognition of the irreconcilability of opposites, the host of paradoxes that irony reveals, the dizzying sense of 'infinite' possibility, turns the individual back upon himself and recalls him to the most significant possibilities, those that are uniquely his own. In the light of Kierkegaard's repeated emphasis on the role that irony plays in forcing the individual to reflect upon his own being, his own "potentiality-for," it is clear why Kierkegaard insists that no authentic human existence is possible without irony.[11]

The ironic standpoint has a tragic dimension insofar as its very skepticism concerning any absolute seems to preclude subjective commitment to anything. Theoretical nihilism is immobilizing. If nothing can be known, if no metaphysics seems to answer what Schopenhauer and Kant called the "metaphysical need" in man, if there is certainty nowhere, how can I possibly know what I ought to do or what I ought to become? If the quest for certainty (as Dewey called it) cannot be satisfied, does this not affect our capacity for resoluteness? A purely theoretical use of irony as a negating device ineluctably leads to a nihilistic impasse. In the Protean world of the ironist one can accept nothing as true and nothing, therefore, has a secure foundation.

The ironist is concerned with the mere play of possibilities, with the entertainment of a multiplicity of hypothetical explanations of a variety of phenomena. In regard to this characterization, it is interesting to note the importance that hypothesis played in Socrates' approach to philosophical questions. For a hypothesis is always a *possible,* tentative explanation, a conjecture that is acceptable (at least *pro tempore*) insofar as it "saves the phenomena." Whenever Socrates seems to be answering a specific question or providing an explanation for some phenomenon he couches his answer or explanation in a hypothetical form. Socrates rarely expresses himself in the assertoric mode. When dealing with the most pressing philosophical issues, Socrates invariably chooses to speak in the modality of possibility. To speak of a Socratic "thesis" (i.e., that knowledge is virtue) is misleading,[12] since the nature of the 'knowledge' he is referring to is by no means clear. To be sure, Kierkegaard also believed that a positive ethics underlies his irony, even though he disagrees with others about the precise meaning of the Socratic ethics.

In his phenomenology of the being of Socrates in *The Concept of Irony,* Kierkegaard was concerned with the negative or ironic phase of his ethical transformation. Socrates is pictured—as Kierkegaard will later describe him in his *The Point of View for My Work as an Author*—as the arch-dialectician who was concerned with an ironic consideration of theoretical possibilities.[13] Kierkegaard tries to uncover the "hidden" Socrates, to discern the existing individual beneath the enigmatic mask. That this phenomenology of Socrates' being was an imaginative, hermeneutic analysis colored by Kierkegaard's own ironic nihilism goes without saying. It was the latter's view that Socrates had used irony both to bring others to self-reflective moral consciousness and to cut away all support for any conceptual, objective certainty. Like the Buddha, Socrates is silent or bluntly skeptical in regard to all questions concerning man's positive knowledge of transcendent reality.

The overall tendency of what Kierkegaard calls the ironic standpoint is to reduce all things to possibility, to negate apodictic certainty, to "level everything," to become engrossed in the mere play of logical analyses or destructive criticism. For the ironist there is no objective truth, but only a mutiplicity of possible "truths." From a psychological point of view, the ironist cannot commit himself to anything, cannot be decisive about anything. In *The Concept of Irony* Kierkegaard was trying to extract the polemical kernel from the various portraits of Socrates (he provides expositions of the works of Plato, Aristophanes, and Xenophon in order to elucidate the thought of Socrates) in anticipation of his own polemical approach to speculative philosophy in general and to that of Hegel in particular. In addition, of course, he endeavored to objectify his own nihilism in order to dissect it and, hopefully, to transcend it. His own conceptual-imaginative reflection upon possibilities without any conviction or commitment was clearly projected into his phenomenological portrait of Socrates. Kierkegaard had seen in Socrates the same refusal of certainty and objective truth that characterized his own thinking at the time. In attempting to understand Socratic irony he was trying desperately to understand himself.

For Kierkegaard, the ironic standpoint is a *via negativa,* "not the truth, but the way."[14] What I have called the nihilism of reflection is characterized by the critical analysis of every claim to truth, every philosophical generalization. Insofar as every holding-for-true can be doubted, can be put in question, the dialectic of reflection invariably leads to an "infinite" process. For, what is to bring such critical reflection to an end? Reflection unguided by any subjectively posited *telos,* reflection independent of the influence of a personal or intellectual commitment, will tend to lead to an ironic or nihilistic standpoint. However, so long as irony prevails there is always the haunting suggestion, the possibility, that some "ideality" (some general metaphysical assertion, some universal principle) may be true, even though it may be inaccessible to objective reflection.

The kind of knowledge that Socrates wished to convey was not a dogmatic, metaphysical truth, but what Kierkegaard calls an existential communication. That is, irony is an instrument of a dialogical dialectic that intends to make others aware of the importance of a moral transformation of the self. The aim of Socratic irony is not to transmit objective, eternal truths but to arouse the one to whom it is directed to exist as a reflective, self-critical individual. Socrates' role as an ironic gadfly was not in the service of a doctrine or an abstract, aprioristic truth; it served, rather, to bring the individual to a concern for his own being —to personal knowledge, the kind of knowledge that Socrates felt was essential.

Hermann Diem, in his *Kierkegaard's Dialectic of Existence*, makes explicit the implicit character of Socratic irony when he remarks that the conversation between man and man liberates each of them to live in his own right and suggests, further, a possibility of existence for each.[15] Existential communication, he avers, ineluctably takes the form of possibility. The possibilities suggested by Socratic irony are, of course, personal, existential ones, those concernful possibilities that, when acted upon, can change the meaning and purpose of an individual's life. Only by indirection, Kierkegaard later emphasized, can one individual bring another individual to a search for ethical self-being. "Know thyself" is a demanding injunction; but Socrates seemed to believe that the sincere pursuit of self-knowledge was a necessary propaedeutic to the possibility of ethical self-being. In this regard, irony was used in order to bring the other to a search for what Kierkegaard calls "concernful knowledge." When irony is directed to another person the suggestion is that one knows that he ought to be other than he is. As Kierkegaard will write in his journals, ethics is concerned with a communication of a potentiality-for (*kunnen*) becoming a self,[16] of a specific kind of knowledge, self-knowledge. If the ironist is negative in regard to objective truth, he is, by implication, deeply concerned with a subjectively apprehended certainty concerning what one ought to be. This, Kierkegaard suggests, was the aim of the dialectical, nihilating effects of Socratic irony.

In the face of the possibility of an eternal life or nothingness, Socrates retained his irony, entertaining—as Kierkegaard puts it—a syllogistic *aut* . . . *aut* (either/or), a playful consideration of the possibility that either this or that may be true.[17] This attitude of mind is itself doubly ironic insofar as Socrates (or Plato through Socrates) had presented a number of arguments in defense of the immortality of the soul. Objective uncertainty does not disturb Socrates. He seems to possess a subjective certainty that gives him the self-mastery characteristic of an ethically self-conscious individual. There is, as Kierkegaard suggests, an "ideality" that functions as an ideal goal and gives meaning and purpose to Socrates' life; but it is neither an objective truth, nor an ultimate, transcendental reality, nor a knowledge about the nature of the totality of reality.

For Kierkegaard, Socrates represented the individual who had attacked objective knowledge (by virtue of his ironic negations or skeptical uncertainty) in order to make room for the possibility of a search for subjective knowledge (that is, knowledge of the self). The ignorance that Socrates thought leads to immorality or injustice is not ignorance of some objective, universal moral principle; rather, it is ignorance of oneself. The problem with ironic reflection is that it tends to put off decision—to inhibit wholesale commitment to an ideal or a goal. As Kierkegaard describes Socrates, he is an individual who is unable to leap into anything; hence, he leaps back into himself in inwardness (*Inderligheden*).[18] Kierkegaard believed that the "cleansing baptism of irony" not only sweeps away irrelevancies but rejuvenates and regenerates the sense of one's own existence and recalls one to one's essential ethical possibilities. Though he sometimes tries to think of Socrates as a proto-Christian "man of faith," he realizes that Socrates was the paradigm of the critical, self-reflective, existential thinker who endeavored to attain an authentic existence outside faith. In *Concluding Unscientific Postscript* the inwardness of Socrates is described as an analogy to faith, not as faith itself. Irony marks the emergence of self-consciousness and the consciousness of possibility. For Socrates, existence as a human being is not a *fait accompli* but a task to be accomplished. Though it may be the case that ironic tension may be sustained because it leads one to a recognition of the possibility of a higher being, a transcendent reality, and dramatizes the distinction between the conditioned and the unconditioned,[19] it is anachronistic to suggest that Socrates arrived at an intuitive awareness of God. While it is true, as Edmund Husserl says in his *Erste Philosophie*, that Socrates practices a critique or ultimate evaluation of his life's goals and, by virtue of this, his "ways of life and changing means," Kierkegaard would not agree that Socrates was concerned with "clarifying reflections" that culminate in "apodictic self-evidence"[20]—unless that is, Husserl was referring to Socrates' concern to find a basis for certainty and resoluteness in an intense, self-critical reflection upon his own being.

For Socrates, there is no apodictic certainty that there is a transcendental being or realm of perfection, nor is there apodictic certainty concerning the nature of phenomena. Socratic irony comes full circle when it is directed against the self, when it is directed to one's own actuality as a means of recalling oneself to the "ideality" (which is an 'object' of thought or imagination) that one can attempt to realize existentially. There are, for Kierkegaard, three fundamental uses of irony: (1) as an instrument for destroying all objective certainty, all metaphysical absolutes, i.e., a nihilistic irony; (2) as an aestheticism that negates all actuality and projects an imaginative ideality that can never be realized, i.e., romantic irony; and (3) as a means by which the individual posits an ethical *telos* that serves as the ideality that contrasts with the actuality of the imperfect self that one has been or is now, i.e., an ethical irony. The tension produced by constantly juxtaposing the ethical ideal and the present imperfect actuality of the self is central to Kierkegaard's conception of ethical self-consciousness. In this sense irony, since it is described as a "determination of subjectivity,"[21] can be the sign of the possibility of an ethical "turn." Before examining the details of the ethical sphere of existence, however, we must attempt to discover precisely what nihilism meant to Kierkegaard and how his understanding of it is related to some important philosophical conceptions of its nature.

Forms of Nihilism

Though nihilism, as a serious philosophical problem, has only come into prominence in Western thought with the writings of Nietzsche, there has been no general agreement concerning the nature of nihilism, and Nietzsche himself discerned a variety of forms of it. Basically, there seem to be three fundamental forms that nihilism has assumed in Western thought: (1) theoretical or philosophical nihilism; (2) psychological nihilism, often described as decadence; and (3) activistic nihilism, i.e., a sociopolitically motivated nihilism of action as manifested in the Russian nihilism of the nineteenth century (what might be called, after Turgenev's novel *Fathers and Children,* Bazarov's syndrome!), in Nazi Germany, and in the sporadic violent activity of various radical political groups. It is Nietzsche, of course, who has provided the most thorough analyses of theoretical (and psychological) nihilism. Gorgias' sophistic attempts to show that "nothing exists" cannot be classified as a serious form of nihilism, even though some elements in his arguments are compatible with a theoretical nihilism.

Socrates' critique of conventional knowledge certainly had its polemical, nihilistic phase in its relentless attack upon commonly accepted concepts and values in the Greek society of his day. However, as Kierkegaard argued in the *The Concept of Irony,* this negativity was, of course, in the service of an ethics of subjectivity. Socratic wisdom is 'ignorance', the realization that, for man, there is nothing that has objective certainty. His irony was, as I have said, an indirect transmission of the necessity for the transformation of the self, the communication, as Kierkegaard puts it in his journals, of "capability."[22] Socrates' role as a "gadfly" was not in the service of an abstract metaphysical truth; rather, it sought to bring the individual to seek personal knowledge, to attempt to become what he knows he ought to be. Kierkegaard later admits that his phenomenological portrait of Socrates was "one-sided" insofar as he exaggerated his negativity. But, in one sense, he did uncover some aspects of Socrates' existence that have not been discerned by many others. That is, his negation of scientific inquiry, his apparent indifference to his impending death (Nietzsche, psychologist that he was, saw the significance of Socrates' comment before dying—"O Crito, I owe a cock to Asclepius"—insofar as he noted that this was an allusion to a customary offering to the god of medicine when one had recovered from an illness, the illness being, in this case, life itself),[23] his casual humor in the face of important metaphysical questions, and, finally those skeptical doubts of his, which reveal an undercurrent of Pyrrhonism. Both Kierkegaard and Nietzsche branded Socrates (at one time or another) a nihilist.

Ironically, while Kierkegaard thought that Socrates' passionate and reasoned pursuit of moral excellence indicated that he had, for the most part, overcome a nihilistic strain in his personality and thought, Nietzsche criticizes precisely this "lack of objective interest" on Socrates' part, this "moralic acid" that ostensibly "poisoned" Greek consciousness, and sees in the morality that Socrates desired to make instinctive signs of decadence rather than strength. But even Nietzsche could not overcome a sympathetic antipathy for Socrates. At one time he characterized Socrates as "that great ironist, so rich in secrets," the first *Lebensphilosoph*, the master dialectician, and, in almost Kierkegaardian tones, he admired his spiritual courage, his self-control, his self-mastery, or, in a word, his capacity for *Selbstüberwindung* (self-overcoming). It is this affirmative core of Socrates' being and thought that precludes any conclusive charge of nihilism.[24]

In Nietzsche's analysis of "the known" (*das Bekannte*) we can see an aspect of critical philosophy not unlike that of Socrates. Nietzsche argues that what is generally accepted as knowledge is, for the most part, based upon fundamental assumptions uncritically accepted, upon conventionally adopted linguistic forms, and upon the encrusted meanings that traditional concepts acquire. Nietzsche's skepticism (which, ultimately, is in the service of his metaphysics of the "Will to Power") resembles that of Socrates insofar as his critical attacks are launched against hallowed notions and commonly accepted beliefs. To be sure, the knife of his nihilism is double-edged and can be used to negate his own positive philosophical views. Indeed, what he proclaimed the most extreme form of nihilism—the meaningless, perpetually recurring—is nothing but his own notion of the eternal recurrence of "the same." As in the case of Socrates or, for that matter, the early Kierkegaard, his critical attacks on 'will', causality, the Cartesian ego, etc., seemed to have been the means by which he could defend his own affirmation of Dionysian existence, self-mastery, self-overcoming, self-realization, and what, in general, resembles, in some respects, Kierkegaard's own conception of ethical existence.

Nietzsche's central conception of nihilism is that it is the view that existence must not be interpreted in terms of 'purpose', 'unity', 'Being', or 'truth'. For the Nietzschean nihilist there is no 'true' world at all. Or, as Kierkegaard expressed it in *The Concept of Irony,* nihilism means the negation of the meaning of actuality. The "feeling of valuelessness" is at the heart of nihilism as Nietzsche understands it. To be sure, he also describes the psychological effects of nihilism in states of spiritual exhaustion.

In *Either/Or* and in his journals Kierkegaard describes the psychological experience of nihilism as a spiritual incapacity for commitment or action, a subjective sense of emptiness, and a feeling of the senselessness of actuality. While Nietzsche engaged in a critical, rational, analysis of basic concepts in Western thought, Kierkegaard seemed to conceive of nihilism in relation to the transformation of everything into conceptual-imaginative possibilities or a state of unending critical reflection. However, both Kierkegaard and Nietzsche, in entirely different ways, reached the conclusion (later repeated by Unamuno and others) that thought is and ought to be in the service of life. In both instances reflection and thought were to be turned upon concrete existence, to conserve and preserve what Unamuno called "the tragic sense of life" and what Kierkegaard called the "dialectical tension of existence." What is probably not appreciated too much by those who have tried to understand Kierkegaard is that he, too, was radically skeptical in his thinking —that he denied, in effect, that man could have apodictic knowledge concerning history, nature, "the world," or the totality of reality. In the

Concluding Unscientific Postscript (a work clearly described as a "thought-experiment") Kierkegaard maintains that all knowledge about nonexistential 'reality' is an abrogation of its actuality insofar as it is translated into the sphere of the conceptually possible. Objective knowledge is provisional, hypothetical, and experimental for Kierkegaard as well as for Nietzsche. For Kierkegaard, as we shall see, there is an ineluctable asymptotic relationship between conceptualization and actuality that permanently bars objective certitude. In a sense, he, like Nietzsche, regarded our "infinitely complex cathedral of concepts" [*Begriffsdome*] as inadequate for an understanding of the world or "reality." On the other hand, both Kierkegaard and Nietzsche seem incapable of doubting propositions that refer to immediate experiences or to the concrete actuality of the self. Both are skeptical concerning man's rational capacity to attain complete knowledge. Nietzsche, if anything, is not as skeptical in this regard as Kierkegaard. Both have a post-Kantian appreciation of the limits of reason. Paraphrasing Kant, we may say (to put it in simplistic terms) that Nietzsche attacked reason in order to make room for a "religion of life," and that Kierkegaard attacked reason in order to make room for an authentic ethical existence and a life of faith.

While Heidegger's conception of nihilism is peculiar to his own ontological reformation, his generalization concerning the "planetary, all-corroding, many-faceted irresistibleness" of nihilism today is by no means exaggerated. For the crisis in the question of truth that Heidegger has wrestled with is central to contemporary nihilism. The reduction of all truth to tautologies, analytic statements, and empirical propositions (that have been or could be verified or confirmed) may seem to be an improvement upon the grandiose claims of metaphysicians. However, it has created a psychological and conceptual vacuum that has been filled (and that is continuously being filled) in this century by a variety of fanatical ideologies. Furthermore, Heidegger's attempt to discover the ontological ground of propositional truth (especially the correspondence theory of truth) is a heroic attempt that is desperately needed in a time of restrictive, dogmatic concepts of truth. Even those who have attempted to delimit the range of truth and meaning—for example, the Wittgenstein of *Tractatus-Logico Philosophicus*—have found themselves in the position of negating in their conclusions the very assertions that led them to their conclusions. Or to put it another way, they have negated the truth of those propositions which asserted the limits of meaning or truth.[25] How Kierkegaard would have relished such paradoxes!

For Heidegger, at any rate, nihilism means "the forgetfulness of Being," the loss of the understanding of the "Being of beings [*Seiendes*]."[26] And it is said that nihilism has been implicit in Western philosophy since Plato and has found its overt culmination in Nietzsche.[27] Such a grandiose claim is practically impossible to substantiate, and it robs the concept of nihilism of much of its meaning. Moreover, the projection of the recognition of the "presence" (*Anwesen*) of Being back to the pre-Socratic philosophers smacks of nothing so much as philosophical romanticism. Heidegger makes of nihilism not, as Stanley Rosen has called it in his study of *Nihilism*, "a permanent possibility for man,"[28] but the underlying theme of Western thought and experience. To hold that nihilism is subjectivism, and to find this "subjectivism" in philosophers as diverse as Plato, Aristotle, Descartes, and Nietzsche, is not "orginating thought" but philosophical idiosyncrasy. While many have seen in Heidegger's *Being and Time* the very subjectivism that he identifies as nihilistic, I would hold that insofar as Heidegger is concerned with authentically existing *Dasein*, with the individuating aspects of human existence, his fundamental ontology is not nihilistic. For *Dasein* is the discoverer and sustainer of meaning. In the authentic existence of an individual *Dasein* 'truth' comes to be in time. To ground all meaning and significance in Being (*das Sein*), as the later Heidegger has done, to abandon the 'essence' of man to the mysterious *Abgrund,* to believe that the mission of Being (*das Geschick des Seins*) is "fate" (the ancient Greek *Moira* in Heideggerian disguise) as the "the confrontation of Being and the being of man" (*Der Satz vom Grund*),[29] is to betray the spirit of existentialism and is, in effect, to negate the intrinsic meaningfulness of human existence as it is painfully won by authentic individuals or in the authenticity of human lives. If Kierkegaard were alive today, he would have to attack the later Heidegger in the same spirit as he attacked Hegel. Heidegger criticizes one form of nihilism (anthropocentric subjectivism), but simultaneously surrenders his defense of authentic subjectivity.

An alien, inhuman, transcendent Absolute has returned to haunt Western thought, an Absolute that mysteriously manifests itself in time, history, *Dasein*, and works of art. What is the individual *Dasein* in relation to this secularized Absolute? He is virtually nothing. In Heidegger's attempt to penetrate the ineffable and to say the unsayable we have the closest analogy in Western thought to *Śūnyavāda*.[30] Against those philosophers who are sympathetic to Heidegger, this does not seem to be a discovery of new wisdom; it is a sign *not* of philosophical rejuvenation but of cultural and philosophical exhaustion. Let Kierkegaard's remark in his journals stand as a commentary on some of Heidegger's later philosophical utterances. There are times, Kierkegaard writes, when one experiences a spiritual phenomenon that may be described as a kind of oriental revery in the infinite in which everything appears to be reconciled—the being of the entire world, the being of God, and my own being itself. All the disparities of life, the sheer multiplicity of actuality—everything is reconciled in a misty, dreamy state. "But then . . . *I wake* up again, and . . . the tragic relativity in everything begins worse than ever, the endless questions about *what I am* . . .what I am doing . . . [and one suspects that] at the same time perhaps millions are doing the same."[31]

The only absolute that the nihilist can tolerate (Kierkegaard tells us) is infinite negativity itself. For both Kierkegaard and Nietzsche the category of Being is empty or, as Nietzsche put it, it is a "cloudy streak of evaporating reality."[32] The emphasis of the theoretical nihilist is upon radical change, impermanence, the insubstantiality of all phenomena, the negativity that Hegel described (in his *Science of Logic*) as immanent in finite beings.[33] When the nihilist asserts that "nothing *is*," he means that nothing is permanent, that there is no being (whether an *ens rationis* or an actual being) that is exempt from the nihilating effect of temporality. Buddhist dialecticians had often appealed to the relativity of experience (as Gorgias himself did), the impermanence of actuality, the radical contingency of all existence, the unending flux of phenomena, in order to show the unreality of phenomenal actuality (in any absolute sense). However, aside from the *nāstika* philosophers,[34] even Buddhists who argued for the impermanence of actuality (Nagarjuna) postulated the possibility of the transcendent, the *Sunya* ("void"), which is not nothing, but is that ineffable, ultimate reality that rationalistic categories are unable to describe.

A consistent nihilism is a rare phenomenon. It is rare because it is ultimately self-negating and self-refuting. What is curious about the nihilist is, as Nietzsche saw, that he would rather have nothingness as his purpose than have no purpose at all. In the case of Kierkegaard, at least, his own nihilistic tendencies, his theoretical skepticism, led him to seek self-knowledge in order that he might have a constructive, subjectively apprehended *telos.* Ironically, Nietzsche, in his metaphysics (i.e., in the doctrine of eternal recurrence and in the notion of an impersonal cosmic will to power), undermined his central existentialist standpoint. If life, as he said, affirms itself through me, if the will to power acts through the individual, then the I-consciousness that he ostensibly defended is obliterated.[35] In this respect, Kierkegaard was more consistent in his existentialist emphasis on the primacy of individual being. His conception of nihilism is, in general, compatible with that of Nietzsche even though he thought that only an ethical or religious existence could overcome its uncanny negative power.

Whereas Nietzsche examined, in an almost exhaustive manner, the various modalities of nihilism—religious nihilism (typified, he thought, by Christianity and Buddhism), pathological nihilism, the nihilism of action, sociopolitical nihilism (which was primarily identified with Prussian militarianism, socialism, communism, etc.)—Kierkegaard characterizes nihilism as the end-product, as it were, of critical reflection or the purely polemical use of reason. Corresponding to this persistent critical reflection in the psychological realm there is a personal sense of pointlessness, purposelessness, and meaninglessness. The contradictions of a multiplicity of metaphysical beliefs or systems seem to leave only a series of unresolved antinomies. This understanding of nihilism can only emerge after a recognition of the historical perspective, a sense of alternative systems or methods of philosophy, a sensitivity to a multiplicity of conceptual possibilities. The much-heralded historical consciousness that Hegel (more than any other single thinker) introduces into Western thought proved to be a mixed blessing. It led, as we can see in the case of Wilhelm Dilthey, to a sense of the "chaos of relativities," to the destruction of "the belief in the absolute validity of any one philosophy," to the type of historicism that is a prelude to dogmatic ideology.[36] Kierkegaard had already understood Dilthey's later discovery of the "liberation" of human consciousness from rigidity and tradition. But he saw, psychologist that he was, that this liberation exacted a cost that one might not be willing to pay. What is the individual to do when faced with the chaos of relativities that historical consciousness and the history of philosophy reveals? It was Kierkegaard's daring that allowed him (before Nietzsche) to see in his own skeptical dialectic of reflection a sphere or stage in human existence that could be "lived-through" by anyone, that had already been experienced (perhaps) by Socrates, and that would no doubt be experienced by many. What *The Concept of Irony* signified, I believe, was the recognition of the "nihilistic standpoint" as a possibility for man in any age. The first path on the dialectic of life is not the aesthetic sphere of existence but a nihilistic sphere that, for Kierkegaard, must be lived through for some meaningful *telos* to be discovered or created by the individual.[37]

Contrary to the view of Stanley Rosen (in his philosophical essay on nihilism), I would hold that there *are* a diversity of forms of nihilism. In one sense, he is right in averring that, for the nihilist, "everything is permitted"—that the nihilist can attribute value to anything by an "arbitrary resolution."[38] But this is only one side of the nihilistic coin. We must supplement it with the correlative psychological aspects of a sincere (and not a superficial) nihilism. We are dealing with a phenomenon that is a cognitive-affective state, not merely a purely theoretical "standpoint."

The gradually emerging challenge to what have been the traditional religious *Weltanschauungen* of the Western world tended to undermine all metaphysical beliefs. The nihilism of reflection that Kierkegaard examined in *The Concept of Irony* is a late cultural product, a sign of both intellectual fertility as well as of theoretical syncretism. The dramatic influence that oriental thought had on Schopenhauer (and others of the nineteenth century) was only one case in point. In a mutiplicity of forms, the underlying malaise of nineteenth-century European thought was revealed in a kind of spiritual exhaustion, the dissolution of the rationalist tradition. Even in Hegel one sometimes senses that there is a looking backward upon something that has already been accomplished—that the end of a tradition has come, that a summary of the evolution of Western thought can now be made, that, in effect, reason can do no more. This is epitomized in his much quoted remark in the *Philosophy of Right* that "when philosophy paints its grey in grey [an allusion to Goethe's *Faust*], then has a form of life grown old. By philosophy's grey in grey it cannot be rejuvenated, but only understood. The owl of Minerva spreads its wings only with the falling of the dusk."[39]

As the nineteenth century comes to a close, there are numerous dithyrambic attempts to preserve the notion of the infinite, the eternal. But the oppressive, negating analytical force of reason is overpowering. The *Weltschmerz* of romantic poets and novelists infiltrates philosophy. Schopenhauer counsels the extinction of the will, and Mainländer and von Hartmann advise the cessation of procreation: since human existence is obviously so painful, one must negate the unconscious will to live, one must see that it is better that nothing come into being at all. The total intellectual-psychological atmosphere of Germanic pessimism must be seen as at least the central background for Kierkegaard's conception of nihilism. The pessimism of the nineteenth century was not only, as Nietzsche called it, "a preliminary form of nihilism." Rather, it was already one of its covert manifestations. Psychologically, what seems to underlie nihilistic pessimism is a deep-seated despair, a subjective sense of spiritual emptiness, a disdain for, if not a hatred of, finite actuality.

It is in the writings of the Italian poet Leopardi that we find the ultimate crescendo of nihilistic pessimism. In his *Zibaldone* he exclaims: "All that exists is evil; that everything exists is an evil. Everything exists only to achieve evil; existence itself is an

evil. . . . There is no other good than nonexistence." Such an extreme pessimism is not unknown to Kierkegaard; it is expressed
in some of his last journal entries, in his charge that one comes
into existence by means of a crime, that existence itself is a
crime, that the world is a prison-house from which the only
escape is death.[40] Temperamentally, Kierkegaard was at one
with the romantic pessimists even though his conceptions of
authentic existence and the possibility of faith saved him from
the lure of nihilism. If Kierkegaard often verges on an ethical
or religious position resembling what Albert Schweitzer called
"world-and-life-negation," he is rescued from such extremism
by virtue of his faith in the capacity, which some men have, of
endeavoring to achieve an authentic, individual existence. In
addition, of course, he could never lead himself to deny the
reality of the concrete immediacy of particular existence. This, as
I shall try to show, played an important role in his description of
the ethical sphere of existence. For Kierkegaard, nihilism did
not mean (as Stanley Rosen claims it does) "discontinuity" but
rather the dissolution of the sense of actuality, of the meaning of
concrete actuality. In the *Concluding Unscientific Postscript*
Kierkegaard remarks that skepticism is a form of idealism; he might
just as well have said that, in a sense, nihilism is a peculiar form
of 'idealism', for it suggests that one is already, for better or
worse, a part of a peculiar 'identity', and that one can "let go."
Translated into the language of Buddhism, it is the recognition
that *saṃsāra* is *nirvāna*.[41] But the recurring question that Kierkegaard raises is: if actuality *is* meaningless, is not then my own
concrete, immediate existence meaningless, unreal? But this is
impossible! I know that I am actual, that I exist. If I know anything at all, I know this. I cannot assert the denial of my own
existence without implicit self-refutation. The heart of all of
Kierkegaard's writings is his emphasis upon the existential reality
of individual existence. Everything else may be objectively uncertain, but I cannot seriously deny the actuality of my own existence. Man, for Kierkegaard, is the only actuality that can know
itself in its own concrete reality in and through its consciousness
of its immediacy. He denies the formula of Descartes, *cogito
ergo sum,* but expresses his own: *sum ergo cogito.*

Kierkegaard, like Socrates, could not wield his critical, polemical intelligence against his own actuality. This certitude of his
own existence—even in moments of despair or hopelessness—was
the cornerstone upon which he built his conception of the dialectic of life. To be sure, he did have the kind of temperament
that led him to be sensitive to the relativity of his own experiences, the endless flux of phenomena, the diversity of forms
of life, the mutability of all finite entities, the transience of all
phenomena. Like all thinkers who have a proclivity toward
skepticism, he was keenly aware of multiplicity, diversity, various
points of view, and the variety of forms of explanation. More
importantly, perhaps, he was sensitive to his own mutability, to
the complexity of his own being. In *Either/Or* he remarks
that "When I consider the different periods into which [my life]
falls, it seems like the word *Schnur* in the dictionary, which means
in the first place a string, in the second, a daughter-in-law. The
only thing lacking is that the word *Schnur* should mean in the
third place a camel, in the fourth, a dust-brush."[42] This self-
conscious, self-reflective recognition of the multiplicity within
the apparent unity of the self in an indication that there is,
indeed, a relationship between the subjective sense of meaninglessness and subjectivism. In this regard, Kierkegaard is quite
correct in relating the ironic standpoint to subjectivity. It is
surely the radical contradictions in one's own life experiences,
the sheer multiplicity that one experiences in existence (the
confusing aspects of life that are either ignored by most philosophers or are shunted aside as irrelevant phenomena that "reason" does not deign to consider), the sensitivity to various points
of view, that tend to nullify the attempt to "fit" experience into
rigid categories of a pure rationalism or logical analysis.

Concrete, immediate experience or existence is neither unintelligible nor transparent to reason; rather it is, as Kierkegaard
suggests, the most difficult phenomenon to understand. The
dissimilarity of individual experiences and modes of thought (as
Gorgias had already suggested) is one of the fundamental bases
of philosophical nihilism. When one emphasizes continuity, the
immutable, the permanent, the constants of thought, the unities
discernible within multiplicities, the patterns or *Gestalten* of

experience, the universal, the repeatable, the nomological, the nihilistic standpoint seems to disintegrate. But once we reflect upon oppositions, contradictions, paradoxes, dialectical relations, the gratuitous nature of empirical events, the complexity of even the most apparently simple act or process, the apparently stochastic aspects of existence, the complex unity of specificity and multiplicity, the subjective sense of the chaotic character of "the world" emerges again. Radical change, specificity, and apparently random multiplicity seem to undermine the unifying tendency of human reason, the need for order.

While Kierkegaard sometimes allows himself the luxury of a misanthropic nihilism, his occasional sense of what Nietzsche called the "in vain" never entirely destroyed his faith in man's potentiality-for authentic existence. Ultimately, nihilism entails the negation of reflection or thought as an end in itself since its affirmation is its own negation. The paradox of nihilism is that it can never be 'true'. Dialectically, as in Kierkegaard's case, it turns the individual back upon himself, upon his own immediacy. Psychologically, the individual who has lived through nihilism, who has felt its corrosive power, can neither return to a pre-philosophical position of naive realism nor to a state of pervasive hopelessness or despair. He is now open to the possibility of faith. I do not mean by this religious faith alone, but a faith in himself, in morality, in existence, in the immediacy of actuality, in the capacity to understand. William James rightly remarked that rationalism itself is based upon a *faith* in the power of reason.[43] Insofar as nihilism awakens the individual to a realization of what Heidegger will later call the uncanniness of existence it has had a productive function, it has cleared away the inessential and the trivial, the commonplace and the conventional, it has, in effect, led the individual to seek a mooring for his own existence that will have meaning for himself, if not for others as well. The transcendence of the nihilistic standpoint is made possible by virtue of the capacity for the negation of this theoretical negation. For Kierkegaard, this is the basis for the 'movement' of the self toward the openness of the future.

Nihilism is not, as is often said, an irrationalist position; rather, it is the result of careful, critical, rational analysis. It is the ultimate by-product of skepticism and doubt. Through the negative, destructive use of reason, reason itself is undermined. The antinomies of conceived possibilities negate each other and there is a subtle erosion of the concept of truth. Theoretically, nihilism means *the impossibility of objective knowledge.* That is, knowledge of "the" world is impossible because the world that is "known" is a phenomenon derived from interpretation, a construction of what is ostensibly 'given' in terms of a variety of conceptual schema that are themselves subject to revision. The attempt to arrive at a wholly objective understanding of a world interpreted on the basis of historically conditioned human thought, language, and experience—a world that is ostensibly known in its independent being—by relying on culturally, historically determined thought, language, and experience is presumably not possible. Heidegger, perhaps more than any contemporary philosopher, has instructed us in the contingency of every previously accepted ontology of "the world," has shown us that our relationship to "the world" (i.e., how we think of it and experience it) has been conditioned by dominant ontological, conceptual schema that have been inherited from the past. Unfortunately, the questions he raised about such ontological schema suggest that there has never been (and may never be) *a* world in which man lives, but rather a variety of "worlds."

It may be asked whether any philosopher (other than Nietzsche, perhaps) has ever realized that if a *Weltanschauung* that has dominated the thought and experience of millions of individuals is shown to be false (or is conceived of as false) or is put in question, then the possibility emerges that no *Weltanschauung* (no matter how convincing it may seem at present) is valid. This does not, of course, apply only to questionable metaphysical systems, for this kind of skepticism affects every holding-for-true, every hypothesis, presupposition, assumption, or logically primitive concept. In this sense, nihilism is the negation of the possibility of attaining the truth—the negation of truth, knowledge, and certainty is itself negated in the very process of asserting it. Hence, the philosopher or the reflective individual must begin again from another standpoint. Ultimately, what the nihilist finds most difficult to deny is his own actual existence.

The ironic nihilist whom Kierkegaard describes in the guise of Socrates is able to reduce every objective possibility to negativity (e.g., perhaps there is a moral world order or perhaps there are no moral phenomena, as Nietzsche said, but only a moral interpretation of phenomena; perhaps language pictures the world or perhaps language constitutes a linguistic 'world' that bears no relationship to the world of actuality), to convert every objective 'truth' into a mere possibility. However, neither Socrates nor Kierkegaard turn their critical analysis upon the self in its concrete actuality. The pursuit of self-knowledge is the beginning of an ethical existence. For Socrates, as well as Kierkegaard, the question "What am I?" is already an ethical question, a signification of concernful knowledge. The examined life is the best life that a man can live—a life of self-examination, a search for self-knowledge, a scrutiny of the self. The negation of every conceivable or imaginable theoretical possibility leaves only existential, spiritual possibilities, which only the individual can realize. Knowledge of the good is indeed a necessary and sufficient condition of right action (as Norman Gulley says in his *The Philosophy of Socrates*); but this knowledge is not primarily an objective knowledge of an a priori truth; rather, it is a subjective knowledge, a knowledge made possible by a critical analysis of the self. And it is this that Socrates sought to attain by means of *elenchus,* irony and indirection in his existential communication with others. Socratic skepticism (like Kierkegaard's skepticism) affects almost everything except the ethical resoluteness and self-existence of the individual. This, at any rate, lies at the core of Kierkegaard's understanding of Socratic irony (and its nihilistic implications) and is a conviction that plays a central role in his account of the essential form of ethical existence.

Whereas the nihilistic orientation is understood by Kierkegaard as a possible mode of being for any human being at any time (even though he, like Nietzsche, thought that the death of religious consciousness would carry in its wake the sense that life has become a "whirlpool, meaninglesness, and either a despairing arrogance or a despairing disconsolateness"), Heidegger conceives of nihilism as an anthropocentrism that proclaims that there is only a multiplicity of beings (*Seiendes*) in a constant process of becoming and implies the "oblivion of Being." The Nietzschean will to power and the contemporary emphasis on 'technicity' are two sides of the same coin. Nietzsche's metaphysics is thought by Heidegger to be the culmination of a conceptual process that had been inherent in Plato's thought. The underlying meaning of this metaphysical tradition is, as he puts it in his Nietzsche, "anthropomorphy—the shaping and viewing of the world in accordance with man's image."[44] In such a standpoint man plays the role of the unconditioned measure of all things and of their value. What is surprising about such attacks on what he calls humanistic metaphysics is that they seem to apply to his hermeneutic, phenomenological analysis of the being of *Dasein* in *Sein und Zeit*. To be sure, Heidegger does explicitly say that this exhibition of the constitution of *Dasein's* mode of being is only one way to approach the question of Being: "Nevertheless, our way of exhibiting the constitution of Dasein's Being remains only *one way* which we may take. Our *aim* is to work out the question of Being in general."[45] But it is clear that *Dasein* is characterized, in general, as the center of meaning, purpose, and interpretation of phenomena. In some of his passionate remarks Heidegger comes quite close to the kind of humanism he identifies as nihilism. Thus he denies, at one point, that there are eternal truths *because Dasein* had not yet been shown to be eternal:

> That there are 'eternal truths' will not be adequately proved until someone has succeeded in demonstrating that Dasein has been and will be for all eternity. As long as such a proof is still outstanding, this principle remains a fanciful contention.[46]

Such a view may be compared with his later assertion, in *Gelassenheit,* that "man on his own has no power over truth and this [i.e., truth] remains independent of him."[47] While Kierkegaard's conception of ethical existence and his general emphasis on the primacy of subjectivity would presumably be branded as nihilistic (even though Kierkegaard himself regards ethical subjectivity as the overcoming of nihilism as he understands it), there is a sense in which there is a tension in Heidegger's thought concerning the centrality of subjectivity. In his *Vom Wesen des Grundes* he does not hesitate to speak of the being that we are as *Subjekt* and to maintain (in almost the language of Kierkegaard) that to be a subject means, essentially, to be a being in and *as* transcending—transcendence is the basic structure of subjectivity (. . . *die Transzendenz bezeichnet das Wesen des Subjekts, ist Grundstruktur der Subjectivität*).[48] While Kierkegaard, too, may be said to have made the individual (in the religious sphere of existence) subservient to "the eternal," he never truly abandons the centrality of subjectivity and, in fact, may be understood as presenting an inchoate philosophical anthropology that is based upon the personal, subjective perspective of human life. Heidegger, on the other hand, sometimes seems to characterize, by implication, his earlier *Sein und Zeit* as subjectivistic, humanistic, and hence, according to his definition, nihilistic.

Rosen argues in his study of nihilism that Heidegger's attempt to overcome European nihilism (as Nietzsche understood it) was a failure because *Sein und Zeit* is itself nihilistic insofar as "Heidegger radicalizes the absence of all gods into a denial of the presence of the eternal; as a result, the present has no enduring status in his thoroughly temporalized Being-process." Furthermore, it is argued that Heidegger's "development of an ontology of historicity" represents a "resignation in the face of nihilism."[49]

The nihilism to which *Sein und Zeit* leads is, we are told, a position that is ostensibly "implicit in [the] ontological analysis of human existence." This charge is primarily made because of Heideggers' insistence upon the dominance of temporality (*Zeitlichkeit*) in the human world. Presumably, Rosen would have to raise a similar criticism against Kierkegaard as well, since he, too, emphasizes that existence is only possible insofar as movement is possible and is, therefore, restricted to temporality (*Timeligheden*). Though it is a mistake to assume that Heidegger's conception of authentic existence is an *ethical* requirement (despite the fact, as I shall suggest, that many of his descriptions of such an existence are closely related to Kierkegaard's existential ethics), his description of *Dasein's* projective movement towards Being-one's-self—the selfhood of *Dasein* being a way of existing—is a positive conception of what *Dasein* ought, in an ontological sense, to be. Though Heidegger's phenomenological analysis is, to be sure, primarily descriptive, it is also, in a sense, hortatory. Like Rilke, he implies that "it is necessary to change one's life." His attack on the inauthenticity of the realm of *das Man* (which, of course, is reminiscent of Kierkegaard's attack upon "the crowd") is a necessary corrective to the tendency in this century to deify society and collectivities. Certainly Heidegger's emphasis on individuating states of being is an echo of Kierkegaard's stress upon the accentuation of subjectivity in ethical self-existence.

I believe that Rosen is correct in discerning a nihilistic tendency underlying *Being and Time,* but I do not believe that it is related to Heidegger's conception of the temporality of the Being-process or to his emphasis upon the primacy of the temporal modality of the future. It is found rather in his notion (borrowed from Hegel) that there is nonbeing or nothingness in the being of *Dasein.* By averring that in uncanniness *Dasein* is confronted by its unvarnished negativity ("In uncanniness *Dasein* stands together with itself primordially. It brings this being face to face with its undisguised nullity . . ."),[50] that man, for the most part, is "lost in the they," in irresoluteness (*Unentschlossenheit*), that "being-guilty" is an unsurpassable characteristic of *Dasein,* that there is a "lack of totality"—of the not-yet (*noch-Nicht*)—that "belongs" to *Dasein* so long as he is. Heidegger has presented a negativistic portrait of man that is practically anomalous in Western thought. At times, in his implicit portrayal of the abandonment and hopelessness of human being, he seems to echo, in philosophical language, the nihilism of Hölderlin's *Hyperion*—the sense that we are "in the grip of that Nothing which rules over us . . . thoroughly conscious that we are born for Nothing, that we love a Nothing, believe in a Nothing, work ourselves to the bone for Nothing, until we gradually dissolve into Nothing."[51] Against such a background one can see the positive and urgent significance of the *possibility* of the transformation of the self, of an asymptotic approximation to authentic self-being. That the universal determination of all thought and experience is, as Kant had implied in his *Kritik,* temporality

(*Zeitlichkeit*) does not mean that man cannot discover meaning
in phenomena, cannot create a temporally conditioned and hence
finite meaning for his existence, that he cannot endeavor to transcend the limitations of his natural being and strive to realize
a spiritual existence that may justify his having been. If this
temporally circumscribed process of individual becoming is, as
Rilke said, "only for once" (*nur ein Mal*), then this "once,"
once having been authentic or "lived truth," can we not agree
with Rilke that:

> Just once,
> everything, only for once. Once and no more. And we, too,
> once. And never again. But this once,
> having been once on earth—can it ever be cancelled?[52]

For Kierkegaard, nihilism is not the ultimate culmination of
a long, gradual metaphysical process that reaches its nadir in
Nietzsche's *Will to Power* and is manifest in a technicity characterized by an endless attack upon the earth, a quantitative reduction of all phenomena (including man) to things for use, a
dynamism that seems to be sweeping Western civilization to a
counterfinality that mocks man's increasing power over nature.
In the material objectification of the will to power the individual is
caught up in a technocentric, mechanomorphic world in which
his own personal existence is made senseless. Kierkegaard, of
course, has little to say about such tendencies (unless one exag-
gerates his claim that scientism will end by corrupting man).
Rather, nihilism is primarily a kind of theoretical dissolution
that has its existential correlate in a subjective sense of emptiness
and meaninglessness. The individual feels alone in a chaotic
world, unable to seize upon a certainty or a purpose that would
give meaning to his life. Heidegger's conception of nihilism as
"subjectivism" or "subjectism" would surely apply not only to
Kierkegaard's emphasis upon the centrality of the becoming of
the individual but also to Socratic humanism (as Kierkegaard understood it) as well. Kierkegaard would certainly have agreed
with Heidegger's claim (which undermines his condemnation of
humanism) that "all representation of the whole of what is, all
interpretation of the world, is, . . . inescapably humanization."[53]

Nevertheless, nihilism meant, for Kierkegaard, a psychological-reflective condition, a mode of being, that can only be transcended through resoluteness by virtue of the attempt to realize one's own "oughtness-capability," one's potentiality-for (*kunnen*) ethical self-existence. As he puts it in his journals, one does not overcome a stultifying state of being by more knowledge or more thought; what is required is a transformation of the self—a "movement" of the self towards possibilities that one endeavors to realize in actuality. The circle of the nihilism of reflection can only be broken by "choosing oneself," by choosing the ethical possibility as one's own, by treating it as a form of "concernful knowledge" and not merely as one more hypothetical possibility. Before turning to an analysis of the relationship between possibility and existence, I would like to discuss another mode of nihilism that is tangential to my central concern here, i.e., to describe the nature of nihilism as Kierkegaard understood it.

Aestheticism and Nihilism

Though activistic forms of nihilism are not directly relevant to my central concern and call for a separate treatment,[54] some are appropriate in this context. For, this form of nihilism is encompassed in Kierkegaard's Hegelian phenomenology of romantic irony and aestheticism in general.

The analysis of romantic irony in *The Concept of Irony* was a a prolepsis of Kierkegaard's fuller analysis of the aesthetic sphere of being in *Either/Or*. Needless to say, romantic irony emerges in terms of the dominance of imagination (a fundamental source of idealities) over reason. This mode of irony comes into being in terms of the contrast between the actual and the ideal, the finite and the infinite, the imperfect and the perfect, the prosaic and the poetic, the limited and the unlimited. An underlying trait of the romantic ironist is a despairing disillusionment generated by the juxtaposition of an ideal possibility and prosaic actuality.

The refinement and cultivation of taste and an exquisite aesthetic sensibility (which is paradigmatically encouraged in Walter Pater's *Studies in the Renaissance*) has, of course, some value. If it becomes obsessive and dominates a personality, how-ever, it provides the psychological precondition for a pandemic disillusionment with all that is not beautiful or perfect—for the boredom that constitutes, as Kierkegaard puts it, the only con-tinuity of a purely astheic existence. The painful evanescence of immediacy, no matter how pleasurable it may be, convinces the romantic ironist of the transitory nature of human existence, of the nihilating power of temporality. The project of the ro-mantic ironist is radically paradoxical because he desires to eternalize finite immediacy. It is not suprising, then, that he has a proclivity for experiences of emptiness—of nothingness. In his journals Kierkegaard (and not the aesthete he portrays in *Either/Or*) gives vent to a typical romantic sentiment when he remarks that "there are . . . insects that die in the very moment of fertilization; so it is, after all, with all joy—life's highest, most splendid moment of enjoyment is accompanied by death."[55]

Although the romantic ironist seeks to attain exalted states of being, a profound sense of ego-expansion, he is, in fact, engaged in a process of losing his self in the dissolution of a life of imag-ination dominated by moods; he is, that is, losing contact with concrete actuality. Like the dialectician of reflection, the ro-mantic ironist is inclined to negate the meaningfulness of actu-ality. Although the ironic romanticism of the nineteenth century was, in some of its manifestations, distinctly religious in its form, it tended to become a kind of self-idolatry—a narcissistic self-pre-occupation that retained, nevertheless, some of the categories of religious experience (e.g., the longing for the infinite or the eter-nal, the depreciation of finitude in relation to a quasi-religious realm of immutable perfection) without ethical restraint or hu-mility. Quite often, as Kierkegaard understood so well, the ro-mantic striving for endlessness (what the German romanticists called *Unendlichkeitstreben*) tended to lead to a longing for no-thingness.

Disillusionment seems to underlie romantic irony since such irony involves a consciousness of the radical discrepancy between an elusive ideal and imperfect actuality. The romantic ironist denies himself a center or a central goal or project for his life. Romantic desire is indeterminate, diffuse, a nostalgia for what always seems to elude one. The romantic ironist is subject to rapid shifts of mood (*Stimmungsbrechung*) and is restless and unstable.[56] Unable to commit himself to an absolute *telos*—insofar as the infinite for which the romantic longs is contentless and vague and hence is not an absolute *telos*—the romantic may turn his irony back upon himself.

In this regard, Kierkegaard was impressed with Solger's understanding of irony, the realization that:

> True irony derives from the point of view that so long as man lives in the present world, it is only in this world that he can fulfill his determination, and this in the highest sense of the word [vocation]. The striving for the infinite does not actually lead man beyond this life . . . but merely into indeterminateness and emptiness. It is inspired by . . . the feeling of earthly limitation to which we have been restricted once and for all.[57]

There is an aspect of romantic irony, then, which can be used as an instrument to deflate the pretention and hurbis of the romantic aesthete. There is the suggestion, as it were, that transcendence for a finite individual is towards the future, towards possibilities which can be actualized in time. Romantic irony can be construed as itself a signification of the decline of romanticism in its original form in the sense that it suggested that it is in actuality (not in imagination) that existence acquires validity, that "action . . . must have an apriority in itself so as not to become lost in vacuous infinity."[58] If the romantic ironist could turn his corrosive irony upon himself, upon his own self-defeating mode of being, if he could expose the contrast between what he is in fact and what he imagines himself to be, then he might be able, in Hegel's phrase, to negate the negation implicit in his life. What Kierkegaard calls "mastered irony" may be seen as the condition for the possibility of making significant choice, of choosing to become a self rather than a manifold of desires, drives, impulses, moods, cravings, and romantic longings. The nihilism that threatens the romantic ironist can be overcome if irony is turned against oneself insofar as one is continuously aware of the discrepancy between what one is and what one implicitly knows one ought to be. It is this sense of dialectical opposition that intensifies subjective concern. One who has developed a capacity for mastered irony has already made a movement towards "the ethical."

The aestheticism that Kierkegaard understood so well is, of course, not a new phenomenon: its roots can be found in the literature of ancient Greece, in some decadent Roman literature, and in various periods of Western literature. However, aestheticism came to full bloom (notwithstanding the fact that it lingers on today in the cinema, in various "life styles," and in aesthetically conceived political stances) in the nineteenth century. Kierkegaard, as the phenomenologist of romanticism or romantic aestheticism, has, more than anyone else, managed to extract the "essence" of aestheticism in his discussions of romantic irony in the *Concept of Irony* and in his description of the aesthetic sphere of being in *Either/Or*. It is quite clear that aestheticism, as a way of life, is inclined towards a form of nihilism. For, in terms of the ineluctable devolution of the pursuit of pleasure in "immediacy," in the shipwreck of a purely hedonistic orientation in life, an aesthetic mode of being seems to entail an implicit denial of the meaningfulness of life as well as the suspension of moral judgment or the bracketing of moral distinctions.

Romantic irony has both a negative and positive aspect, the latter of which clearly plays a role, for Kierkegaard, in terms of his conception of man's oughtness-capability. The paradoxical process of relating an ideality to one's own actuality is not only a signification of existential subjectivity, but has a fundamental ironical aspect as well. The danger of asetheticism or romantic irony is its tendency to lead to passive despair, inactivity, irresolution, and a sense of hopelessness in the face of an imaginary ideality that one realizes cannot be attained in finite existence, and cannot even be approached in an approximation-process.

In *The Birth of Tragedy*, Nietzsche expresses the central characteristic of one form of aesthetic nihilism when he avers that "only as an aesthetic spectacle is life and the world justified eternally." As in the case of Nietzsche, Kierkegaard conceived of the aesthetic mode of life as one in which the finite is eternalized, in which a paradoxical condition of a pleasurable eternal present is sought. What the aesthetic sphere of life indicates, as Kierkegaard describes it, is its self-negating insufficiency.

All forms of aestheticism venerate the "form" of phenomena, the surface brilliance of phenomena (no matter how disastrous or destructive they may be). The aesthete wants "to burn with a hard, gem-like flame," as Walter Pater put it, setting uncomfortable moral questions aside. Aestheticism is nihilistic not so much because it posits a supramoral value (which, indeed, it does) but because it ignores or positively avoids moral questions. The cultivation of an exquisite, refined aesthetic taste is all; the creation or appreciation of beauty is all; the pleasure of the reflection or of the moment is all. As in the case of *soi-disant* political nihilism, aesthetic nihilism is, strictly speaking, a misnomer. For the aesthete does indeed value something; in point of fact, he absolutizes a temporal, fleeting actuality. On the other hand, by implication, all moral questions or moral values are shunted aside in a wholesale pursuit of pleasure or aestheticism. As in the case of the Italian lyric poet Leopardi, aestheticism has often been linked (as Kierkegaard points out in his *Either/ Or*) with a nihilistic pessimism. Leopardi, the psychologist of his own aestheticism, explains one of the reasons for this. In his *Zibaldone* he notes that "the man most subject to falling into indifference and insensibility is the sensitive man, full of enthusiasm and mental activity. For such a man, just because of his unusual sensibility, exhausts life in a moment. And when he has done so, he remains profoundly disenchanted, for he has experienced everything deeply and intensely . . . has embraced everything and rejected it as unworthy and trivial. There is nothing more for him to see, to experience, or to hope."[59]

In *Either/Or* Kierkegaard describes the spiritual exhaustion of the aesthete, the narcissistic self-enclosure that characterizes his life, the suicidal tendencies that are generated by a terrible "apathy." Although there seem to be many people who can go on living a purely aesthetic existence year after year, an existence that is usually a blend of erotic excitement and aesthetic appreciation, Kierkegaard sees in this mode of being (as an exclusive mode of being) an intrinsic, underlying despair that tends to negate the possibility of the very enjoyment the aesthete seeks.

A fascination with "glittering transitoriness" is not enough. The aesthetic perspective begins to narrow and the pleasure one seeks in immediacy seems more and more elusive. In his phenomenology of aestheticism—which could just as well be described as a phenomenology of romanticism—Kierkegaard, in the manner of Socrates, draws out all of the implications of such a form of life and sketches its psychologically self-negating *dénouement*. To be sure, the aesthetic orientation toward life ought not to be entirely eliminated; rather, it must be *aufgeheben* in the ethical and the religious spheres of existence.

Aestheticism, insofar as it is characterized (as it usually is) by moral indifference or indifference to moral distinctions, is itself a kind of moral nihilism. For the aesthete, too, everything is permitted, and he cannot legitimately condemn any action or behavior (provided that it can be transformed in the prism of the aesthetic point of view) from the standpoint of a violation of moral law. A purely aesthetic existence, dominated as it invariably is by imagination, tends towards the dual process of the dissolation of the self and a suspension of moral judgment. In a letter to Woodhouse, written in 1818, John Keats described the "poetic character" in the following way: "it is not itself—it has no self—it is everything and nothing—it has no character—it enjoys light and shade; it lives in gusto, be it foul or fair, high or low, rich or poor, mean or elevated . . . What shocks the virtuous philosopher delights the chameleon poet."[60]

What Kierkegaard understood was the vulnerability of the aesthete to insensibility and moral corruption. To view all phenomena, even the sufferings of others, even the most despicable human actions, from a purely aesthetic perspective is itself a species of moral nihilism. What he tried to indicate in his impressionistic, imaginative, psychological portrait of the aesthete was that he is open to the same sense of emptiness, meaninglessness, and hopelessness as the reflective dialectician who cannot commit himself to no truth, who can find no mooring for his polemical analyses. While the nihilism of reflection and the exclusive aesthetic mode of life lead to the same psychological impasse, they reach this negativistic state of being by different paths. There are many roads to nihilism.

The Ethical Possibility

For Kierkegaard, the "nihilistic standpoint" can only be overcome by virtue of a resolute transformation of the self, a subjective inwardness that holds fast to a truth for which the individual can live. The end of the nihilism of reflection is a subjective commitment to an ethical goal or a resolve to make what Kierkegaard calls the "movement" of faith. If one waits passively for the resolution of the encounter with nihilism one must remind oneself that one has a potentiality to exist and that one is accountable (to oneself if to no one else) for what one is becoming. Whether we will it or not, the momentum of life carries us forward, carries us towards that ultimate possibility that is, so far as we know, the impossibility of possibility. The "movements" toward the realization of one's own unique possibilities, or those possibilities that enable one to become a self, require decisiveness and not merely a theoretical deliberation about alternative choices, decisions, or actions.

What I would call the nihilistic sphere of life (Kierkegaard does not describe the nihilistic standpoint in these terms in *The Concept of Irony*) is a permanent possibility for a man so long as he lives. While irony is indeed central to this mode of being, it can, as mastered irony, play a significant role in ethical existence. For a reflective irony suggests the possibility of an "ideality" that transcends the realm of actuality. If this ideality is understood in terms of what Max Scheler described as *Idealfaktoren* ("ideal factors"), in terms of a *telos* guiding the realization of spiritual possibilities, then irony can be understood as the process of constantly relating the ought to the is—the ideal self that one ought to be to the actual imperfect self that one is.

Neither the basis of this subjective certainty that provides a purpose for one's life nor *arete* ("excellence") can be taught—directly. For *arete* was thought of as something that proceeded from within, as a moral transformation that affected the entire, integral personality.[61] To become a moral being, knowledge alone is insufficient; rather, reasoning, reflection, and deliberation must be paired with a passionate concern with becoming virtuous, with one's own existence. Without *pathos* or feeling,

Kierkegaard insists, there can be no ethical decisiveness. To be able to turn irony back upon ourselves is to realize the gap between what we ought to be and what we are. A mastered irony reveals the contradictions in our own existence—existence begins, as Kierkegaard puts it, in contradiction—and humbles us before our subjectively apprehended potentiality-for.

Ironic tension, when incorporated in moral self-consciousness, calls us back to a concern with our own existence, reminds us that we ought to seek to realize those 'spiritual' possibilities that are an expression of what is best in ourselves. What lies beyond the individual's acquaintance with his own potentiality-for becoming a self is subject to skeptical doubt. Although the ethical possibility for an individual arises in doubt, one cannot doubt that possibility for oneself. Kierkegaard understood the ethical commitment of Socrates not as a condemnation of actuality and life (as Nietzsche describes it in his *Wille zur Macht*) but as the one certainty to which Socrates clung. Perhaps, as Johannes Climacus will insist in *Concluding Unscientific Postscript,* the ethical self-existence of the individual is the only true certainty we have. Perhaps, as Socrates suggested before Nietzsche, a repetitious striving for self-mastery, for *Selbstüberwindung*, is the highest spiritual possibility that a man can endeavor to realize.

Socratic irony, when it is turned back upon the individual, is the generator of the tension of opposition, is a means by which one juxtaposes the finite and the infinite (whether it is a possible infinite being or infinite nothingness). To exist in a paradoxical relationship to a subjectively posited ideality, in objective uncertainty, in the face of one's own spiritual, existential possibilities, is to exist authentically. The individual who has become aware of the opposition between ideality (what could be or what ought to be) and actuality (immediate actuality) is one in whom I-consciousness has come to fruition, for it is precisely this juxtaposition of immediacy (which is nonlinguistic, nonconceptual) and ideality (conceptualized or linguistically expressed possibility) that entails the recognition of possibility. This confrontation of possibility in relation to the development of the self is an encounter with, as Kierkegaard puts it in *The Concept of Dread*, "the dreadful as well as the smiling,"[62] for the attempt to actualize one own's spiritual possibilities is a means by which to escape from the *cul de sac* of theoretical nihilism. But the sheer indeterminacy of possibility holds also the possibility of losing myself, of falling into the emptiness of immorality, or of endlessly seeking pleasures impossible to attain. Possibility is a double-edged sword because it not only "opens up" the hope of realizing my own unique spiritual potentialities but also generates an anxiety concerning what I *might* become. Socratic irony, as an instrument for critical analysis of the self, recalls us to what Heidegger calls "the silent power of the possible" (*die stille Kraft des Möglichen*). But, as Kierkegaard himself knew so well, the transition from conceptual-imaginative possibility to existential possibility is one of the most difficult "movements" to make, for the resolute choice to attempt to realize one's own spiritual, existential possibilities entails the assumption of full responsibility for what one is becoming. No longer does one evaporate responsibility by converting it into a theoretical question for which there are a multiplicity of alternative answers or by placing the question of responsibility at a "psychic distance," diffusing it in the colorful light of the aesthetic perspective. An ethical existence or a moral self-consciousness is precisely a condition in which one has become fully aware of a potentiality-for becoming a self by virtue of choice, decision, and action. The virtue that Socrates spoke about, Kierkegaard believed, could not be taught because it is not a doctrine, a teaching, a subject-matter; rather it is "a being-able, an exercising, an existing, an existential transformation."[63]

Kierkegaard's phenomenology of Socratic existence served as a means of interpreting the meaning of irony, of representing the nihilistic sphere of existence, of analyzing the significance of Socratic subjectivity—what Hegel described as a mere "negative moment" in the development of consciousness. Kierkegaard attempted to penetrate the underlying meaning of this *soi-disant* negative moment, this nihilism, in order to indicate the role it played in the generation of I-consciousness, inwardness, and the search for meaning through a pursuit of "concernful knowledge." He understood that theoretical nihilism was fused with a subjective sense of meaninglessness that, in turn, stimulated an

unending process of reflection that returned again and again to
the zero point of doubt. A journal entry dating from three years
before he completed his master's thesis indicates his understanding of his situation:

> What I have often suffered from was that all the doubt,
> trouble, and anguish which my real self wanted to forget in order
> to achieve a view of life, my reflective self sought to impress
> and preserve, partly as a necessary, partly as an interesting
> stage, out of fear that I should have falsely ascribed a result
> to myself.[64]

What Kierkegaard lived through is, to some extent, partially
described by Hegel in his account of "skeptical self-consciousness." While Hegel denigrates such a "confused consciousness"
as one caught in a "giddy whirl of a perpetually self-creating
disorder," he admits that skeptical self-consciousness discovers its
own freedom and knows itself as a consciousness that contains
contradictions within itself.[65] For Kierkegaard, it is precisely at
this point of the recognition of the duality of consciousness that
concernful consciousness (i.e., reflection having relevance for
one's personal existence) emerges. To be sure, the whirlwind of
the nihilism of reflection can be overcome, but not by extending
human reason beyond its limits—not by constructing a universal
rationalistic system that pretends to explain everything. The
duality of consciousness does not have only the negative meaning
that Hegel attributes to it; rather, it is condition of finite consciousness that can never be surpassed. The contradictions in the
thought and existence of a finite individual can never be mediated
or synthesized. Human existence *is* paradoxical—*is* characterized
by dialectical tension.

Corresponding to the unending dialectical reflection of skeptical self-consciousness is a subjective "absolute spiritual incapacity" characteristic of a nihilistic stage of life. The only "movement" that Kierkegaard (or the reflective nihilist) is capable of
is the ostensible movement of thought. Hence he sees Socrates
as the archetypal dialectician who "conceives everything in terms
of reflection." The phenomenology of the existence of Socrates is
an indirect communication of Kierkegaard's own nihilism, a por-

trayal of the nihilistic stage of life that, it is suggested, is perhaps a necessary stage in the personal and intellectual development of the individual. As Kierkegaard conceives of it, nihilism is, in one sense, liberating: it frees the individual from the accumulated categories of the past, and from the conventional beliefs of his own time and place and thus opens the way for a renewed reflection upon life, experience, the world, and the self from the perspective of a critical self-consciousness. In another sense, of course, nihilism is dangerous—an abyss from which the individual may never escape. Unfortunately, one of the most common ways in which human beings attempt to find a cure for their encounter with nihilism is through irrational action. A persistent, honest, and consistent "living in" a nihilistic mode of being is something that few individuals (even individuals with the spiritual strength of a Nietzsche or a Kierkegaard) can long endure. What Kierkegaard says about irony could just as well be said about a "lived" nihilism: "Irony is an abnormal growth . . . it ends by killing the individual."[66]

The ironic or nihilistic sphere of existence is a *via negativa*. It is a form of being that is a contingent possibility for any individual in any historical period in which reflective human beings live. It can have the positive function of stimulating a passionate search for meaning, purpose, and significance in regard to what is an 'object' of profound concern: one's own existence and the direction of one's own life. Nihilism dramatizes the question of the meaning of one's own life and generates a search for a firm foundation of one's existence.[67]

2
Existence and Possibility

"If I were to wish for anything, I should . . . wish for . . . the passionate sense of the possible."—Søren Kierkegaard, *Either/Or.*

"Das Dasein versteht sich selbst immer aus einer Existenz, einer Möglichkeit seiner selbst, es selbst oder nicht es selbst zu sein."—Martin Heidegger, *Sein und Zeit.*

The central category by which individual existence can be understood is that of possibility (*Mulighed*). If the realm of necessity is mathematics or logic, the realm of the probable, empirical phenomena (as in Peirce's fallibilism), then the dialectical existence of human beings falls within the realm—which of course encompasses *entia rationis,* imaginary being, and all finite entities—of the possible. The factical being (*faktisk Vaeren*) of man is characterized by contingency. Since there is contingency and potentiality in the being of man, Heidegger is correct in maintaining that "*Dasein* is its possibility" and that by virtue of this man may or may not be, may choose to become himself or not, may gain his self or lose it. The language Heidegger uses to describe *Dasein* in relation to possibility is, for the most part, that of Kierkegaard. To be sure, Kierkegaard does not say, in so many words, that man *is* his possibility. But the notions of man's fundamental potentialities—his being-possible, his projection of himself towards the realization of possibilities—are central to Kierkegaard's understanding of human development, of the "movements" of the self compromising the dialectic of life. His usual formulation is that man is a being who *has* possibilities or who is capable of encountering what he describes, in typical dramatic terms, as "the nothingness of possibility." This formulation is a conception of human spiritual possibilities that lies at the heart of Kierkegaard's philosophy of man.

Existential Possibility

The concept of existential possibility, as developed by Kierkegaard, has its philosophical roots in the Aristotelian notion of potentiality. Moreover, his account of ethical existence is a synthesis of his own conception of Socratic "inwardness" and Aristotle's accounts of choice, the relation between desire and reason, teleology, and the superimposition of Aristotle's metaphysical account of possibility and actuality upon the dialectic of man's moral development. Before discussing this neglected aspect of Kierkegaard's thought, we must first determine how he arrived at the notion of what Rosen calls (in reference to Heidegger, but the phrase is even more appropriate to Kierkegaard) "the eminence of possibility."

Contrary to William Barrett's assertion that Kierkegaard accepted the "traditional and Aristotelian" notion that actuality is prior to possibility,[1] it is clear that Kierkegaard emphasized the priority of possibility in the dialectical development of the individual. This emphasis had its roots in his attacks upon certain aspects of Hegel's thought.

One of the reasons for his attack on Hegel's systematic rationalism was his belief (a correct one, in my opinion) that a systematic, rational essentialism such as Hegel's negated or destroyed possibility. Kierkegaard contended that human existence and human actions are comprehensible only in terms of the possibility of possibility. Although he maintains that one form of possibility, that of "conceived reality," is "higher" than actuality from the standpoint of thought, he did not hold that actuality (*Virkelighed*) is prior to possibility (*Mulighed*) in the concrete, existential development of the individual. To be sure, he did obviously recognize that actuality, in one sense, is prior to possibility. That is, that actual beings are temporally prior to the generation of possible beings or that a being that 'has' possibilities is actual insofar as he 'has' being or is 'in' being. What he insists upon, however, is that in the dialectic of an individual life, in the becoming of a self, possibility is prior to actuality in the sense that one becomes (for better or worse) what one is by virtue of repeated 'movements' from possibility to actuality in temporality. On a purely ontological level, of course, an entity must already be in order to discover, encounter, or attempt to realize possibilities; but in terms of the "persistent striving" characteristic of *existence* as Kierkegaard understands it, possibility *is* prior to actuality.

Kierkegaard's conception of possibility (which is, I feel, his most important contribution to philosophy as such) must be understood in terms of his own interpretation of Aristotle as well as his appropriation of F. A. Trendelenburg's commentaries on, and interpretations of, Aristotle's writings. In his *Elements of Aristotelian Logic* (1837), *Logical Investigations* (1840), and *Historical Contribution to Philosophy* (1846/1867), Trendelenburg had been concerned not only with reviving the philosophical heritage of Aristotle but with an implied attack on Hegel. In particular, Trendelenburg emphasized the concept of motion or *kinesis* in his Aristotelian studies in direct opposition to the Hegelian dialectical principle and, in addition, he stressed the importance of purposive activity in terms of the Aristotelian teleology. More specifically, Trendelenburg argued that movement is the common essence of existence as well as of thought. In his attacks upon Hegel, Trendelenburg pointed out that Hegel tended to mistake the ostensible 'movements' of thought for "existential movement," the concrete actuality of the becoming of particular beings. As James Collins remarks, Kierkegaard was attracted to Trendelenburg not only by virtue of his criticisms of Hegelianism, but because Trendelenburg reinforced his own latent appreciation of the reality of empirical actuality.[2] Trendelenburg not only supported Kierkegaard's break with Hegel, but sent him back to a study of Aristotle, a study that provided the theoretical basis for his conception of the nature of human existence.

Kierkegaard's basic objection to Hegel's logic (ostensibly a "logic of contradiction") was that the use of the term 'transition' in logic is, strictly speaking, "chimerical." The term 'transition' refers primarily to historical phenomena or the concrete, temporal, process of becoming. Hegelian logic could not (as much as Hegel seemed to think it could) account for the process of becoming or *genesis*, and was especially unable to account for the transition from possibility to actuality in an individual being's development. In the writings of Trendelenburg and in those of Aristotle himself Kierkegaard found the existential 'categories' (what Heidegger will later call *existentialia*) by which he could attempt to provide an existential analysis of human existence. In effect, what Kierkegaard did was to appropriate and transform many of Aristotle's basic conceptions and to apply them exclusively to man.

In his *Physics* Aristotle had conceived of movement in general as a transition from possibility to actuality. Kierkegaard appropriated this notion, related it to Aristotle's conception of qualitative change or *alloiōsis*, and gave it a purely anthropomorphic meaning. For the specific kind of 'movement' that Kierkegaard was concerned with, of course, was the mode of transition from possibility to actuality that characterizes qualitative change since this could be accommodated to "historical freedom" or the capacity that the individual has to become, to change, to act in accordance with (not a universal immanent teleology over which he has no ultimate control) a subjectively posited *telos*. This mode of change, which is manifested in becoming, is an 'actual' change—a change in existence, not merely in thought. For Kierkegaard, "becoming is a change in actuality brought about by freedom."[3] It is the 'category' of movement that enables Kierkegaard to describe the activity of *existence* as a dialectical process of striving (*Straeben*) and becoming (*Vorden*). Hegel was wrong, Kierkegaard charged, in holding that necessity is a synthesis of possibility and actuality[4] insofar as the terms "possibility" and "actuality" properly refer to a "being-in-act," a being capable of action or of change. Furthermore, it is not necessity that characterizes the being of such existing individuals, but contingency and, hence, possibility. With his prowess for eclectic appropriation Kierkegaard will reintroduce the notions of necessity and possibility, relating them to the actuality of contingent individuals. That is, he will describe the existing individual as a paradoxical synthesis of necessity and possibility.

Although there are those who might believe that Kierkegaard's use of Aristotelian terminology is idiosyncratic, I do not believe there is any justification for such a view. To be sure, he does borrow concepts from Aristotle's *Metaphysics* and applies them to human existence exclusively, and not to natural beings in general, or to a large class of finite entities. However, his assertion of the priority of possibilty to actuality is not entirely foreign to some of Aristotle's formulations of this relationship. Thus, for example, Aristotle does suggest that possibility is prior to actuality in some of his references to movement and qualitative change. For, in a discussion of becoming, it is said that it is "between" being and nonbeing insofar as "what is coming to be is always intermediate between what is and what is not." How closely Kierkegaard follows such Aristotelian formulations of the process of becoming can be seen in his comments on this question in his journals. Kierkegaard avers that change—i.e., coming into existence—this actualization of a project or a possibility is a 'movement', as it were, not *between* being and nonbeing, but,

> from nonbeing to being [*ikke at vaere til at vaere*]. But this nonbeing from which it is changed must also be a kind of being [*en Art af Vaeren*], because otherwise we could not say that the subject of coming into existence remains unchanged in coming into existence. But such a being which is nevertheless a nonbeing we certainly could call possibility, and the being into which the subject of coming into existence goes by coming into existence is actuality [*Virkeligheden*].[5]

The individual's coming to be *is* intermediate between what is and what is not yet. The very futurity of the becoming of an individual suggests that the present being of that individual is not exhaustive of what he is. Hence one can say that an individual "is" what he is (what he has been up to the present and what he is at present) and is also what he is not yet, but what he is becoming. In this sense, then, the possibilities of an individual are significant aspects of his total being. The various formulations of the becoming of an individual in the forms of 'existentialism' are not only compatible with Kierkegaard's analysis of "coming-to-be" (and, ultimately, with Aristotle's conception of the genesis of any finite being), but are clearly derived from it.

In his discussion of qualitative change or *alloiōsis*, Aristotle argues that "everything that changes changes from what is po-

tentially (*on dunamei*) to what is actually (*on energeia*)."[6] This
analysis from Aristotle's *Metaphysics* is, of course, appropriated
by Kierkegaard (again, it is applied not to change in all finite
beings but to the transformations in human existence) and transformed into what he calls the "qualitative dialectic" that characterizes the becoming of an individual in terms of changes in
attitude, comportment, feeling, belief, or action. Since the individual is, according to Kierkegaard, constantly in a process of
becoming (*Vorden*), the activity of an individual (whether mental or physical) is characterized by a continuous number of actual
transitions that are possible because of the volitional self-pro-
jection of individuals toward the openness of the future by virtue
of a 'movement' from possibility to actuality in temporality.
Every decisive, significant change in an individual's life is
brought to fruition by the reflective recognition of conceptual or
imaginative possibilities and the endeavor to actualize a possibility (or a number of possibilities) *in concreto*. If one merely
reflects upon alternative possibilities without interest or concern
(as in ironic reflection), if one entertains possibilities as curious
hypotheses, then decisive choice is precluded. To be sure, those
alternative possibilities upon which we deliberate are those that
are within our power to bring to actualization. Although Kierkegaard himself does not, so far as I know, explicitly describe the
kind of possibilities that are the 'objects' of concernful reflection,
I believe that he thinks of them, for the most part, as *imagined*
possibilities. For, when an individual is reflecting upon alternative modes of choice, states of being, or action, he tends, in
general, to imagine what condition he will be in or to imagine
what he will do. Before we act, of course, the alternatives we
are imagining are, in a manner of speaking, theoretical possibilities. In this sense, there are no such things as *concrete* possibilities; that is, unless we mean by this the *actual* conception or
imagination of a possibility by an individual. But in such an instance, it is not the possibility itself that is concrete (i.e., a particular, temporal occurrence in the life history of an individual)
but the consciousness of the possibility.

The concept of movement refers to the *nisus* of the self that
is characteristic of the qualitative dialectic of life, whose mo-

mentum is sustained by the *pathos*-filled, volitional self-commit-ment of the psychophysical individual. Here, again, Kierkegaard follows Aristotle insofar as he argues that action requires desire and deliberate choice. Since for Kierkegaard there are real, not merely apparent or illusory, choices open to man, the refusal of a possibility that is one's own (what Heidegger calls an *eigentlich* or "authentic" possibility) is a refusal to take up responsibility to become oneself or is a yielding to an irresolution that will, in turn, make resolute choice more difficult on a fresh occasion of choice. Since "everything is uncertain" in finite existence, we can never know with apodictic certainty that the possibility we attempt to actualize is the 'highest' possibility for us. In this sense, existence entails risk and even in faith the only certitude the individual has is a "subjective" certainty.

The process of existence can be described in general terms as a 'movement' of the individual towards the realization of unique possibilities by means of qualitative transitions from possibility to actuality in temporality and uncertainty. The contingency of the future is the condition for the possibility of finite freedom and for the "freedom of possibility." Kierkegaard emphasizes not so much 'freedom of choice' as what may be called man's primor-dial freedom—that is, his freedom for possibility. For a choice, before it is made, is a possibility. Finally, this freedom for possi-bility is rooted in human existence insofar as rational, reflective human beings have a potentiality-for (*kunnen*) the self-deter-mined realization of possibilities.

It is clear, I believe, that Kierkegaard did not accept the view that actuality is prior to possibility in the subjective teleology of human existence. In the spiritual development of man possibility is prior to actuality insofar as the movement of the individual is towards the future or the realm of possibility. William James, in his *Essays in Pragmatism*, makes an allusion to the Danish thinker who held that life is understood backwards, but it must be lived forward; the allusion was, of course, to Kierkegaard.[7] In any event in regard to what Kierkegaard calls the "teleological dialectic" of the becoming of the individual, the 'category' of the possible is essential. However, this is not the extent of the role that possibility plays in what may be called Kierkegaard's philosophical anthropology. For, the concept of existential possibility ultimately has its origin in Kierkegaard's interpretation (and transformation) of Aristotle's concept of potentiality or his onto-logical understanding of possibility.

Potentiality and Possibility

In the Homeric age the Greek term *dunamis* basically meant power or might in the sense of bodily strength. In time, *dunamis* came to mean power in the sense of political or economic influ-ence. In the *Theatetus* Plato uses the same word to refer to "bodily faculties." There is, however, a more interesting use of this term in the *Sophist* (247e), where it is said that

> everything which has by nature the capacity of either doing something else or undergoing the action of some other thing however insignificant, infinitesimal or infrequent—really exists. I therefore propose this definition: beings, inasmuch as they are, are naught but potentialities.[8]

Since finite beings are, in their process of becoming, "poten-tialities," they *are,* insofar as they are beings-in-act, actualities as well. The general notion that a finite individual, especially a self-conscious being, is a synthesis of potentiality and actuality is one that will appear and reappear throughout the history of Western thought (in different guises to be sure), up to and including the present. Even a philosopher who prefers to talk about "intelligent capacities" is still fundamentally dealing with concepts that arose out of the writings of Plato and Aristotle.

Whereas Plato does not develop an overt metaphysics of po-tentiality and actuality, he certainly left to Aristotle the puzzling problem of change, a problem that Aristotle dealt with in terms of the categories of possibility (or potentiality) and actuality. While Aristotle confined the notions of possibility and actuality to his *Metaphysics* (and did not apply them where it would have been likely for him to do so, that is, in his *Nicomachean Ethics*), he did at times relate the concept of potentiality to morally rele-vant action. Thus, for example, in his *Topica* (126a–126b) he remarks that

You must also see whether your opponent has put anything blameworthy or to be avoided in the category [*kategoreitai*] of capacity [*dunamin*] or capable [*dunaton.*] . . . a capacity is always among the things worthy of choice [*aireton*].[9]

At other times, Aristotle seems to fall back upon more traditional concepts of potentialities, those that referred to gratuitous goods or values that the individual acquired without his own initiative. In his *Magna Moralia,* for example, he refers to "potentialities" (*dunameis*) such as authority, riches, strength, and beauty that the morally good man can make use of in his life. Such "goods" or potentialities, however, are those that are "conferred on us by fortune [*Magna Moralia,* 1183b–1184a]."[10] Quite naturally, Aristotle does not emphasize this arbitrary granting of potentialities in his ethics (though he does make passing reference to them). One reason for this is that it seems to undermine an ethical exhortation to strive to acquire moral and intellectual virtues. It is obvious that the gratuitous inheritance, as it were, of what Aristotle calls (in his *Nicomachean Ethics*) "the faculties given us by nature" gives some human beings an arbitrary advantage over others.[11]

As I shall try to indicate, this reference to man's "original" capacities is one that is central to Kierkegaard's emphasis upon what he assumes to be man's primordial potentiality-for. To my mind, Aristotle's stress upon the acquisition of moral virtues (*aretai*) through repeated practice, his view that our moral dispositions are formed (basically) as a result of corresponding activities, had a profound effect upon Kierkegaard's general understanding of the ethical development of the individual. Indeed, I believe that it could be argued that the paradigm for Kierkegaard's conception of the centrality of repetition for ethical existence is found in Aristotle's assertion (in the *Nicomachean Ethics*) concerning the role of repetition (*anapalin*) in acquiring moral virtue.[12]

The point, at any rate, of referring to some of Aristotle's uses of the term "potentiality" is to show that Kierkegaard's appropriation of this notion (especially in regard to what he calls man's primitive potentially-for ethical self-realization) is neither peculiar nor idiosyncratic. In point of fact, the following passage from the *Nicomachean Ethics* indicates, I believe, the *point d'appui* for two of Kierkegaard's basic assumptions about man, namely, the concept of the moral indeterminism of the individual and the notion that man can return to possibilities that have already been 'there' in the being of man. In discussing the acquisition of *aretê* Aristotle remarks that "the virtues . . . are engendered in us neither by nature nor yet in violation of nature; nature gives us the capacity to receive them, and this capacity is brought to maturity by habit."[13] As we shall see, this is only one instance in which Aristotle influenced Kierkegaard's conception of the role of the category of possibility (or potentiality) in human life and his general conception of the nature of moral development in the teleological dialectic of human existence.

Before we discuss other relationships between Aristotle's concept of potentiality and Kierkegaard's concept of possibility, a digression must be made in order to indicate how Kierkegaard believed that the question of subjective, existential possibilities arise in terms of his schematic phenomenology of individual development.

With the dissolution of the aesthetic mode of life or the self-negation of the nihilism of reflection the individual is forced to look within himself for positive, affirmative, meaningful goals for his life. So long as an individual is engaged either in the constant pursuit of an impossible eternalized moment (as in aestheticism) or in the unending (or apparently unending) dialectical process of reflection that brackets or ignores concernful possibilities, a subjective commitment to any one possibility is precluded. To be sure, both the nihilist and the aesthete can continue to live on, to be engaged in a variety of activities, to live without direction, purpose, or meaning. But Kierkegaard believed that there is a price to pay for such modes of being. That price is a profound feeling of despair or hopelessness. Furthermore, the nihilist and the aesthete are losing what is no doubt the only opportunity they will have to become a self. And it is what Kierkegaard calls the "physical-temporal urgency of actuality" that does not allow individuals the luxury of an indefinite postponement of decisiveness in regard to their own existence. Not to have been decisive in regard to one's own life is to lose a possibility, as Kierkegaard puts it, that, if death is imminent, may be lost forever. While Kierkegaard understood that the reflection upon one's death can be enervating at times—in his journals he laments: "what is this life, where the only certainty is the only thing one cannot with any certainty learn anything about: death; for when I am, death is not, and when death is, I am not"[14]—he also believed that reflection upon the possibility of death can serve the function of recalling one from casual nihilism, from an inauthentic refusal to endeavor to become a self. Ironically, the possibility of our death intensifies the meaning of our present existence, generates an 'interest', a concern with what we are doing with our lives. Kierkegaard seems to have agreed with Schopenhauer that death is the X-factor in human life, without which man would scarcely philosophize.

A disinterested use of reason, a speculative use of reason, is a detached consideration of a variety of conceptual possibilities, a theoretical mode of reasoning that carries the individual from the realm of the personal to the realm of the impersonal. While a disinterested use of reason is an important activity for man, a means by which his thought can range over the vast, complex panorama of diverse phenomena, Kierkegaard thought that a corrective to the speculative use of reason (or, today, the analytical use of reason) was necessary. The subjective perspective is not, by any means, the only one that man can or ought to adopt. Kierkegaard indicated this in his *rational* phenomenology of the various modalities of despair in his *The Sickness unto Death* and in his rational, analytical description of the 'movements' of faith and the meaning of faith in his *Concluding Unscientific Postscript.* If it is maintained that in these works he approaches the questions he deals with from the perspective of his own personality, the same could be said, with almost equal justice, of a work such as Wittgenstein's *Philosophical Investigations,* in which it is said that the problems that arise by virtue of a "misinterpretation of our forms of language" have "their roots . . . as deep in us as the forms of our language."[15] While Wittgenstein and his followers are, of course, primarily concerned with the forms of our language (*die Formen unserer Sprache*), Kierkegaard was more concerned with the form of life (*Lebensform*) or the activity (*Tätigkeit*) of which the speaking of language (*das Sprechen der Sprache*) is a part.

What is lacking in *objective* thinking (despite its obvious value) is subjective concern, the turning of reflection upon one's own immediate existence. What is especially needed in order to choose a life of ethical self-consciousness is "concernful knowledge." "Concern," Kierkegaard says in *The Sickness unto Death*, "implies relationship to life, to the reality of personal existence."[16] The question is, how does this concern emerge in the life of a reflective individual?

The key to understanding Kierkegaard's concept of self-reflective existence is found in his *Johannes Climacus or, De Omnibus Dubitandum Est*. In this work he is again opposed to Hegel's treatment of actuality or actual life (*Virkelighed*) as merely a moment that is incorporated into an abstract dialectic. For, an existing individual has an interest (*interesse*) in his existence, in his decisions and choices, in the concrete specificity of the actuality in which he finds himself. To paraphrase the Heidegger of *Sein und Zeit*, man is a being who, in his being, has that being (*not* Being) as an issue for himself. This self-concern Kierkegaard describes in terms of the 'category' of interest. Now, the basic meaning of *interesse* is "to be between." In another sense, it can mean "to be present" insofar as a consciousness attends to or heeds something at hand. This use of *interesse* corresponds to recent intellectualistic conceptions of "concern" as heeding or paying attention to something. Thus Gilbert Ryle, in his *The Concept of Mind*, equates care with "attending" to something, as one attends to a task at hand. Care means to think about what one is doing. Ryle's account of care does not even mention emotional modes of care, or what I would call the emotional basis of care.[17] Kierkegaard, at any rate, finds this mode of 'interest' in mathematics, science in general, aesthetics, and speculative philosophy. That Kierkegaard included aesthetics in this category seems somewhat odd. Perhaps this might be explained in terms of the influence of Kantian aesthetics on his thought. That is, the general notion that aesthetic appreciation is a kind of "disinterested interest." Or perhaps he was thinking of his own characterization of the aesthetic point of view as one that involved the cultivation of aloofness, detachment, and the absence of commitment to anything.

Aside from these two meanings of *interesse* there is the concept of *interesse* as "to be concerned." This mode of interest refers to an individual's concrete existence and to ethical or religious decisions. In an intellectualist sense of the term, interest applies to a kind of curiosity about something, or a purely contemplative, detached mode of intellection. In contemporary terms this mode of 'interest' may be described as the chess game theory of philosophy, the 'moves' one makes in an argument being compared to moves in a chess game, *et cetera*. Nevertheless, it is clear that the category of interest applies primarily to a reflective concern with one's own being, with what one is and what one is becoming, with alternatives that matter to the individual. Insofar as *interesse* is taken to mean "to be concerned" (the meaning that Kierkegaard, as we might expect, emphasized) it is obvious that it is the source for Heidegger's conception of concern (*Sorge*) as a fundamental *existentialia* of *Dasein*.

Although Karl Löwith remarks that, for Kierkegaard, *interesse* refers to that which is between "theoretical thought" and "reality,"[18] this is not completely accurate in terms of Kierkegaard's interpretation of the being of an existing individual. While I will have occasion to refer to this question later, I may mention here that, for Kierkegaard, *interesse* does, in one sense, refer to the relationship between consciousness and "ideality" (what Löwith calls "theoretical thought") and actuality (not reality). However, the meaning of this relationship is not quite so transparent as Löwith seems to suggest, for it is the existing self that is "in between" ideality and actuality, that is the *locus* of a specific interest. Before exploring this issue further we must continue to elucidate the conceptions of interest, consciousness, ideality, and actuality.

Phenomenologically, the emergence of consciousness occurs when there is an awareness of the disparity between ideality and actuality. This sense of opposition (which, as we have already seen, is characteristic of irony) is generated by virtue of the juxtaposition of concrete, empirical immediacy (practically corresponding to C. S. Peirce's phenomenological category of second-ness) and the universality of conceptual-linguistic ideality. Consciousness is fundamentally an intentional act of relating diverse relata. Specifically, consciousness (in its phenomenologically most primitive mode) relates actuality and ideality, the immediacy of experience and the conceptualization (or linguistic expression) of that experience. Immediacy is essentially an encounter with non-conceptual, extralinguistic "beings." Again, in C. S. Peirce's terms, it is the irrefragable sense of actuality, the preconceptual, prelin-guistic sense of contact with alterity.[19] However, a caution must be introduced here insofar as Peirce conceives of secondness in terms of the ego's encounter with the nonego. For Kierkegaard, the existing individual himself is a lived actuality that is conscious of itself in its own actuality. The brute facticity encountered in sensory experience is not in itself intelligible, except insofar as it is 'mediated' by conceptual or linguistic determination. However, the actuality of the self is that which is 'in between' linguistic-conceptual ideality and sensory actuality. The actual, for Kierkegaard, is the "particular instance" ("this here man," as Aristotle would put it, rather than 'man'). Since we have not yet "reflected" upon it, what Kierkegaard refers to as the "actual world" is neither true nor false. It is, as Kierkegaard puts it, simply "here." From a phenomenological standpoint, according, to Kierkegaard's account of the matter, there is no *ego* that encounters (as in Peirce's view) the other. I-consciousness follows upon what Kierkegaard describes as the emergence of consciousness; indeed, it is not even entailed by consciousness; as *reflection* alone, it is disinterested, impersonal.[20] The process of relating the ego to the nonego already presupposes the emergence of *self-consciousness.*

Contrary to the expectations or prejudices of those who associate the name of Kierkegaard with irrationality, Kierkegaard himself was quite clear concerning his own conception of consciousness. Indeed, it is a conception that is central to his concept of the self and what he calls the "intermediary" mode of being of the existing individual. Although the question of Kierkegaard's understanding of consciousness or 'mind' (*Bevisthed*) will be dealt with in my attempt to show the relationship between

Kierkegaard's conception of self-consciousness and the ethical mode of existence, a number of details in his treatment of the emergence of consciousness and its fundamental nature must be touched upon here because they are closely related to the concept of possibility.

Whereas Kierkegaard uses Hegelian terminology in his *Johannes Climacus* (a name he will use as one of his pseudonyms, probably derived from the name of the author of a sixth-century book entitled *Scala Paradisi,* by one Johannes Climacus or "John the Climber"), he is concerned to make some important distinctions that serve to provide a philosophical basis for his conception of the consciousness of the individual. Thus, for example, Kierkegaard is concerned with the relationship between actuality (or the immediacy of the actual world encountered in prereflective perception) and ideality (the "thought world" or the realms of conceptualization and speech). Basically, he maintains that consciousness emerges, as it were, by virtue of bringing actuality and ideality together in contradistinction. Thus, in talking about actuality an individual brings together the ideality of conceptualization (as expressed in overt speech acts) and the immediacy of actuality. Consciousness is not identical with reflection, for Kierkegaard, since reflection implies that phenomena *can* be brought into relationship; we may say, then, that reflection is the *possibility* of consciousness. Reflection may be described as a rather diffuse generalized awareness that could be called, for want of a better expression, a 'prephilosophical consciousness.'

Kierkegaard avers that neither actuality nor ideality are, in themselves, consciousness. However, consciousness is not, strictly speaking, present without the awareness of the opposition between actuality and ideality. Consciousness is the activity of relating these two categories of relata. Although Kierkegaard does not explicitly refer to intentionality, I believe his interpretation of consciousness implies that there is, in the act of consciousness he describes, the implicit notion that consciousness intends the 'objects' of ideality and actuality. Furthermore, it engages in the intentional process of relating the two relata that are intended by what Kierkegaard calls its "energizing force." At one point, Kierkegaard formulates the "classifications of consciousness" in terms of a propositional analysis. Thus he remarks that when I say "I was conscious of such and such a sense-impression" we can discern references to "consciousness," "I," and the actuality that is an object of consciousness (i.e., the sense impression). Now, while reflection (as Kierkegaard understands it) is disinterested, consciousness, by virtue of its relational being, entails an interest or concern. The intensification of consciousness occurs when the relational activity of consciousness involves personal interest. Concernful knowledge involves a heightened sense of self-consciousness, a sense of the contradiction between the two relata.[21] Although all existential thinking is characterized by this dynamic tension in consciousness by virtue of the attempt to relate ideality to actuality, the paradigmatic instances of concern, for Kierkegaard, are found in ethical self-consciousness and religious consciousness. The intensification of ethical consciousness is brought about because of the dialectical tension between the conceptual or imaginary ideality (what one ought to be) and the actuality of the present self or, as Kierkegaard will call it in *Either/Or*, one's own imperfect actuality. It is by means of speech that man is able to transcend immediacy; if man were unable to speak, he would be immured in immediacy. By implication, he seems to collapse the distinction between conceptualization and speech. This would seem to be too hasty since (despite the difficulty of the question) one may hold that concepts are not identical with speech (or the inscription of a natural language) but are expressed in speech and written language. By implication, Kierkegaard does sometimes seem to say that language is the expression of a "thought world" or of conceptualization. At any rate, it is clear that whether we are referring to ideality in terms of concepts or of language, Kierkegaard is committed to the view that there is not only a relationship of opposition between an ideality (e.g., 'man') and an actuality (e.g., "this here man" in a spatiotemporal context), but there is an implicit asymptotic relationship between language and the concrete immediacy of the world. Because of this, as Kierkegaard was forced to admit, there cannot be, strictly speaking, a "philosophy of the concrete" or an existential science (*Existentiel-Videnskab*). Thus all existential thought is an approximation-process, an impressionistic, phenomenological (though not, of course, in the Husserlian sense of the term) activity that is essentially paradoxical. For Kierkegaard neither logic (not even a 'contradictory' Hegelian logic) nor language can "picture" the world of actuality.

When we attempt to translate our experiences of actuality into concepts or language we are confronted with opposition or paradoxical relationship. Thus there is an opposition between what is experienced or encountered and our linguistic description of what is experienced. This is regarded as an opposition by Kierkegaard because he held that when I express concrete actuality or immediacy in language I am not truly expressing that immediacy at all. Language does not and cannot picture immediacy because it transforms concrete specificity into linguistic universality. No proposition that is a putative truth-claim about "the world" or any phenomenon can convey this information without using universal terms. And, as Heidegger has pointed out in *Sein und Zeit*, our simplest assertions employ a form of the verb "to be" and hence entail an implicit understanding of Being.[22]

Language is a form of ideality, an expression of concepts that is clearly not identical with actuality or immediately experienced phenomena. If we assume that a picture is a thought and that an assertion is an act of saying or outwardly thinking that such and such is the case in actuality, we can only stipulate or assume that there is a relationship of correspondence between language and actuality; strictly speaking, we do not *know* this at all. Kierkegaard raises the question of the relationship between language and the "world" of actuality in such a way as to undermine the claim that there is, in fact, a correspondence between language and the immediately experienced presentations to which language refers. Perhaps we can say that only by projecting an "ideality" into the realm of actuality would we then be able to say that thought or language pictures that actuality. Of course, from Kierkegaard's point of view this would be illicit.

It would seem that language is not experienced actuality; rather, it is that by which we describe, classify, label, and order our experiences. Although we inevitably endeavor to talk about

immediacy, about what is there, this does not mean that the
actual ontological structure of what is there (or what is encountered) is conditioned by, or determined by, how we *talk* about
the world. If language is an expression of a form of life, then
this 'ideality' would, in all probability, reflect or preserve the way
in which beings engaged in this *Lebensform* interpret the actuality they experience. In this regard, it seems that generally accepted ontologies of a historical epoch seem to influence per-
vasively how man understands himself and the world in which
he finds himself. Kierkegaard's skepticism concerning the relationship between language and the world is one that was shared
at one time by Moritz Schlick, who remarked in his *Allgemeine
Erkenntnislehre* that

> the judgment is something completely different from that which
> is judged. . . . It is not like that which is judged. . . . For the
> concepts occurring in the judgment are certainly not of the same
> nature as the real objects which they designate, and the relations
> among concepts are not like the relations of things.[23]

Despite the asymptotic relationship between thought (and
consequently language) and actuality, Kierkegaard, of course,
sought to transmit his existential communications by means of
language. In this regard, as I have mentioned, he was quite
aware that a philosophy of the concrete is not literally possible,
that "no theory can adequately embrace the concrete." Hence
he was engaged in the paradoxical task of trying to 'show' what
language would tend to hide or disguise. He did this by virtue
of Hegelian phenomenologies of the various stages of life, existential 'categories', and an impressionistic literary description
that seems so offensive to official philosophers. He avoided a systematic approach to an analysis of the dialectic of existence, at
tempting to convey, as best he could, the specificity of the modes
of being that are possible for an individual. Language can be
used to point to concrete existence, but it cannot literally describe that existence because it universalizes whatever it describes.
A philosophy of existence must ineluctably bear an asymmetrical
relationship to existence itself.

If neither concepts nor language can be said to picture actuality in a literal sense, this is also true, *a fortiori,* of logic as well. Specifically, Kierkegaard charged, Hegelian logic was inadequate for a description of the historical becoming of particular actualities. To be sure, he admitted (in *Johannes Climacus*) that there is an identity of being and thought in mathematics and logic. But neither mathematics nor logic have anything to do with "existence in the sense of daily life." In the case of a Hegelian 'dynamic logic' it only appears that logic is appropriate for a description of the "contradictory" tendencies in actuality. For even if one were to grant to Hegel the possibility of describing some natural process (e.g., chemical synthesis) in terms of a logic of contradiction, it would seem odd to equate or fuse cognitive synthesis and material synthesis. Nevertheless, Kierkegaard charged that man in his complex being-in-process can never be completely subsumed under the simple unity of the abstract notion. Even a Hegelian logic cannot be used to explicate the historical phenomenon of the becoming of an individual. The ostensible transitions of logic are chimerical. Movement or repeated transitions from possibility to actuality in time is not possible in logic.[24]

The dialectical process of movement in the actuality of an individual's life is a qualitative dialectic; it is unlike the quantitative dialectic of logic (if such it can be called). Kierkegaard notes in his journals that the absolute distinction between qualitative and quantitative logic must be borne in mind because logic is a quantitative or modal dialectic whereas existential becoming is a qualitative dialectic.[25] Logical relations are essential relations and not actual, concrete relationships. Kierkegaard charges that it is sheer superstition to assume in logic that from the continuation of something purely quantitative something qualitatively new could emerge. The Hegelian inference from quantity to quality can only be made within the circle of his logic alone and cannot be the basis of a transcendence of conceptual being to actuality. To be sure, Kierkegaard does not deny that conceptual thinking is dialectical; but he does insist that it is basically hypothetical, dealing with conceptual possibilities. *Kinesis* cannot be characterized by necessity insofar as it "belongs" neither to possibility as such nor to actuality as such. The contingent actuality of an individual precludes his being encompassed, as it were, by an ostensible dialectic of necessity. In regards to an existing individual, he is a being whose being is characterized by contingency or possibility not necessity; the 'movements' he makes are themselves contingent or possible; his projective 'movement' toward the future is a 'movement' toward the possible and toward the realization of possibilities. As in the case of Aristotle's account of moral development, there is no necessity that the individual realize his potentialities; there is no necessity that he acquire a virtue that it is possible for him to acquire. For Hegel, however, the movements characterizing the development of an individual are phases in a process that is dominated (ultimately) by necessity. Kierkegaard's basic question is, how can the progressus of the historical development of an individual be contingent and, in some mysterious way, necessary as well? Kierkegaard avers that "the change of coming into existence [of what was possible] is the change of actuality. In coming into existence the possible becomes the actual . . . everything which can come into existence shows in this very way that it is not the necessary."[26] While this does not, of course, demonstrate the logical impossibility of the necessitarian form of the becoming of an individual, it does suggest that the changes that man can initiate in his own self-development have the form of contingency.

While Kierkegaard's notion of possibility is, I believe, basically derived from that of Aristotle, there are, of course, some echoes of the Hegelianism that he never successfully purged from his thought. Thus Hegel's view (found, for the most part, in his *Science of Logic*) that the real is initially conceived of as contingency (*Zufälligkeit*), that the real contains within itself the negation of its immediacy (i.e., possibility),[27] is consonant with some of Kierkegaard's assertions about possibility. It must be pointed out, however, that Hegel conceives of the process of actuality as the realization of an inherent necessity. For Kierkegaard there is no inherent law that determines the self-development of the real. Hegel's notion of contingency seems to be merely a kind of conceptual illusion; if we *truly* understood the dialectical 'movement' of thought, we would see that, in fact, there is no contingency at all. Futhermore, he disagrees with

Hegel in regard to the notion that the *knowing* subject is the true actuality. For the cognitive-emotive existing subject, a being who acts or is a being capable of action, is the only real actuality. To be sure, Kierkegaard does generally agree with Hegel insofar as he holds that it is only by the negation of the negations in one's self that one is capable of self-development. However, he avers that possibilities are not realized by some immanent rational process nor are they made actual by virtue of an immanent dialectical process governed by necessity. The existence of an actual being (i.e., a self-reflective actual being) is itself suffused, as it were, by possibility: its coming-to-be was not necessary, its present existence is not necessary, and its future being is, though possible, not necessary. The possibility that Hegel refers to in his *Science of Logic* is ultimately only a mode of conceptual possibility. Although Hegel *wanted* to talk about lived actuality, about the dialectical relationship between possibility and actuality, he invariably tended to diffuse his analyses in terms of what he called the "essentiality of thought." The contingencies and possibilities of individual existence are continually annulled by virtue of the necessitarian form of dialectical thinking. While Kierkegaard made use of the notion of conceived possibility—declaring, in fact, that all conceptualization is a transformation into conceptual possibility—he also desired to analyze the nature of one's own possibilities—one's own immediate relationship to the multiplicity of open possibilities. He desired to view possibility not only from the standpoint of abstract thought, but from the perspective of lived experience, from the perspective of the individual who is a synthesis of possibility and actuality.

The "movements" characterizing the self-development of an individual (in the limited sphere in which he is capable of effecting that development) are contingent, not necessary. The potentialities that an individual has may not, of course, be realized in the life history of that individual. Indeed, the central potentiality that a rational individual has—the potentiality-for-being-itself—is not necessarily realized in the lifetime of this individual. As in the case of Heidegger, Kierkegaard tended (a) either to collapse the distinction between potentiality and possibility or (b) to derive possibility from potentiality. In *Sein und*

Zeit Heidegger remarks: "In terms of its *possibility*, *Dasein* is already a potentiality for-Being-its-Self."[28] The decision to strive to become a self is the realization of a possibility that one has already had. However, one could not act upon this fundamental possibility if one did not have the potentiality-for such a possibility. For a reflective, self-conscious individual capable of understanding, possibility is rooted in a primitive sense of indeterminate potentiality. Such a notion is by no means alien to Aristotle's implicit conception of the ontological structure of finite beings. Indeed, Kierkegaard's view that the possible emerges from the "sphere of potentiality" is, in all probability, derived from his understanding of Aristotle's concept of potentiality. In order to see how Kierkegaard could have applied Aristotle's metaphysical categories to the dialectical development of an individual life, it is necessary to read certain passages in the *Metaphysics* and the *Nicomachean Ethics* as if one were reading a palimpsest.

While there is in both Greek and Latin an etymological basis for the assumption of an intimate relationship between potentiality and possibility (e.g., Aristotle uses the term *dunaton* for both the "possible" and the "potential" and the Latin *possibile*—which Quintillian equates with *dunaton*—is derived from *posse* or *po* + *esse*, "power to be"), the philosophical support for this assumption is found in the writings of Aristotle. However, the relationship between the spiritual or moral potentialities of man and the metaphysical concept of potentiality is one that is not emphasized by Aristotle himself even though it can be extrapolated from his writings. Kierkegaard himself, of course, did seem to understand the implications of many of Aristotle's metaphysical analyses for a description of the subjective teleology of human existence, especially ethical self-development.

In his *Metaphysics* Aristotle makes a distinction between what he calls "rational potencies" and "irrational potencies" in his general analyses of the meaning of potentiality.[29] Inanimate entities are possessed of irrational potencies insofar as they produce only one result (e.g., heat produces heat, the salutary produces health, etc.) or passively undergo various processes. Beings that possess rational potencies, on the other hand, are those that have not only the kind of potentiality that Aristotle characterizes as "the power of being affected" by something (what may be described as an empirical, dispositional property) but are also capable of producing contrary effects and of acting in accordance with a rational principle or a *logos*. Although Aristotle does not explicitly say that the paradigmatic being possessing rational potencies is man, many of his illustrations of beings capable of bringing such potencies to fruition refer to human action. To be sure, he refers to physical action (and, hence, to what it is empirically possible for an individual to do) or a capability for overt physical behavior. But what he does say about beings that have 'rational potencies' is interesting in the light of the language used to describe the being of man in the writings not only of Kierkegaard but of Heidegger and Sartre as well. Thus, for example, when describing a rational being capable of intentional action or 'movement', Aristotle remarks that it is possible that a being may be capable of being and yet not be and may be capable of not being and yet be. The ambiguous character of the becoming of an individual as well as the projective *nisus* towards the "not-yet" find their origins not in what is usually described as "obscure" German philosophy but in Aristotle's attempt to describe the nature of entities possessing rational potencies. The philosophical language of Kierkegaard's existentialism and Heidegger's phenomenological ontology would not have been possible without Aristotle's *Metaphysics*.

In numerous specific references to beings capable of intentional action in the *Metaphysics* one can find the source for Kierkegaard's analysis of the becoming of an individual. In his *Journals* Kierkegaard practically appropriates *in toto* assertions such as the following: "A being is capable of doing something if there is nothing impossible in its having the actuality of that of which it is said to have the potentiality." Even Kierkegaard's analysis of possibility (or potentiality) and choice is one that can be discerned in Aristotle's writings by means of a conflation of assertions in the *Metaphysics* (especially Book Theta) and in the *Ethics*. Despite some of his remarks in the *Metaphysics*, Aristotle himself was led, *mutatis mutandis*, to attribute rational powers or potentialities to man alone. This is clear, for example,

when he discusses the activity of beings that can produce movement rationally or in accordance with a reasoned teleology.
Whereas nonrational potencies appear to be subject to necessity
(*anagke*), this is not the case in regard to beings possessing rational powers. For rational action requires that something be
decisive, namely desire (*orexin*) or deliberate choice (*pro-
airesin*).[30] Now we know that Aristotle cannot attribute rational
powers or rational 'potencies' to finite beings other than man
because he explicitly states in his *Ethics* that only a rational,
mature man is capable of choice (*proairesis*); neither irrational
animals nor children are truly capable of choice.[31] Indeed, Aristotle not only maintained that man alone is capable of choice (and
hence of rational action) but in the *Magna Moralia* he held that
'true action' can be ascribed only to man.[32] One can see that Kierkegaard's emphasis upon man's fundamental potentiality-for
(*kunnen*) possibilities, rational choice, and rational action is not,
as is sometimes suggested, based upon an irrationalistic concept of
freedom, but is a recrudescence of Aristotle's conception of the
finite freedom of man. Although there are a number of other
parallels between Kierkegaard's description of the ethical development of the individual and specific assertions in Aristotle's
Nicomachean Ethics, I will refer to them in the context of an
analysis of what Kierkegaard called the dialectic of choice.

A reflective individual has the capacity to understand that he
has possibilities (not only what Heidegger calls the "worldly"
possibilities that dominate practical life) that are uniquely his
own and that are significant insofar as their realization (or the
pursuit of their realization) can bring continuity, history, and
meaning to one's life. Man has, Kierkegaard believed, a fundamental sense of a capacity for moral excellence.[33] In order to
become a self the individual must cultivate a potentiality for
moral self-consciousness; he must repeatedly strive to become
the 'ideal' self he knows he ought to be. Kierkegaard argued, by
indirection, that the attempt to evade the ethical (*ethisk*) possibility is a turning away from one's own highest possibility, a
falling into nihilism, aestheticism, despair, cynicism, a mode of
being that the individual knows to be that of a "false self." Even
within what R. D. Laing calls the "false-self system" the indi-

vidual cannot entirely escape the subjective knowledge that he has allowed himself to become what he ought not to be.[34]

As is the case in Heidegger's ontological transformation of Kierkegaard's conception of ethical self-existence, an individual who falls into inauthenticity can never entirely escape the realization that it is possible for him to become an authentic self. The ethical possibility can indeed be evaded or avoided; but, as Kierkegaard insists, once the question of the possibility of becoming a morally self-conscious individual is raised, one cannot doubt this possibility. To paraphrase Kant's dictum, if one knows that he can be what he ought to be (from a moral point of view), then he ought to endeavor to be what he ought to be. A morally self-conscious individual should not attempt to take upon himself a global sense of moral responsibility; it is difficult enough to become an authentic self. The beginning of the recognition of the ethical possibility is, then, a subjective self-knowledge of one's potentiality for becoming a self.

Basically, Kierkegaard agrees with Aristotle insofar as he maintained that moral virtues are neither implanted in man by nature nor in violation of nature. Aristotle held that 'nature' only provides the capacity for virtue, a capacity that can be brought to fruition only by *praxis*. Kierkegaard focuses his attention upon our possibility (or potentialities) for ethical development because it is in morally relevant behavior and (more importantly) in choice that the character of the individual is formed. In the limited sphere in which we are capable of choosing what it is within our power to do, our 'movement' toward self-realization is manifested. Kierkegaard also agreed with Aristotle that authentic moral self-being is, despite the contingency of our existence and despite our hedonistic proclivities, a potentiality that every rational man can seek to realize in a finite existence. To attempt to deny our potentiality for an ethical existence is to fall into what Sartre called "bad faith." Our knowledge of our own state of being (*pace* the behaviorists) is intimate and ultimately inescapable. Although there are, indeed, states of consciousness that exhibit some publicly observable behavioral criteria, our own subjective sense of the distance between what we know we ought to be and what we are in fact is an important aspect of the self to which we do, indeed, have privileged access. The reflection that is characteristic of a turn towards the ethical possibility is not a reflection upon an object—is not objective knowledge (*Videns*); it is a reflection, as Kierkegaard put it in his journals, upon the ethical "communication" itself: a communication of existential capability or potentiality.[35] The knowledge required in order to live within the ethical sphere of existence is not objective knowledge but a self-knowledge that Kierkegaard believed was possible at least as an approximation-process.

The essential possibility for Kierkegaard is the possibility of bringing to actualization one's own potentiality-for becoming a self. This might be called man's original possibility or the potentiality that enables one to be free for choice. In self-reflective knowledge one discovers any number of ontic possibilities for oneself as well as a potentiality for good or for evil. The concernful knowledge characterized by *interesse*, the concernful reflection upon what I am and what I am becoming, turns the individual back upon himself and a process of dialectical deliberation emerges. Although one deliberates, as Aristotle said, about the possible, deliberation in itself is insufficient for commitment or a decision to live in accordance with a subjectively posited *telos*. Indeed, excessive deliberation tends to lead to doubt. But, as Kierkegaard puts it, reflective doubt is necessary for resolution insofar as it heightens an anxious concern about the possibilities one can choose to actualize. Again, all resolution in relation to a life-project is a risk, since by choosing this or that spiritual possibility I negate other possibilities that may never again be encountered as existential possibilties (even though they may, of course, be reflected upon disinterestedly as imagined or conceivable possibilties). The notion that man has an original potentiality-for or an original possibility that he can retrieve since it has already been there (a view found in Heidegger's *Sein und Zeit*, but traceable to Kierkegaard) is one that had been foreshadowed in Aristotle's *Ethics*. For Aristotle, too, there is an original potentiality-for excellence ('virtue') that may or may not be brought to realization in a man's life. Even in regard to our dispositions it is said that "we can control their beginnings." Moreover, the unjust man and the profligate could, at the outset,

have avoided becoming so, since it was possible for them not to
be so. Aristotle and Kierkegaard suggest that an individual may
lose his potentiality-for moral excellence, his freedom for possibilities, or his 'original' potentiality-for ethical existence.[36] What
is required in order to retrieve one's original potentiality-for is an
acceptance of despair over the loss of oneself, a choice of guilt
for what one has done (or has neglected to do), and the taking
over of one's entire being. Since man has 'rational powers' or the
capacity to understand, he can understand not only nature and
the world but himself as well; he can understand his own state
of being. He cannot evade the implicit self-understanding that
he is false to what he ought to be—that he is not, from a moral
point of view, what he can be.

Kierkegaard assumes that the most fundamental potentiality
(or possibility) that a rational human being 'has' is a potentiality
for ethical self-existence, for authentic self-being. An ethical
existence is a repetitious striving to become a spiritual being or a
self. While the realization of our other potentialities contributes
to the totality of our existence, it is an ethical existence that is
important for the becoming of a self since, as Aristotle puts it, "it
is our choice of good or evil which determines our character."[37]
Although there are a multiplicity of causal factors impinging
upon our lives over which we have little or no control, we do have
the power or potentiality for (a) determining what it is possible
for us to do and (b) performing, in Aristotle's terms, through
our agency what it is possible for us to do. Kierkegaard suggests
in *Either/Or* that our primal potentiality is a potentiality to
strive persistently to become the "ideal self" that we are capable
of positing as the goal that gives purpose and authenticity to our
lives and that which is itself the ethical task. It is not surprising,
in light of the relationships between Aristotle's conceptions
of potentiality and/or possibility and Kierkegaard's concept of
possibility, that Kierkegaard formulates the becoming of the self
in Aristotelian terms. Thus he avers in *The Sickness unto Death*
that "a self, every instant it exists, is in process of becoming, for
the self *kata dunamin* [potentially] does not actually exist, it is
only that which it is to become."[39] The indefinite striving (*Straeben*) to become an integral self is the central, though by no

means the only, characteristic of the act of existing (*at existere*).

Kierkegaard does not agree with Aristotle in regard to the ultimate end or goal of ethical existence (and here he depends upon what may be called the Socratic ethics of individuation) insofar as he believes that the aim of existence is not a *bios theoretikos*, a "theoretical life," that imitates the activity of the Aristotelian god ("thought thinking itself"), but is an activity in which the 'ideality' of the self is realized, so far as this is possible, in the concrete finite existence of the individual. By virtue of the acquisition and practice of moral excellence and intellectual excellence the Aristotelian self is, in a manner of speaking, deindividuated. Whether or not *nous* or 'mind' is conceived of as the immanent presence of divine mind in man, it is clear that for Aristotle the final goal of an ethical existence is one that is attained, as he puts it, "not in virtue of [one's] humanity" "but in virtue of something within [man] which is divine [*theion*]."[40] Although Aristotle describes the highest mode of being as one characterized by self-sufficiency, it is certainly not a mode of being in which one is engaged in a pervasive reflection upon the becoming of the finite self. In point of fact, it is a form of life that is the paradigm of the intellectual life, the disinterested interest that Kierkegaard describes as typical of speculative thought or of objective consciousness. While the self-sufficient life of the intellect is, for Aristotle, the realization of one's highest potentialities, it is also a life (as Kierkegaard notes in his journals) that is isolating.[41] This is a paradoxical conclusion, when one considers that Aristotle had stressed, in his *Nicomachean Ethics*, the social dimension of ethical existence. The isolating phase of the dialectic of moral development for Kierkegaard is the intensification of the search for concernful knowledge, the critical examination of oneself as a synthesis of necessity (the characteristics of the self that were acquired by the individual independent of his will and those characteristics that comprise the actual, imperfect self up to the present) and possibility. To be sure, there is a similarity between Kierkegaard's prescription of the cultivation of 'inwardness' (which, as in Aristotle's conception of the best life for man, is characterized by seriousness) and the self-sufficient intellectual activity that Aristotle prescribes for man. However, it is doubtful that Aristotle would have agreed with Kierkegaard that the best life is one in which there is a concerted effort to intensify a sense of subjective individuation. In this regard, as I have mentioned, Kierkegaard reverted to what he conceived of as the Socratic ethics of subjectivity.

In general, Kierkegaard's conception of the significance of possibility in human existence is ultimately derived from his interpretation of Aristotle's conceptions of possibility and potentiality (which is itself a form of possibility). The description of the projective 'movement' of the individual towards the actualization of possibilities having relevance for the formation of one's character or personal existence (*personlige Existents*), the conception of the moral indeterminacy of the individual *ab initio,* the notion that choice is possible only for beings having 'rational powers', the view that man is the only being whose potentialties can be realized by (or not realized by) the intentional activity of the agent, the implied distinction between the subjective teleology of human action (in the *Ethics*) and an impersonal, immanent teleology pervading nature (in the *Metaphysics*), all play a significant role in Kierkegaard's inchoate philosophical anthropology and are, of course, central to his concept of the ethical sphere of existence. Needless to say, many of Heidegger's descriptions of the essential characteristics of *Dasein* are ontological formulations of Kierkegaard's existential (*existentielle*) description of the dialectic of life. Heidegger's notion that there is a "primordial" potentiality-for (*können*) in the being of *Dasein* is similar to Kierkegaard's appropriation of an implicit Aristotelian view that there is a fundamental capacity-for or potentiality-for (*kunnen*) authentic self-existence in the being of man. In Kierkegaard's terms, the ethical can be lured out of the individual "because it is *in* the individual," and that one who communicates, by indirection, the possibility of an ethically self-conscious existence presupposes that *kata dunamin* each man is 'the same'.[42] Furthermore, Heidegger's conception of *Dasein's* "potentiality-for-Being-one's-Self" (*Selbstseinkönnen*) is an explicit appropriation of Kierkegaard's conception of the initial awareness necessary in order to begin to live an ethical existence. It is Kierkegaard's interpretation of Aristotle's implicit conception of self-development that has reappeared (in disguise, to be sure) in Heidegger's conceptions of the potentialities of *Dasein*. That Kierkegaard seized upon Aristotle's notions of potentiality (and/or possibility) and actuality in order to describe the form of the 'movements' in the dynamic *nisus* of the dialectical process of human life is not surprising, since these categories are still the best available philosophical tools by which to describe a process of becoming and, as Kierkegaard showed, they are peculiarly appropriate for an understanding of the choices, decisions, and actions of human beings. While it is true that Kierkegaard was the first thinker to emphasize the centrality of the category of possibility in the interpretation of human existence, it is not the case (as has been argued by Nicola Abbagnano) that there is a radical bifurcation between Kierkegaard's conception of possibility or potentiality and Aristotle's fundamental understanding of the meaning of potentiality.

In Nicola Abbagnano's *Critical Existentialism* questions touching upon the existentialist concept of possibility and Aristotle's notion of potentiality are raised that are relevant to the present discussion. While Abbagnano follows Kierkegaard quite closely in regard to the status of the category of possibility in relation to the description and interpretation of the mode of being of man in the world, he holds a number of views that run counter to the claim that I have been concerned to make here, namely, that Kierkegaard's concept of existential possibility has its philosophical roots in the writings of Aristotle. In an essay translated from a chapter in his *Possibilità e Libertà* Abbagnano remarks that the term 'possible' means that which can be or not be. "The possible," he continues, "refers to every condition, state or mode of being which in some way includes indetermination, instability, uncertainty, precariousness, transience, danger, or risk."[43] I believe that each of these descriptive terms, with the exclusion of indetermination, accurately conveys the fundamental meaning of possibility, and they certainly are terms that Kierkegaard associated with the concept of possibility.

The reason that I would question the use of the term "indeterminism" as descriptive of 'the possible' is that, although there are some phenomena that are possible and indeterminate, it does

not follow that the possible is in every case that which is unpredictable or "uncaused." To be sure, we may say that certain
states of an electron or other subatomic particles are both possible and characterized by indeterminism insofar as the possibility
of determining precise values for the "positions" and "momenta"
of such entities is precluded by virtue of the uncertainty relations. While quantum theory has determined statistical variables
of state, it is unable to predict the specific or detailed "behavior"
of elements in subatomic processes. In regard to such micro-
physical phenomena we may indeed refer to the stochastic character of possibility.[44] But aside from this rather limited domain
of physical processes we are not by any means led to claim that
all possibilities are characterized by indeterminism. Certainly
this is not the case in the analysis of human choice or action as
either Aristotle or Kierkegaard understand them.

For Aristotle, as well as for Kierkegaard, the 'cause' of a choice
or action is the psychophysical individual. If an individual is
acting upon a conceived or imagined possibility, and if a man is
the author of his own actions, and, furthermore, if we cannot
trace our conduct back to any origins other than the origins
within ourselves, then such actions are voluntary. Again, for
Kierkegaard, the 'cause' of a choice or an action is the psychophysical individual insofar as the individual has the power to
act upon one of a number of alternative possibilities. Although
Kierkegaard does emphasize volition as the ultimate ground of
choice (as does Aristotle in his *Magna Moralia*), he insists that
it is the individual as such who is the 'cause' of his choices and
actions. In the realm of human behavior, then, possibility and
determinism are clearly compatible. In a choice situation an individual is confronted by a number of posited possibilities any one
of which, presumably, he *can* choose. If he chooses A rather than
B, C, or D, he is himself a causal agent of his choice and/or
action. The actual self of the individual is *the* causal factor in the
realization of possibilities that are within the power of the individual to realize.

To say that an event (e.g., a choice or an action) is possible
means that it may or may not be actualized. An agent has the
capability, as Aristotole puts it in the *Metaphysics*, of realizing

a possibility insofar as he has a capability of acting in certain circumstances in which no external hindrances prevent such action. While I will have occasion to refer later to the question of the origin of choice, decision, or action in both Aristotle's and Kierkegaard's account of the matter, the point I want to make here is that the concept of possibility does not entail that of indeterminism (though, in isolated instances, it may be understood in such terms). In addition, of course, there is no evidence that either Aristotle or Kierkegaard would hold that possibility requires indeterminism; indeed they cannot do so since they both desire to attribute full responsibility to an individual for deliberate choice and voluntary action. To be sure, possibilities are in themselves indeterminate, in a sense, insofar as they *are not*. But in another sense possibilities are determinate insofar as one is referring to human choice or action since an individual must first conceive of or imagine possibilities (which are, then, determinate objects of consciousness) *before* he chooses or acts. There is no independent "realm" of unfulfilled possibilities that, in some magical sense, *exists*. Possibilities, even the hypothetical possibilities that are considered in scientific speculation or prediction, *are* in relation to some human consciousness. Even if we say that man exists within a field of possibilities, what we seem to mean is that man exists within a world in which a multiplicity of possible events, states, occasions, actions, or occurrences is conceivable or imaginable. In the strictest sense of the term, it seems to me, only man can *have* possibilities or *know* that something is or is not possible; what Heidegger calls "innerworldly beings"[45] do not "have" possibilities in the sense in which man conceives of, imagines, or encounters an indefinite multiplicity of possibilities, including both those that are within his power to realize and those that are not.

In Abbagnano's conception of possibility is included the notion of the structure of problematic conditions that, in turn, find their foundation in possibility—ultimately in what is called transcendental possibility or the possibility of a possible. For one who refuses to postulate the ground of possibility in an eternal being, or for one who is unable to accept such a postulate, it is difficult to know what the ground of transcendental possibility is.

Abbagnano's illustration of what he means by this notion does
not clarify things very much, for he notes that if a hypothesis
would be verified, it propounds, in effect, a set of confirmations,
measurements, and tests that constitute the observation, O.[46]
First of all, the scientific hypothesis can be understood as transcendental possibility only if one limits oneself to this particular
schema. But this is not an illustration of what the transcendental
condition for the possibility of a possible would be. In this instance, all that has been shown is that a hypothesis can (and
does) function as a means by which one can predict possible effects *in futuro*. If we have confirmation of these possible effects
in experiment we are not referred back to a transcendental possibility. For a hypothesis is itself derived from prior collections of
facts or from a more general theory. The notion of transcendental
possibility may refer either to the view that the actual is 'pregnant' with possibility or that the ontological basis for possibilities
is the openness of the future. Even Kierkegaard's hyperbolic
phrase "the nothingness of possibility" is closer to what Abbagnano seems to be seeking in his conception of the possibility of
possibles. Or, again, we may revert to Aristotle's notion that the
possible is intermediate between being and nonbeing. The problem of analyzing the ontology of possibility or the conditions for
the possibility of possibilities is that we are inclined to think of
possibilities as having a kind of independent being in a nebulous
realm between being and nothingness. But this is a fruitless
approach to the question because of the tendency to speak of
possibles as if they were in fact actualities. To use Abbagnano's
phrase "consistent possibilities"—it is used in reference to acquired
possibilities or capacities—does not really resolve the problem
because we cannot know whether someone "has" a given possibility (e.g., whether in regard to a specific sphere of activity, he
knows *how*) unless he is capable of realizing that possibility *in
concreto*. Psychologically, it would seem (as Kierkegaard suggests) that the understanding of possibility is itself based upon
imagination insofar as it is imagination (as Sartre has argued)
that enables us to have consciousness of what is not.[47] Onto-
logically, possibility seems to be founded upon the present actuality of entities capable of motion or transformation. Or, again,

possibility may be conceived of in terms of the ambiguity, uncertainty, and amorphous character of the future. If the lives of men are enclosed in finitude, then the possibilities open to them are also finite. And yet Kierkegaard is not wrong in describing the *concept* of possibility in terms of the indefinite, the unlimited, or the infinite. From the subjective perspective of an individual, however, the notion of transcendental possibility, as I have already suggested, may be said to refer to a primordial freedom for possibility that is an immanent capacity in reflective beings capable of self-consciousness. To attempt to speculate about the origin of this primitive freedom for possibility (apart from theological speculation) is to be led beyond the limits of rational human understanding, to encounter the ineffable or what Heidegger calls *das Geheimnis* ("the mystery," which is the hidden source of openness or *Offenständigkeit*),[48] or, perhaps more appropriately, it is an attempt to talk about what Wittgenstein calls *das Mystische*.[49]

The most questionable aspect of Abbagnano's analysis of possibility is, to my mind, his assumption that Aristotle, insofar as he is concerned with the virtual (*dunamis*), must exclude the category of the possible. Abbagnano holds this view because he believes that potentiality is, for Aristotle, a "preformation and predetermination of the actual." Again, he assumes that a potentiality that is not realized was not in fact a potentiality.[50] Now it would seem that this is a basic misinterpretation of Aristotle's conception of potentiality. First of all, it is false to assume that Aristotle holds that every potentiality *must* be realized. Thus, in his discussion of the question whether the elements (*ta stoicheia*) exist potentially or in some other sense, Aristotle remarks that "potentiality is prior to the actual cause, and the potential need not necessarily always become actual."[51] Again, things are described as "potent" because they might happen or might not happen. To say that X has the potentiality of becoming Y means that it may, barring destruction, prevention, or the interference of unforeseen factors, become 'Y' or that it has the capability for becoming 'Y'. Though Aristotle assumes that there is a universal teleology pervading the development of beings, the process of development from potentiality to actuality is non-

necessary. To be sure, he does hold that there is a 'natural' tendency for beings to have their potentialities realized or (in the
case of men) to realize their potentialities. While the realization
of potentialities in nonhuman beings is itself not a necessary
process of development or evolution, this is even more obviously
the case in man insofar as he has rational potentialities or has a
consciousness of his potentialities. For the realization of an intentional action is itself conditional. As Aristotle puts it: "In
those cases in which the change from potentiality to realization
is brought about deliberately, the process takes place as willed
[boulethentos] on condition that nothing external hinders it."[52]
Whatever has potentialities is perishable and, hence, contingent.
As Aristotle expresses it in his *Metaphysics*: "everything that is
potential (*dunaton*) may fail to be actualized. Therefore, that
which is capable of being may both be and not be. The same
thing is capable of being and of not being. But that which is
capable of not being may possibly not be; and that which may
possibly not be is perishable."[53]

There is sufficient evidence in Aristotle's writings to discount
Abbagnano's claim that "potency is such because it is realized
and the *necessity* of the actualization defines potency"[54] and to
indicate why he was unable to see any relationship between the
centrality of the concept of possibility in Kierkegaard's existentialism and Aristotle's conception of potentiality (or possibility).
While Abbagnano maintains that Aristotle held that insofar as
the potential can be and not be it can be conceived of as itself
possible and thereby generated a "confusion" by surreptitiously
introducing a category (*to endechomenon*, 'the possible') that
is not found in the *Metaphysics*,[55] I believe that he is mistaken.
While it is true that the concept of the possible is not explicitly
dealt with in the *Metaphysics*, it is clearly implicit in many of
Aristotle's analyses. Indeed, many who have translated the *Metaphysics* into English (including recent translators such as Richard
Hope and H. G. Apostle) often translate *dunaton* or *dunatos* as
"possible."[56] Moreover, even Aristotle's logical analysis of the
concept of possibility or the possible is, in many respects, compatible with his metaphysical analysis of potentiality. Thus in his
account of *endechesthai* or "to be possible," he maintains that

something is possible if it is nonnecessary. Again, he remarks in *De Interpretatione* that basically possibility means that "if a thing may be, it may also not be." In at least one of his uses of the modal concept of possibility he avers that it may be contrasted with necessary in an ontological sense. That is, a given being is possible if it is perishable; or, on the other hand, a being that is imperishable is necessary. One of the central meanings of the possible (*endechomenon*) for Aristotle is contingency. Fundamentally contingency and possibility are homonyms for Aristotle insofar as a contingent event is one that is properly possible but not necessary. To say that it is possible for someone to do something means that an individual has the capability, capacity, or potentiality to do that something. In Aristotle's typical illustration (in the *Metaphysics*), to say that a builder has the potentiality to build something may mean that it is possible for him to do so or that he 'has' the possibility to build something. It is clear, I believe, that Kierkegaard's tendency to conflate the notions of potentiality and possibility (in terms of his exclusive application of these concepts to fundamental aspects of human existence) is neither idiosyncratic nor based upon a misinterpretation of Aristotle's use of these conceptions. Before entering upon a discussion of the description of the dialectic of choice and the nature of authentic ethical existence, I must briefly concern myself with the relationship between Kierkegaard's notion of existential possibility and other modes of possibility.

Possibility, Imagination, and Choice

While Kierkegaard did implicitly concern himself with what Heidegger calls "empty logical possibility" (*leeren logischen Möglichkeit*), especially in regard to the postulate of the God-idea as a conceptual possibility[57] and in regard to his notion that if a being such as God existed, then it would be logically possible that for such a being everything would be possible,[58] his primary concern was with existential or spiritual possibiltiy. Although he sometimes expressed the hyperbolic view that "everything is possible," he usually means that "for God" (*for Gud*) it is possible that everything is possible. In human existence, which is neces-

sarily conditioned by temporality, the possible is either a subjective possibility that an individual has the capacity to realize or
an objective possibility (whose paradigm is death) that can
occur or one that an individual can endure or undergo. Again,
a subjective possibility (as in Aristotle's *Ethics*) is one that can
be an 'object' of deliberation or that can be performed by an
individual's agency. For Kierkegaard, as for Aristotle, choice is
concerned with what is within our power. To be sure, Kierkegaard also maintains that the self is a synthesis of necessity and
possibility, necessity being the limiting or finite factor in the self
and possibility being the "expanding factor" or the paradoxical
"infinity" of the self.[59] Basically, as I have mentioned above, it is
imagination (which, in *The Sickness unto Death*, Kierkegaard
describes as "the faculty *instar omnium*," "for all faculties")[60]
that is the origin of the sense of infinite possibility. What Kierkegaard seems to mean here is that man, as an imagining being,
has the capacity to entertain an indefinite multiplicity of possibilities and to imagine infinite possibility. That is, man, in the
productive activity of imagination, can project an unlimited
number of possibilities and, in this sense, there is, in a manner of
speaking, infinity 'in' his being. In actuality, of course, an individual can only realize that possibility which it is within his
power to realize. To be unable to relate possibility to one's own
immediate actuality or to realize a possibility *in concreto* is to
lose one's self, to become unreal, to see a flattering but false
image of oneself in "the mirror of possibility." Kierkegaard does
not by any means say that man *has* infinite possibilities; rather,
he can *imagine* infinite possibilities (and infinite possibility).
But he has, by virtue of his actuality in finitude and the limiting
factor of the necessity in his being, finite possibilities that he has
the capacity to bring to fruition.

Obviously, whatever it is possible for an individual to do is,
per necessitatem, logically possible. Kierkegaard would have
agreed with Wittgenstein that, from the point of view of human
understanding or reason, the paradigm of necessity is logical
necessity (*logische Notwendigkeit*) and the only impossibility
that exists is logical impossibility (*logische Unmöglichkeit*).[61]
It is clear, however, that the notion of logical possibility, which

is so popular amongst analytical philosophers, is practically ir-relevant in regard to an individual's attempt to understand what choices, decisions, and actions it is possible for him to realize. A reflection upon logical possibility exclusively seems to be para-digmatic of what Kierkegaard regards as an indefinite dialectic of reflection. While it is true that conceptual possibility does play a role in our anticipation of our actions, it seems to me that imagination plays a more significant role in our anticipations of specific self-transformations or behaviors.

When an individual reflects upon his own possibilities (or po-tentialities) he usually rehearses what he might or might not choose or do. Even in regard to ordinary actions (e.g., driving an automobile down this or that road) we usually tend to imagine ourselves doing one thing or another. To take a favorite illustra-tion from some Anglo-American philosophers—i.e., the move-ments in a game of chess that are so often appealed to as models for intelligent behavior that one might readily refer to the chess-game theory of human action—it is clear that, for the most part, we imagine what possible moves we can or may make. To be sure, we do have an implicit understanding of the rules of the game, which limit the number of legitimate moves that can be made; but the moves that we do entertain as possiblities are not only conceptual possibilites but would more accurately be described as imagined possibilities. In human action (including, of course, choice or decision) we are concerned with what Sartre calls, in his *L'Être et la néant*, possibles, or the concrete act to be per-formed in a concrete world, and not with the abstract idea of possibility or conceptual possibility.[62] Although Kierkegaard seems to hold that we can *understand* what our own possibilities are—and especially those possibilities that are relevant for an authentic existence—he suggests that it is in imagination that we anticipate specific possibilities. Although it is tempting to refer to 'concrete' possibilities in this regard, it is clear that, strictly speaking, there are no concrete possibilities at all. Every possi-bility is either a hypothetical or conceptual possibility or an im-agined possibility before it is realized and appropriated. To be sure, the appropriation (*Tilegnelse*) of a specific possibility ne-gates it as a possibility even though an individual who has

actualized a particular possibility intensifies his capacity to realize a similar possibility *in futuro*. While Kierkegaard sometimes
refers to possibilities that are related to an individual's reality as
"conceived reality," this does not seem sufficient to distinguish
such possibilities (as Kierkegaard wishes to do) from "aesthetically and intellectually disinterested possibility," since a conceived reality is itself, prior to its realization, a possibility. Although I believe that Kierkegaard did not think out the question
of how possibilities that are intimately related to an individual's
self-development are attended to (i.e., whether such possibilities
are conceived or imagined possibilities), it is clear that it is
concern (*interesse*) which signifies that the individual is entertaining possibilities that are important for his own becoming. As
Kierkegaard puts it in *Concluding Unscientific Postscript*: "when
I think that I will do this or that, this thought is not an action,
and . . . it is qualitatively distinct from action; nevertheless, it is
a possibility in which the interest of action and of reality already
reflects itself."[63]

Although it is certainly true that overt human action is circumscribed by empirical possibility (that possibility which is compatible with presently *known* laws of nature), Kierkegaard's
conception of existential possibility is not reducible to empirical
possibility. Empirical possibility has reference to overt action, to
physical action, or to publically observable behavior. An empirical possibility is clearly a conceptual possibility that can be enter-
tained by one who has sufficient knowledge of the physical laws
to enable him to predict, with varying degrees of probability,
what may or may not occur. Empirical possibility, then, has
reference to what it is possible for man, as a physical being, to do
or to undergo. However, when the question is raised concerning
the initiation of an action (and, of course, we are primarily concerned not with *adiaphoric* actions or trivial actions but with
morally relevant ones), we are not asking a question about physical possibility or what it is empirically possible for an individual
to do. To be sure, this does not mean that the physical well-being
of an individual is entirely irrelevant to the spiritual capacities of
an individual. But most discussions of responsible action, including that of Aristotle, presuppose individuals who have a capa-

city or potentiality for choice, decision, and action. When Aristotle (and later Kierkegaard) refers to the fact that, within a limited range of phenomena, "a man is the origin of his actions" (*anthropos einai arche ton praxeon*)[64] he is not primarily referring to what it is empirically possible for a man to do. In the case of Kierkegaard, of course, what he calls an individual's "oughtness-capability" is not a purely physical capability. Existential possibilities are those that have direct relevance to the self-being of an individual, to the development of character and personal being; as such they can be described as "spiritual" capacities or possibilities. It is an individual's spiritual capacity that gives him his possibility for choice. For Aristotle as well as for Kierkegaard choice requires a capacity for deliberation and self-conscious intentionality.

Deliberation in relation to that which is a spiritual possibility for man is a manifestation of what Kierkegaard calls concernful consciousness or the pursuit of concernful knowledge. A spiritual capability can only be apprehended in subjective knowledge and is something that is by no means ascertainable by virtue of the methods of empirical psychology. If it were possible (which it is not) to determine and describe 'objectively' all the empirical facticities comprising an individual at any particular stage of his life history, this description would omit something essential: it would neglect the projective capacities of this individual in terms of his spiritual potentialities and possibilities. And it is precisely these spiritual capacities that, for the most part, provide the intensity and depth of personality. The individual can, in imperfect self-knowledge, understand his spiritual or existential possibilities since, as Heidegger expresses his paraphrase of Kierkegaard, "to my state-of-mind or mood, understanding [*das Verstehen*] belongs equipriordially." In this way, *Dasein* "knows" what it is capable of "doing or becoming."[65] The positing or projecting of these possibilities is, for the most part, an imaginative activity.

I believe that what Bertrand de Jouvenal has recently said about assertions having reference to possible actions is substantially correct. He remarks that this reference to future possibility (for myself) places this statement outside the realm of

attested or verified fact and projects it "beyond the domain of the
true or false." "This 'beyond,'" de Jouvenal continues, "constitutes another domain, where I can place images that do not
correspond to any historical reality. An image of this kind is not
a mere fantasy if I have the will and feel I have the capacity to
bring about at some . . . time a state of affairs that corresponds
to the image. The image represents a possibility because of my
power to validate it it in this way, and represents a *project* because of my will to do so."[66] The future is the field of imagined
(or conceived) possibilities in which an individual may realize
spiritual capacities or existential possibilities.

The recognition of, or awareness of, one's potentiality for an
ethical existence (which means, for Kierkegaard, the potentiality
for becoming a person or a self) is an instance of the emergence
of an intensified subjective consciousness and is also the simultaneous recognition of the possibility for choice. Phenomenologically, once concerned consciousness arises in an individual,
choice and responsibility are unavoidable insofar as an individual
can no longer *doubt* the possibility of an ethical existence but can
only choose to strive to attain such a *telos* (or not to do so, as
the case may be). In regard to moral self-development, as John
Dewey put it in his *Theory of the Moral Life,* it is "the possibility of a desirable *modification* of character and the selection
of the course of action which will make that possibility a reality
[that] is the central fact in responsibility."[67] Since we are responsible only for the deliberate choice of what is within our power,
the central focus of our analysis of Kirekegaard's existential
ethics will be the 'dialectic of choice' or the "movements of
choice." As is the case in Kierkegaard's interpretation of subjective possibility or spiritual potentiality, we shall see that his
conception of choice is not (as is often charged) an irrationalist
notion but is one that has affinities with that of Aristotle. The
prototype for Kierkegaard's existential category of "choice" is to
be found in Aristotle's analysis of choice or forechoice in the
Nicomachean Ethics. The transition from possibility to actuality,
at any rate, is a movement made possible by reasoned choice
that is itself possible by virtue of man's primitive potentiality-for,
his capacity, *kata dunamin,* to become the self that it is his task
to become.

3

Existential Choice

". . . choice . . . appears to be intimately connected with virtue, and to afford a surer test
of character than do our actions."—Aristotle,
Nicomachean Ethics (III, ii, 1.)

Although it has become traditional to describe Kierkegaard's
practical ethics as based essentially upon the model of Kantian
ethics, it is questionable that this is, in fact, the fundamental
basis for his conception of ethical existence. While there appears
to be an emphasis upon an ethics of duty or "duty for duty's sake"
in some passages in *Either/Or*, the conception of a fundamental
duty towards oneself in terms of a subjectively posited goal to become a self or a person—a view which can be found in *Either/Or*,
The Sickness unto Death, Concluding Unscientific Postscript, and
in numerous journal entries, but which must be synthesized with
other aspects of authentic existence in order to provide an ex-
tended schema for the form of an ethical existence—is central to
Kierkegaard's phenomenology of ethical existence. Kierkegaard
has sometimes been said to have put forward a Christian ethics
that emphasized the absolute relationship between the individual
and the absolute being of God. While there is some evidence
that he did propose an ethico-religious mode of existence,[1] it is
also the case that a religious mode of existence requires the
aufgeheben (or paradoxical negation and preservation) of ethical
consciousness or the notorious "teleological suspension of the
ethical." However, the basic conception of an existential ethics
(or an ethics of subjectivity) is itself neither necessarily nor
essentially a Christian ethics. This is not to deny that Kierkegaard presumably held that a religious mode of existence (which
would, of course, appropriate aspects of aesthetic and ethical

existence) was the "highest" possibility for man, since he believed that it offered the individual the consolation of faith, an absolute, transcendental *telos*, and the hope that the spiritual trials (*Angfaegtelser*) of existence would be resolved beyond the ineluctability of death. However, the various presentations of the ethical sphere of existence (*Existents-Sphaerer*) comprise a conception of ethical existence that is one for which Christian faith is not required, although it is, of course, one that is compatible with the essential teachings of Christian ethics.

While it is understandable that Henriksen, in his commentary upon Bohlin's *Søren Kierkegaard etiska åskådning*,[2] should hold that a "new ethic" was required in terms of Kierkegaard's notion of a subjective commitment to faith, such a view is basically mistaken since Kierkegaard himself explicitly remarks that an authentic ethical existence is possible outside of Christianity. Since his conception of an ethical mode of being is modeled upon his interpretation of Socrates' subjective ethics of self-mastery, self-control, and self-transformation and upon Aristotle's account of the acquisition of moral virtues, as well as his own conception of the individuating states of being which intensify personal existence, it is not surprising that his account of the ethical sphere of existence is not necessarily based upon Christian faith.[3]

If Kierkegaard's notion of the meaning of an ethical existence is not essentially based upon Christianity, neither is it merely built upon the foundation of Kantian ethics. Although there are some echoes of Kant's ethics in Kierkegaard's portrayal of an ethical mode of being, it is not the case, as James Collins avers in his *The Mind of Kierkegaard,* that "Kierkegaard's view . . . must be reconciled with the Kantian theory of moral law, upon which his notion of ethical personality ultimately rests."[4] To be sure, the relationship between some of the themes of Kant's ethics and Kierkegaard's phenomenological description of ethical existence is complex and is one that I will attempt to deal with (at least tangentially) in my explication of the relationship between universality and subjectivity in Kierkegaard's practical ethics.

The Dialectic of Choice

The insufficiency and self-negating character of a purely aesthetic or nihilistic standpoint leads an individual to seek a meaningful mode of being that will provide both a justification for his life and a sense of purpose. One of the general characteristics of man is his need for purpose; as Nietzsche once remarked, man would rather have nothingness as his purpose than have no purpose at all. Purposiveness is a pervasive quality of human behavior, whether it is manifested in the practical concerns of daily life or in an individual's spiritual aspirations. Even the theoretical nihilist (at least in Western thought) who is willing to proclaim that everything is without meaning or purpose finds it difficult, if not practically impossible, to apply this generalization to his own life. No sooner does Nietzsche assert the total meaninglessness of the world than, in almost the next breath, he proposes a goal, a purpose, or a meaning for human existence (e.g., live in such a way that you would will that your life be repeated eternally, make possible the sociocultural conditions for the possibility of the emergence of the *Übermenschen* ["overmen"] of the future, strive repeatedly for "self-overcoming," etc.). If there is purpose nowhere, if the cosmos is no more than a vast field of phenomena that is nothing but a pulsating multiplicity of energy systems revealing no purpose whatsoever, there is a tendency for man to believe that *his* existence, at least, *must* have some meaning. And if his reason can provide no basis for his belief, his passion will force his reason to create such a basis. What psychiatrists such as Viktor Frankl call "the will to meaning"[5] is a recurring phenomenon in the existence of both individuals and groups. It is something similar to this that seems to underlie Kierkegaard's view that the "living through" an aesthetic or nihilistic standpoint makes the question of the meaning and purpose of one's existence a more urgent question, a question for which the individual craves an answer. It is possible to doubt everything, perhaps, but Kierkegaard maintains that true "self-doubting" (*Selvfordoblelse*) is impossible and that any "self-doubting existing" is either an illusion or a thought-experiment.[6] Ultimately, there is only one way out of the impasses of aesthetic despair, nihilism, or theoretical doubt: a resolution to commit oneself to a subjectively posited *telos*. Since, as Kierkegaard expresses it, in order to doubt we must will to doubt, we must also will to stop doubt, for doubt cannot be transcended by knowledge since knowledge is based, as Wittgenstein put it, upon a tacit presupposition (*einer stillschweigenden Voraussetzung*). In effect, doubting has an end, *Das Zweifeln hat ein Ende.*[7]

While there is no immanent necessity in the dialectic of human life, the psychological negation of a purely aesthetic mode of being and the theoretical negation of a consistent nihilism tend to leave the individual open for the possibility of seeking concernful knowledge, of discovering in his own being a primitive potentiality-for that he has not yet attempted to realize. In reflecting upon this being-possible or this potentiality-for the individual's concern or interest in his own being is revealed to him. Since, according to Kierkegaard, there is no action without interest, the individual must encounter this subjective sense of *interesse* in order to begin to make what Kierkegaard calls the "movement of choice." Replacing Heidegger's expression in the existential context from which it was taken, one may say that man is that kind of being who, in his being, has his being (not Being or *das Sein!*) as an issue insofar as his existence is an 'object' of *actual* concern. In his concernful, subjective consciousness the individual is, as Kierkegaard puts it, "in between" ideality and actuality. The intensification of consciousness that occurs by virtue of doubt and uncertainty is itself an initial phase in the relational activity of consciousness in which ideality and actuality are brought together in a dialectical tension. Only when, as Kierkegaard says in *Johannes Climacus*, "ideality is brought into relationship with actuality does *possibility* appear."[8] Ethical consciousness requires this intentional act of relating ideality and actuality. Unlike epistemic doubt—where one is interested in the question of truth or the possibility of truth—in the consciousness of the disparity between ideality (the *ought*) and actuality (the *is*) in reference to my own existence "what I am interested in is myself." The questions that are raised in relation to one's own being (e.g.: Can I become other than I have been? Can I realize my potentiality for ethical existence? Can I become an intergrated self?) cannot be resolved by reason or by additional objective knowledge because these turn the individual back upon himself in search of subjective knowledge—a knowledge of what he is capable of doing or being. In a sense, then, doubt is the starting point for ethical self-existence since, as soon as it is a question of acting, "interest or concern is present to me, because I take the responsibility for myself and thereby acquire significance."[9] When one raises questions about one's own "being-possible" (or what Heidegger calls *das Dasein als Möglichsein*), this mode of doubt is distinguished from a purely theoretical, epistemic doubt (e.g., do we directly perceive sense data or physical objects?) by virtue of the interest or concern that accompanies this activity.

Ethical questions are not concerned with speculative or objective knowledge or *Videnskab* (corresponding to the German *Wissenschaft*) insofar as they are questions about the self, questions concerning what an individual is or what he can be. Kierkegaard held that once questions concerning what an individual is or can be are raised one can no longer be indifferent to them since they are intimately associated with one's being and are, hence, matters of concern. In his journals Kierkegaard remarks that it is in questions of ethics that skepticism founders. For "since Descartes they have all maintained that during the time in which they are doubting, they might not make any definite statement with regard to knowledge, but they certainly might act, because with regard to action we can be content with probability."[10] Kierkegaard regards this as a monstrous "contradistinction," since it is far more terrible to act or to do something that one is doubtful about (since this involves responsibility) than it is merely to say something or make some claim to knowledge. In regard to an individual's heightened self-consciousness about the ethical possibility, "there is after all something which doubt cannot touch!" One cannot doubt a subjectively apprehended potentiality-for or possibility-for an authentic ethical existence, although one is of course free not to act upon this potentiality or possibility. In subjective consciousness, at any rate, one realizes that one is at a distance, as Kierkegaard puts it, from what one knows that it is possible for one to be. Intellectually, this is a form of ironic understanding (hence, in *The Concept of Irony*, Kierkegaard remarks that "an authentic existence is not possible without irony"); psychologically, it is an irrefragable sense of responsibility to endeavor to become what one ought to be. The attempt to avoid this understanding of one's own potentiality-for an ethical existence (which, for Kierkegaard is the paradigm of an authentic existence) is what Heidegger calls, in a slightly different context, "a *flight* of *Dasein* in the face of itself as an authentic potentiality-for-being-its-self" (*eine Flucht des Daseins vor ihm selbst als eigenlichem Selbst-sein-können*).[11] This "flight" from this disclosed possibility of being a self is in effect an attempt to escape from a subjective understanding of one's responsibility for what one has been, is, and is becoming. In this regard, there is no question of what the ancient skeptics described as "retiring doubt" (*epochē*) or a refusal of intellectual assent (*metriopathein*).[12] For the apprehension of possibility, either as conceived possibility or as imagined possibility for oneself, involves a confrontation with what William James calls (in his *The Will to Believe*) a "live option" that entails a 'forced' and 'momentous' choice.[13] There is, as Kierkegaard might say, a dialectical tension between one's understanding of one's possibility for ethical self-consciousness and self-existence and one's potentiality-for choice. One can, of course, engage in deliberation about what it is possible for one to do or to become; but deliberation, since it is without limits, cannot in itself resolve this subjective tension. To be concerned only with a deliberation about what it is possible for one to become is, of course, to be trapped in the labyrinth of dialectical reflection, to postpone choice for the sake of a disinterested consideration of a multiplicity of conceptual or imaginative possibilities. But this is itself, as Kierkegaard understands it, a return to the dialectic of reflection and a futile attempt to escape from a concernful consciousness of one's own potentialities or possibilities. This endeavor is by its very nature paradoxical since "reflection is disinterested." But subjective consciousness is, on the other hand, a relational activity which "brings with it interest or concern, a duality," as Kierkegaard puts it in *Johannes Climacus*, "which is perfectly expressed with pregnant double meaning by the word 'interest' [*interesse,* "to be between," "to be a matter of concern"]."[14] Once something is a matter of *interesse,* the individual cannot, in effect, avoid a choice. Either he will choose to be himself or he will choose not to be himself. In regard to this "either/or" (*aut . . . aut*) there is no facile mediation (*Vermittlung*).

Since both the aesthete and nihilist are not inegrated individuals but are multiplicities or centers of a diversity of moods, feelings, needs, and desires, they are, in a sense, disintegrated beings subject to impulses or fantasies over which they have no control. Or they are stultified by the apprehension of conceptual or hypothetical possibilities that replace each other with increasing rapidity. Their mode of being is fragmented, disunified, and lacking in direction. By submitting oneself to a multiplicity of possibilities of pleasure or by entertaining a multiplicity of hypothetical possibilities one's own existence and one's own spiritual possibilities are obscured or are covered with the film of ambiguity. The individual loses his sense of his own actuality, his own temporal reality. Only by recognizing and accepting the failure or shipwreck of a purely aesthetic or nihilistic standpoint can the individual become open to the possibility of an ethical existence that can give meaning and purpose to his life. Only in a *chosen* despair of an emotional aestheticism or a *chosen* despair of a life of theoretical nihilism can the individual begin to be aware of the possibility for choice or, as Kierkegaard puts it, the possibility of a choice to choose. This is a return to a possibility that has already been 'there' as a possibility. It is, in effect, a recovery of a primordial possibility for being a self. The loss of one's own actuality is the loss of the subjective consciousness of the opposition between ideality and actuality. If every possibility is construed as an aesthetic or speculative possibility, there seems to be no existential possibility that an individual might conceivably seek to realize. The etherealization of possibility entails its derealization.

In order for the pathos-filled transition to an ethical existence to come to fruition, an individual must be confronted with a subjective concern for his own being—a serious concern for what he is becoming. That is, he must realize that he and he alone must accept responsibility for what he has been, for what he is, and for what he is becoming. The ethical movement is not merely an intellectual change, not merely a matter of knowing how one ought to live; rather, it is a subjective, emotionally conditioned *nisus* toward a transformation of the self (*a metabasis eis allo genos*) that is passionately desired. Indeed, the "movement" towards choice is not possible without what William James called the "passional" aspects of the self. In what Kierkegaard describes as "spiritual movement" the state or condition of the individual is essential since spiritual possibilities are only attainable or appropriated in freedom, in the interiority of the self in which the motivation for significant (as opposed to trivial) choice is found.

A skeptical doubt in regard to what one is or what one ought to be cannot be transcended by the acquisition of objective knowledge or by deliberation per se. In resolute choice alone is self-reflective doubt overcome insofar as, by means of choice, the individual asserts his own being and brings to realization his possibility for choice. Although Kierkegaard's analysis of the content of the existential category of choice or of the "movements" of choice does have features that are uniquely based upon his interpretation of the meaning and nature of choice, it is also similar to many aspects of Aristotle's account of choice in the *Nicomachean Ethics*. Indeed, there are many specific statements in Kierkegaard's journals and in *Either/Or* that indicate that he was intimately acquainted with a number of Aristotle's works (and especially with the *Ethics*) and was prone to paraphrase many of Aristotle's key assertions concerning the moral development of the individual. Insofar as Kierkegaard's conception of ethical existence appropriated at least some of Aristotle's views concerning the ethical becoming of man this may serve to indicate that two rather common interpretations of Kierkegaard's analysis of choice are basically false. That is, the assumption that Kierkegaard defends a conception of absolute freedom (à la Sartre) and that he propounds an irrationalist conception of choice.

While a kind of abstract or disinterested deliberation is by no means foreign to the aesthete or the reflective nihilist, what is lacking in their modes of being is a sincere commitment to something, a willingness to choose to realize a possibility that has meaning for their own personal existence. What is lacking for individuals who are absorbed in a consideration of romantic or aesthetic possibilities and those who are engaged in a skeptical, dialectical reflective process is a purposive, subjective teleology and a recognition of limitation in themselves. When a sense of purpose is lacking and when the individual is unwilling to understand the necessity in his being he seems to lose himself in the indefinite, the fantastic, or the unlimited. In terms of a purely aesthetic or hypothetical consideration of possibilities in relation to oneself the individual appears to be engaged in an "infinite" or unlimited process of deliberation. In Kierkegaard's terms, there is a movement of thought or of imagination but the 'self' is unmoved, remaining, from a spiritual point of view, where it had been before. In *Either/Or* the individual immured in the aesthetic mode of being (the character 'A') is the arch-deliberator par excellence, the paradigm of the irresolute man. If the *aut . . . aut* the individual contemplates is not related to the individual in concernful consciousness, then there is a disinterested contemplation of imagined or hypothetical possibilities. If one is entertaining a choice (or the possibility of authentic choice) that has direct relevance for one's life, the individual, obviously, continues to live in the meantime, balancing the alternative possibilities in constant deliberation, falling further into the habit of irresolution. From the point of view of imagination and dialectical reflection alone deliberation is infinite. If, as Aristotle says in the *Nicomachean Ethics,* we continue the process of deliberation about each particular point (or every possible alternative), it can continue ad infinitum.[15] Deliberation can only be brought to an end by a decision to choose or the actualization of the possibility of choice. Deliberation is the condition for the possibility of choice, but it neither entails nor initiates choice. For Kierkegaard, as well as for Aristotle, we deliberate not about the eternal, the necessary, or the impossible, but about the possible (*dunaton*) or that which we believe or know to be within our power to perform.[16] However, for Kierkegaard, the most fundamental possibility discernible in self-reflective deliberation is a possibility *for* choice. For beings who, in Aristotle's terms, have "rational potencies" there is a capability that distinguishes them from other beings and that is the basis for intentional decision and action, namely a capacity for, or potentiality for, conscious or deliberate choice. The possibility for choice is the basis for the finite freedom of the individual. In his journals Kierkegaard notes that Aristotle maintains "that free action lies . . . in man's power."[17] The freedom for the possibility of choice is itself fundamentally derived from man's potentiality-for (*kunnen*). Or, from the standpoint of the relational activity of the self in subjective or concernful consciousness, freedom is the dialectical element in the relationship between possibility and necessity. Although Kierkegaard sometimes (e.g., in *Either/Or*) equates freedom and choice, this is neither his basic notion of freedom nor is it consistent with what must be his implicit position in regard to this question, i.e., that choice is a manifestation of freedom as a potentiality-for that is accessible to an individual capable of self reflective understanding. Further discussion of Kierkegaard's understanding of freedom must be postponed until we attempt to analyze his conception of the self and its relationship to his description of ethical existence.

Since an ethical movement can only be realized existentially (*realiseret existentielt*), the individual must be passionately concerned with his own possibilities for choice, decision, and action. In order for what Kierkegaard calls an existential communication (*Existents-Meddelelse*) to have a relationship to existence it must be presented in the form of possibility (*maa vaere i Mulighedens Form*). An existential communication (whether it is directly related to an individual by himself or indirectly related to another) is, as Kierkegaard puts it in his journals, a communication of capability, capacity, or potentiality.[18] Hence, before one attempts to actualize a possibility for choice one must intensify one's self-conciousness and endeavor to attain an understanding of what one has been and is. Aside from a search for self-knowledge (which, in *The Sickness unto Death*, involves the attempt to discern the "necessity" in one's being) there is what might be called a concernful deliberation about one's own possibilities. Concernful deliberation (as opposed, say, to the neutral or indifferent deliberations of the aesthete, which are referred to in *Either/Or*) is tantamount to Aristotle's notion of deliberation (*bouleusis*) insofar as it is a reflective consideration of what it is possible for one to choose or to do. Phenomenologically, Kierkegaard considers the decision to choose (and, thereby, to put an end to the mere reflection upon imagined or conceived possibilities) as fundamental to an ethical existence. As he puts it in *Either/Or*: "It is . . . not yet a question of the choice of something in particular, it is not a question of the reality of the thing chosen, but of the reality of the act of choice."[19] Kierkegaard, unlike Aristotle, emphasizes that in order for the possibility for choice to be actualized the individual must choose to bring to realization *this* possibility. Kierkegaard does not consider a refraining from choice an *act* of choice; rather, an individual falls into what he calls an "aesthetic choice" or a momentary, fleeting, expression of preference that is, strictly speaking, no choice at all.[20]

While there is a tendency in some contemporary analyses of choice to trivialize the problem by reducing all choices to the same basic form, I believe that Kierkegaard intended to emphasize the distinction between relatively insignificant 'choices' and existential choices or spiritual choices that have relevance for the development of the character of the individual. To be sure, many trivial choices may, contingently, turn out to have been 'important' in the sense that subjectively unpredictable events directly impinging upon one's life may occur as a result of a rather casual selection of a possibility (e.g., deciding to fly on this airplane rather than another; drive down one road rather than another, etc.). While a skeptic might suggest that we cannot know what choices may or may not turn out to be significant or important, we do tend to rely upon practical judgment in regard to such questions, or we simply rely upon common sense. In regard to choices having relevance for our own moral or spiritual development we are concerned with the intentional choice of what it is in our power to do. In regard to virtue (moral excellence) and vice (immoral behavior or action), as Aristotle puts it in the *Ethics*, we are responsible for cultivating the one or the other. "For," as Aristotle expresses it, "where we are free to act we are also free to refrain from acting, and where we are able to say No we are able to say Yes."[21] If we are responsible for virtuous behavior (a responsibility that we willingly claim), then we are also responsible for vice. Morally relevant choices, then, are concerned with effects (e.g., the practice of a virtue on a specific occasion or the practice of vice) that it is within our power to attain. In the case of trivial choices having 'important' consequences (e.g., choosing to eat a particular food that later makes one ill; choosing to drive down one road rather than another and becoming involved in an accident; choosing to trust someone who eventually betrays you, etc.), we are referring to possibilities to which we are subject or to empirical possibilities that are counterintentional. Surely we are not responsible for what may or may not happen to us as a result of a casual, *adiaphoric* choice. To my mind, most *soi-distant* 'choices' that are made in an individual's lifetime are, *mutatis mutandis,* insignificant. While one could probably create a schema indicating the various degrees of importance among choices (which, no doubt, would vary considerably from individual to individual), this would be an interesting source of psychological data that would probably not tell us much that we did not already suspect, namely, that most rational human beings have a reasonably clear idea of what choices are important to them. If a society or a group attempts to obscure this practical knowledge, to blur an individual's resonsibility to himself, or if it appeals to common practice to relieve the individual of his responsibility for choices relevant to his own moral development, then this society or group is probably itself immoral or has an ideological reason for undermining the individual sense of personal moral responsibility for what it is within his power to do. An individual's moral responsibility is not global, but personal. In any case, the attempt to conflate *adiaphoric* choices with existential choices is a falsification of a distinction that, for the most part, we *know* to exist, and it results in the kind of trivialization of choice against which Kierkegaard's dithyrambic assertions are directed.

The first "movement" of the self (or, more accurately, the potential self) in the dialectic of choice is choosing to realize the possibility of choice. Kierkegaard considered this a difficult choice to make, believing that "there is nothing of which every man is so afraid as getting to know how enormously much he is capable of" doing or becoming.[22] The question of the possibility of choosing is one that cannot be put off indefinitely since one is, as Kierkegaard puts it, carried forward by the momentum of life, a momentum that is bringing the individual nearer to what Heidegger calls the "impossibility of possibility," which is to say, death. The postponement of significant choices (something with which Kierkegaard himself was quite familiar in his own life) usually means that an individual will passively allow others to make choices for him, or that a pseudo-choice will be made by what Kierkegaard calls the "unconscious" aspects of the individual.[23] Of course, the hypothetical individual in Kierkegaard's phenomenology of choice has already realized possibilities or has had possibilities realized in his factual existence. But one can live without making decisive choices (one thinks, for example, of the passive nihilism of Camus' character in *L'Étranger*, Meursault, who seems to assert his own existence only in the face of death); one can 'drift' with the tide of daily practical life and fall into a state of irresolution. The kind of choice Kierkegaard describes is one that is directly concerned with the self-becoming of the individual and is made in a state of intensified consciousness. Such an 'act' is possible only for a rational, self-reflective, self-conscious individual who is in dialectical relationship to a concernful possibility. The loss of a subjective sense of spiritual possibility, as Kierkegaard remarks in *The Sickness unto Death,* means that the individual believes either that everything is necessary (or that he, like some contemporary philosophers, is a fatalist) or that everything is trivial.[24] Since Kierkegaard believes (following Aristotle) that the capacity for choice can be lost, the important thing, in regard to the ethical sphere of existence, is to choose to realize one's own potentiality for choice. In tracing the further phases in the description of the dialectic of choice, I will attempt to show how specific aspects of this description are related to Aristotle's conception of choice.

Kierkegaard's view that choice is itself already a manifestation of an ethical mode of being (what he typically calls "the ethical" or *ethisk*) may seem idiosyncratic until we read, in Aristotle's

Nicomachean Ethics, that choice (*proairesis*) "appears to be intimately connected with virtue [*aretê*] and to afford a surer test of character than do our actions."[25] Whenever the "either/or" is seriously presented in relation to the subjective concern of an individual, the ethical possibility is involved. It is "the act of choosing" that is the essential and "stringent expression of the ethical." Once the question of the ethical possibility (or the possibility of living in the "sphere" of the ethical) is raised, the individual is confronted with an "absolute" choice or "the choice whereby one chooses good *and* evil/or excludes them."[26] What this means, I believe, is that the individual is free to choose either to live in accordance with ethical 'categories' or not to so live, in which case he chooses to live an aesthetic or nihilistic mode of being in which moral distinctions ought never to be recognized or made. But what Kierkegaard seems to suggest is that if an individual has wholeheartedly and seriously made such a choice he cannot avoid *knowing* the negative character of this choice. Since Kierkegaard holds that authentic choice is individuating, there is a contradictory tension in the spiritual activity of the individuals who choose an extra-ethical mode of being that is itself deindividuating because one who lives in such a mode of being is unable or unwilling to choose, and is, hence, not responsible for what he is or becomes. In point of fact, a self-conscious, self-reflective person will have chosen a mode of being that prohibits his becoming a self. It is as if one deliberately chose to lead an inauthentic life and hoped, in some magical fashion, to escape from one's responsibility for so choosing. If a knowledge that one has chosen an inauthentic mode of being returns (like a spontaneous flashback) at any time in one's life, then one has an authentic understanding of one's inauthenticity and is, therefore, faced with the "either/or" that Kierkegaard describes as absolute. Once an individual has made such an "absolute" choice he has already made an ethical 'turn' even in his deliberate choice to exclude the notions of good and evil. To choose not to live under ethical determinants means, for Kierkegaard, that one has chosen not to become a self, has chosen a life of irresponsibility and irresolution, has chosen not to lead an authentic existence, has chosen, in Kierkegaard's terms, not to *exist*.

Since Kierkegaard seems to regard resolute choice as having *ethical* significance, a choice made concerning what is a matter of 'interest' to an individual is already an ethically relevant spiritual activity. In the face of the 'absolute' choice of the either/or that Kierkegaard describes, the choice between good or evil emerges. And, in this regard, Kierkegaard implicitly agrees with Aristotle that "it is our choice of good or evil that determines our character" (*tō gar proaireisthai t'agatha he ta kaka poioi tines esmen*).[27] That the individual will, in all probability, choose the good is a view for which Kierkegaard has often been unjustly criticized. What I believe he means by this rather optimistic view is that, in most cases, individuals will choose to do what they think or believe is good. Again, as Aristotle's first line of the *Nicomachean Ethics* expresses it, "every practical pursuit or purposive undertaking [or every choice, *proairesis*] seems to aim at some good." While individuals may be mistaken in what they believe is good (e.g., pelasure), the 'principle' guiding their choice and action is basically a principle of goodness. It is rare, at the very least, for an individual who is capable of deliberation and 'forechoice' to choose or to act in accordance with a universal principle of evil. The most immoral actions of human beings who are responsible for their actions are not usually done out of a recognition of some rationally formulated immoral principle, but are done for the sake of some short-range or long-range good. The immorality, in such instances, arises in terms of the *means* that some individuals are willing to use in order to realize some subjectively posited 'good'. There is, however, another reason that Kierkegaard is sanguine about the choice of the good. It is one that is not obvious in his writings, and one that requires a constructive synthesis of various assertions he makes about the 'movements' of choice.

Not only does "momentous" choice serve the same function for Kierkegaard's conception of man's being as Heidegger's conception of *Angst* does for his conception of *Dasein* (insofar as it is individuating); but it is also a complex spiritual act that is characterized by stages or 'movements' that are analyzed seriatim even though they are thought to be in dialectical relationship in the self. An act of choice is one that is, as it were, infused by what Kierkegaard describes as concernful, subjective consciousness. In such a state of consciousness the individual is personally concerned with the ironical opposition between ideality and actuality. The consciousness of the conflict between the conceived or imagined ideality (e.g., it is impossible to effect an 'absolute' choice; it is possible to choose either good and evil or to exclude them) and one's own imperfect actuality (i.e., a consciousness that one has not made such choices, that one has put off authentic choice, etc.) intensifies the significance of the kind of choice Kierkegaard describes. In *Johannes Climacus* Kierkegaard avers that it is 'in' subjective consciousness that the process of relating the opposition of ideality and actuality takes place. Indeed, concernful consciousness is the "energizing force," as Kierkegaard puts it, behind this relational process.[28] In this intentional activity of consciousness the individual himself is concerned with 'the object of choice' insofar as it is an 'object' of concernful deliberation.

Before one makes an absolute, existential choice, as Kierkegaard expresses it, "the personality is already interested in the choice before one chooses."[29] This interest is nothing but a rational, concernful deliberation about the 'object' of choice. In Aristotle's terms, "choice involves reasoning and some process of thought" because "previous deliberation seems to be implied by the very term *proaireton*, which denotes something *chosen before*."[30] Lest it be thought that the attempt to relate Kierkegaard's conception of choice to Aristotle's conception of *proairesis* is arbitrary or capricious, it may be mentioned that Kierkegaard noted with interest (in his journals) that Aristotle's term *proairesis* could mean "purpose" or "forechoice."[31] In Kierkegaard's terms, *proairesis* can be understood as an anticipation of choice in subjective concern, a "movement" of the individual towards a possibility having significance for his own moral or personal development. For Kierkegaard, as well as Aristotle, concernful deliberation is a condition for the possibility of *rational* choice. To be sure, Kierkegaard held, as Aristotle did, that there can be no resolute choice without "desire" or *pathos*. In his *Con-

cluding Unscientific Postscript Kierkegaard remarks that "ethically the highest pathos is interested pathos, expressed through the active transformation of the individual's entire mode of existence in conformity with the object of interest" or subjectively posited *telos*.[32]

Kierkegaard agreed with Aristotle that "the irrational feelings are just as much a part of human nature as reason" and that rational deliberation in itself is incapable of bringing about choice or action. In an assertion that will pervade Kierkegaard's critique of the habit of indefinite deliberation, Aristotle claims that "thought by itself moves nothing" (*dianoia d'aute outhen kinei*).[33] It is for this reason that thought must be brought in relation to desire in order for choice to occur. The Aristotelian notion that *proairesis* is either reason served by desire (*orektikos nous*) or desire served by reasoning (*orexis dianoetike*) is one that underlies Kierkegaard's conception of choice despite his tendency to exaggerate the role of 'passion' in choice. For Kierkegaard, ethical being is concerned with the "pathos of action." He points out in his journals that one should not "misunderstand my talk about passion (*Lidenskab*) and pathos to mean that I am proclaiming any and every uncircumscribed immediacy, all manner of unshaven passion."[34] Passion or desire is the motivating *nisus* in choice for Kierkegaard as well as for Aristotle, but it is not, as some commentators on Kierkegaard have suggested, entirely divorced from reason or rational self-consciousness. Kierkegaard's essential position is that action (of which choice itself is an instance) is not possible without concern or interest—that it stands in relation to resolution consciously thought through. Without what he calls the "clarity of resolution," it could be said that our 'actions' are things that "happen" to us rather than that we act at all. As Kierkegaard remarks in his *Edifying Discourses,* action presupposes at least some self-knowledge in order that we may have assurance that our actions depend upon conscientious reflections and are not "in the service of unclarified cravings."[35] Thus, although Kierkegaard does emphasize the importance of the energy and passion with which an 'absolute' existential choice is made, he did not intend that such a choice would be purely irrational; rather, he has indicated that reason or, at least rational self-reflective consciousness, must interpenetrate passion or *Lidenskab* in order that a choice be truly an act of the individual. As in the case of Aristotle (in his *Nicomachean Ethics*), choice, for Kierkegaard, "necessarily involves both desire and reasoning directed to some end."[36] Since Kierkegaard holds that an "absolute" choice is not possible without a deliberate reflection upon possibilities having direct relevance to one's becoming, without an intensification of consciousness, without an attempt to attain subjective or self-knowledge, it is clearly for him as much an act infused by reason as it is for Aristotle. Kierkegaard's conception of the "dialectic of choice" is not antagonistic to that of the rationalist tradition in Western thought. In point of fact, it is, I believe, specifically derived from Aristotle's analysis of deliberate choice in the *Nicomachean Ethics*. That Kierkegaard refers to the importance of the "baptism of the will" in choice may also be said to be related to Aristotle's occasional references to the importance of will in voluntary choice (especially in *Magna Moralia*). Indeed, there are commentators on Aristotle's ethics (e.g., A. Grant, W. D. Ross, A. K. Griffin, and T. Ando) who claim that Aristotle's discussions of *boulesis* and *proairesis* are attempts to provide an account of the will.[37] The striking similarity between Kierkegaard's informal phenomenology of choice and that of Aristotle is even clearer in St. Thomas' Aristotelian analysis of the act of choice. In his *Summa Theologiae* Aquinas states:

> The term choice expresses something belonging to the reason or intellect, and something belonging to the will . . . it is evident that, in a sense, reason precedes the will and directs its acts . . . insofar as the will tends to its object according to the order of reason; for the apprehensive power presents to the appetite its object . . . choice is substantially, not an act of reason, but of will; for choice is accomplished in a certain movement of the soul towards [what] is chosen.[38]

There are a number of similarities between Aristotle's account of *proairesis* and Kierkegaard's phenomenology of choice. Even Kierkegaard's notion that choice is individuating is not entirely alien to Aristotle's analysis of choice. As I have already indicated,

Aristotle held that choice is a surer test of character than action, that it is our choice of good or evil that determines our character, that it is an act brought about by an individual by virtue of a synthesis of reason and desire, and, finally, that an individual can, through unfortunate choices, lose his capacity for choice and resoluteness. The loss of character and the loss of the capacity for choice seem to correspond to what Kierkegaard regards as the loss of self. In man there is no immanent *nisus* toward complete realization since the actualization of moral and intellectual 'virtues' is dependent upon the repeated choices and decisions of an individual. Indeed, the ethical goal for Aristotle (which, of course, is quite different from that of Kierkegaard), which corresponds to Kierkegaard's conception of an ethical ideality, is a complete self-realization (*entelecheia*) that, we may assume, is a goal that, insofar as it is attained, requires a lifetime of striving and repeated *praxis*. Indeed, one might say that even for Aristotle the movement toward this goal could only be an approximation-process.

While there are a number of similarities between Kierkegaard's account of ethical self-becoming and Aristotle's analysis of moral development, there are, of course, differences that ought to be pointed out. Before briefly considering some of them, I would like to indicate some other relationships between some of Kierkegaard's explicit notions about moral development and Aristotle's implicit description of *how* one becomes a virtuous being.

In general, Kierkegaard accepts Aristotle's implicit conception of the subjective teleology of an individual's moral development (which may be contrasted with the imminent teleology in the *Metaphysics*). In regard to the acquisition of 'virtues' Kierkegaard agrees with Aristotle that one acquires 'virtue' by means of repeated choices, repeated *praxis*, by means of repeated good action (*eupraxia*). In general, too, Kierkegaard adopts the Aristotelian notion of the moral indeterminacy of the individual. This is clear from his understanding of significant choice insofar as choice is possible only for one who is capable of deliberation and intense self-consciousness; hence, even guilt or despair must be *chosen* by an individual in order that he be responsible for what he has become. If one assumes that Kierkegaard, insofar

as he accepted a Christian conception of man, was committed
to the view that man has a natural proclivity towards evil by
virtue of 'original sin', it can be shown, on the contrary, that
this is not his essential standpoint. As Louis Dupré has pointed
out in his *Kierkegaard as Theologian,* Kierkegaard held that
"original sin" is not a sin. Indeed, it is said that he "abandons the
orthodox tradition of the Reformation" and tends to reject "the
thesis that man is no longer free to do good and avoid evil since
the Fall." Kierkegaard does so, as Dupré avers, because he desired to preserve the notion of personal responsibility.[39] It may be
said that man's fundamental potentiality-for is morally indeterminate insofar as it is a potentiality for good or evil. There is an
assertion in Aristotle's *Topics* that is curiously relevant to this
question. In discussing what he calls the "category of capacity or
potentiality," he remarks that "a capacity is always among the
things worthy of choice [*aireton*], for even capacities for evil
are worthy of choice."[40] To be sure, Aristotle held that the touchstone is the use made of potentialities by the good man, and not
the bad.

For Aristotle, as well as for Kierkegaard, there are certain
moments in the lives of individuals when their deliberate choices
are decisive. For the most part, our 'choices' and decisions are not
morally significant, not particularly important for the development of character, but are *adiaphoric* or morally neutral. However, certain choices are, indeed, important since they contribute
not only to the formation (or deformation) of character but to
the direction of our lives or the evolving holistic tendency of our
being. While Kierkegaard does not, so far as I know, explicitly
refer to the acquisition of a disposition (*hexis*) to choose to act
in a specific way in the future by virtue of a repetition of similar
choices in the past, I believe that it is implicit both in his dialectic of choice and especially in his conception of resoluteness.
Since this latter notion is intimately related to Kierkegaard's
account of choosing oneself, I will attempt to deal with it in my
explication of this 'stage' in the phenomenology of choice. In regard to the question of the similarity between Aristotle's account
of the development of morally relevant tendencies in the person
and that of Kierkegaard, it is clear that Kierkegaard's emphasis

upon the decisive moment of choice, his view that an individual "forges the chains of his bondage with the strength of his freedom," do have their origin in Aristotle's account of man's "original" moral indeterminacy. This is manifest in his reference to a passage in Aristotle's *Nicomachean Ethics* that had considerable influence upon his conception of the development of the individual. In a discussion of an individual's capacity to liberate himself from a debilitating moral condition that he himself had 'willed', Kierkegaard, in *Philosophical Fragments,* quotes with approval the passage in Aristotle's *Ethics* that refers to the 'power' an individual has to become virtuous or vicious. Since Kierkegaard apparently quotes this passage from memory he does not present Aristotle's views as completely or as accurately as he could have. Aristotle asserts that "when you have thrown a stone, you cannot afterwards bring it back again, but nevertheless you are responsible for having taken up the stone and flung it, for the origin of the act was within you. Similarly, the unjust and profligate might at the beginning [*ex archēs*, an expression that is somewhat ambiguous in Aristotle's analysis because he hesitated before an attempt to discern the nature or meaning of this original potentiality in man; needless to say, I have endeavored to indicate that Kierkegaard did attempt to deal with this question in terms of nan's original potentiality-for or *kunnen*] have avoided becoming so, and therefore they are so voluntarily, although when they have become unjust and profligate it is no longer open to them not to be so."[41]

Although Kierkegaard does not explicitly deal with the question of the acquisition of habits that dispose an individual to act in this way or that on a fresh occasion, he does tend to interpret resoluteness itself in these terms. Kierkegaard places the accent on resolution or determination because he regards it, as he puts it in *Stages on Life's Way,* as an "ideality" that is the hallmark of a man. A positive resolution has the advantage that it consolidates an individual's life and gives him assurance in his own consciousness. It is the "act of resolution" that is the ethical act par excellence since it is by virtue of it that an individual makes concrete in his actuality an ideality (i.e., a conceptual possibility) that can, through repetition, become—as Kierkegaard suggests in *Stages on Life's Way*—habitual.[42] The energy and *pathos* that interpenetrate resolute choice (whether it is the absolute choice of good and evil—a choice of the *ethisk*—or a choice of oneself) receive emphasis in his phenomenology of choice because he believed, as he expresses it in his journals, that "determination, decision also open up, and therefore it is also called resolving; with resolution or in the resolution the best powers of the spirit open up."[43] Needless to say, the mode of existential choice that involves "choosing to choose a kind of Being-one's-Self which, in accordance with its existential structure" is what Heidegger calls "resoluteness" (*Entschlossenheit*), practically corresponds to Kierkegaard's conception of resolution. Furthermore, when Heidegger avers that the understanding of the "call of conscience" (compare Kierkegaard's remark that conscience (*Samvittighed*) is "but a question . . . for the sake of conscience") reveals itself as "wanting to have a conscience" (*Gewissenhabenwollen*), in which phenomenon lies resoluteness (which is, hence, related to the disclosedness of *Dasein*), one can see what a careful student of Kierkegaard's writings Heidegger was. Indeed, it is not at all surprising that Heidegger states that "resoluteness is a distinctive mode of *Dasein's* disclosedness."[44]

In resolute choice the individual accentuates his own unique individuality and reinforces, as it were, his capacity for resoluteness in the future. As Kierkegaard describes the resoluteness of an 'absolute' choice, it is precisely the kind of action (Heidegger, of course, notes that in resolution *Dasein* "takes action") that is not possible for a psychopath. It is this type of individual who is most often referred to in criticisms of Kierkegaard's stress upon "the energy, the earnestness, [and] the pathos with which one choose,"[45] despite the fact that such individuals are typically described by psychoanalysts as incapable of remorse, guilt, or a sense of responsibility for their actions, and who are, as many psychoanalysts believe, driven by unconscious motivations over which they have little or no control, the usual candidate for such motivation being an unconscious feeling of guilt.

The scrutiny of the self that Kierkegaard counsels as a propaedeutic to authentic choice has the capacity, he believes, to inhibit, if not preclude, immorality. His emphasis upon resolute choice, self-knowledge, and decisiveness is by no means idiosyncratic and, in fact, is one that is tantamount to the views of some contemporary philosophers. Thus, Stuart Hampshire, for example, in his *Thought and Action*, avers:

> A man becomes more and more a free and responsible agent the more he at all times knows what he is doing, in every sense of this phrase, and the more he acts with a definite and clearly formed intention. He is in this sense less free the less his actual achievements, that which he directly brings into existence and changes by his activity, correspond to any clearly formed intentions of his own.[46]

The moment of choice, when it is concerned with a significant moral decision or with what Heidegger, after Kierkegaard, calls one's potential-for-being-a-self, is important because it is the beginning of the establishment of a pattern of behavior or patterns of behavior that will tend to be repeated by an individual and will affect many future choices. There is, for each individual, a significant moment that, although it is transitory, is the "right time" (*kairos*) for the transformation of the self through choice. It is by virtue of the self-conscious repetition (*repetere,* "to seek or to attack again") of resolute choice that an individual becomes a self.

Before discussing the question of what Kierkegaard means by his admonition to "choose oneself," I would like to concern myself with an assertion that seems to offend some philosophers of human behavior or action, namely, Kierkegaard's insistence that the most fundamental choice that must be made in order to attain an authentic ethical existence is a choice to choose. Although I have already indicated that man's possibility of, or potentiality-for, choice is central to Kierkegaard's concept of man, I would like to approach this question from another perspective in order to see whether this notion does, in fact, make any sense.

Since Kierkegaard is not primarily concerned with the 'what' of the activity of choice, but with its *how*, he attempted to present a Hegelian phenomenology of the 'movements' of choice or the dialectic of choice as it is experienced from within. What he calls the choice to choose (that is, to make a significant choice that entails an intense subjective commitment on the part of the individual) originates with the psychic processes of the complex psychophysical individual who posits this choice as a spiritual possibility and subjectively apprehends his own capacity or potentiality for this choice. Unlike some contemporary philosophical psychologists, Kierkegaard held that choice is a voluntary, intentional 'mental act' of an individual. Like Aristotle, as I have already indicated, Kierkegaard maintained that (a) choice is a voluntary act and (b) that it is, in Aristotle's words, "the cause of action," and that the cause of choice "is desire and reasoning directed to some end." Although Aristotle avers in Book III of the *Nicomachean Ethics* that choice is brought about by intellect or reason (a view that Kierkegaard would have had to reject), he corrects this position in Book VI and proclaims that "choice [*proairesis*] may be either thought related to desire or desire related to thought; and man, as an originator of action, is a union of desire and intellect."[47] This interpretation of choice is substantially the same as Kierkegaard's. It must be pointed out, however, that Kierkegaard held that existential thinking (e.g., a reflective analysis of one's own existence) is a process in which thought, imagination, and passion (*eros*) interact in dialectical relationship. Since a consciousness of the possibility of 'absolute' choice would be paradigmatic of existential thought, Kierkegaard would have added imagination as a relevant factor in a choice situation. In this regard, Kierkegaard held that "the power of a person's feeling, knowledge, and will depends in the last resort on his imagination." This is a significant difference between Kierkegaard's account of choice and the becoming of the individual and that of Aristotle. *En passant*, it may be pointed out that Heidegger, who appropriated many specific details of Kierkegaard's analysis of human existence, practically ignores the role of imagination in *Dasein's* existence and hence weakens his analysis of existential possibility. At any rate, what I have tried to suggest is that Kierkegaard's description of choice is, in certain respects, not entirely unlike that of Aristotle. At no point does Kierkegaard deny the role that understanding, self-knowledge, and deliberation play in the act of choice. As James Collins has said (in his *The Mind of Kierkegaard*), Kierkegaard "does not advocate that we *suppress* imagination and intellect, but only that we *integrate* them with will and the sense of concrete conditions of action which it heightens."[48] Against Hegel (and, by implication, against some contemporary "Anglo-American" philosophers), Kierkegaard desired merely that philosophers give imagination and feeling their due since, as he puts it, "it is just as arbitrary to exalt reason exclusively as it is to exalt feeling and imagination. . . . reason is just . . . as deceptive as feeling and imagination."[49]

While the act of "absolute" choice (e.g., the choice to choose, the choice of good and evil or their exclusion, or the choice of oneself) is a dialectical transition, the 'movement' from an aesthetic or nihilistic mode of being requires what Kierkegaard calls a 'pathetic transition' or a transition brought about by *pathos*. It is from Kierkegaard's study of Trendelenburg's works (especially, his *Logische Untersuchungen* and *Geschichte der Kategorienlehre*) that he constructed what he calls a "technique" for the description of the dynamic character of human existence. To be sure, Kierkegaard transforms Aristotle's application of basic concepts (e.g., *kinēsis, kata dunamin, kat' energeian, alloiosis*, etc,) in an ingenious way that would scandalize scholars who are devoted to rigid interpretations of Aristotle's thought. Thus, for example, the conception of a 'movement' effected by an agent is related to *kinēsis kata to pathos*, which is characterized by "qualitative change" or *alloiosis*. Again, Kierkegaard appropriates the notion of *pathos* insofar as it is the quality by which it is possible for a being to undergo *alloiousthai* or "qualitative change." The "pathos-filled transition" to the *ethisk* or what I have called the ethical 'turn' involves a transformation in kind, a qualitative change in the being of an individual. In describing the projective movement of the individual towards the realization of his spiritual possibilities Kierkegaard interrelates many of Aristotle's basic concepts and applies them (as Aristotle, of course, did not) exclusively to the 'becoming' of an individual. In a passage in the *Philosophical Fragments* we can see how Kierkegaard integrated these Aristotelian notions. The

following analysis can be applied to the contingency of authentic
choice, the realization of a possibility, and the 'movements' of an
individual capable of action. In this analysis of coming into existence (not 'originally', but in regard to the realization of possibility) Kierkegaard asks what the nature of the mode of change
that may be designated "coming into existence" is. Qualitative
change (*alloiosis*) presupposes the existence of that

> which changes, even when the change consists in ceasing to
> exist. But this is not the case with coming into existence. For,
> if the subject of coming into existence does not itself remain
> unchanged during the change of coming into existence, that
> which comes into existence is not this subject which comes
> into existence, but something else. Then the question involves
> a *metabasis eis allo genos* [an expression he uses in his journals
> to refer to a transformation of the self in terms of having a con-
> viction which becomes central to the individual's actuality—in his
> illustration Kierkegaard says that a person who is in love does
> not merely want to say "I am in love," but undergoes a *metabasis
> eis allo genos* in pathos] in that the inquirer in the given case
> either sees another change copresent with the change of coming
> into existence, which confuses the question for him, or he mis-
> takes the nature of what is coming into existence and therefore
> is not in a position to ask the question. If a plan in coming into
> existence is in itself changed, it is not this plan which comes
> into existence; but if it comes into existence without being
> changed, what then is the change of coming into existence? This
> change (coming into existence) . . . is not a change in essence,
> but in being and is a transition from not existing to existing. But
> this non-being which the subject of coming into existence leaves
> behind [i.e., negates or transcends] must itself have some sort of
> being. . . . But such a being [which, strictly speaking, appears to
> be intermediate between being and non-being] . . . is precisely
> what possibility is . . . the change of coming into existence is a
> transition from possibility to actuality.[50]

For Kierkegaard the "coming to be" of choice, decision, action,
or, more generally, the becoming of a rational, self-conscious, intentional being, takes place 'through' freedom insofar as there

is no necessity determining the occurrence of such 'effects'. The 'cause' of the 'movement' from possibility to actuality in the historical and temporal development of an individual is precisely the complex psychophysical individual who is, qua causal agent, a synthesis of reason, imagination, passion, and will. While one may question (as I have already indicated) Kierkegaard's attempt to attribute an independent ontological status to possibility itself, and while one may question further the 'artificiality' of his language, Kierkegaard has endeavored to provide a philosophical account of 'self-becoming' that is not (once the Aristotelian terminology is, as it were, softened) radically dissimilar from many recent accounts of intentional action. The transition from the intention to act to the realization of an action is a complex process that, when it is subjected to philosophical analysis, is often expressed in Aristotelian language. One wonders whether this is the case because Aristotle's concept of causality (which has a way of appearing and reappearing, thinly or thickly disguised, in Western philosophical thought) was itself basically modeled on human action. It is quite obvious, at any rate, that Kierkegaard's conception of the subjective teleology of human development and of the voluntary or intentional activity of man (including the voluntary activity of choice) is derived to a great extent from a synthesis of various Aristotelian conceptions. This must be borne in mind, as I have said, when one is confronted by those who believe that Kierkegaard's analysis of choice and action is a paradigm of irrationalism.

Although the 'cause' of choice is the actual psychophysical individual (who is described in *The Sickness unto Death* as a synthesis of possibility and actuality) at a particular stage of his physical, psychological, and spiritual life history, Kierkegaard, of course, emphasizes the role of volition" or an "act of will" in one's choice to choose. The questions of volitions as 'causes' of choices or actions and of the meaningfulness of a choice to choose have a direct bearing upon some recent analyses proffered by philosophical psychologists. It may help to clarify Kierkegaard's interpretation of choice if such analyses are applied to his views.

In *Either/Or* Kierkegaard seems to describe at least three types of crucial or 'absolute' choices: (1) the choice to choose,

(2) the choice of 'the ethical', of good and evil, *or* the choice to exclude these determinants from one's conception of oneself and all actuality, and (3) the choice of oneself. This is not the case, however, since it is said (via Judge Wilhelm) that the "will to choose" or the choice to choose is itself already ethically significant and, hence, by virtue of it "the good and the evil are posited."[51] Kierkegaard holds this view, so far as I am able to see, because he is considering the case of an individual who has not deliberately willed 'evil', but who has been irresolute or lacking in any subjectively significant commitment to a purpose (e.g., the asethete or the nihilist). Since resoluteness itself is, for Kierkegaard, an ethical existential category, the individual has, by choosing to choose, already implicitly become involved, as it were, in the ethical sphere of existence. The decision to choose is itself a *good* action. At this point in his description of the dialectic of choice, Kierkegaard abruptly 'prescribes' that the *object* of choice (once the decision to choose is made) ought to be oneself, even though he had previously said that an individual may choose 'the wrong' and yet still be capable of an authentic existence because the choice was made with the energy and 'inwardness' of the personality. (The reference, in this context, to the person being brought into immediate relation to "the eternal power" whose presence pervades all existence is, as I shall argue, not central to Kierkegaard's concept of ethical existence and is an importation of a characteristic of religious existence that is by no means necessary for the practical ethics of subjectivity that Kierkegaard formulates.)

The reason that Kierkegaard advocates the choice of oneself is that he believes this to be a necessary condition for right choice insofar as it enables the individual, as we shall see, to understand and accept the "necessity" in his being in order to be relatively free from the influence of personal characteristics or tendencies that might prohibit the rational choice of the good. At this stage of my explication of Kierkegaard's phenomenology of choice I would like to focus once more upon the question of the possibility of choosing to choose.

A resolute choice (which is described as absolute in contrast to the relative, momentary 'choices' that are common in daily life) to choose is an 'event' that Kierkegaard describes as extraordinary and one that presupposes, of course, an individual who has already realized possibilities of choice and action. Indeed, "absolute" choice seems possible only for one who is already intensely self-reflective. For Kierkegaard, the possibility of personality lies in self-awareness; indeed, the "self grows out of reflection." The choice to choose may be described as an original project by which a self-reflective individual *begins* to become a self. Now, in regard to the notion of a choice to choose it has been argued that such a view leads to an infinite regress. To say, as Gilbert Ryle does in *The Concept of Mind*, that "if . . . an act of choosing is describable as voluntary, then . . . it would have in its turn to be the result of a prior choice to choose, and that from a choice to choose to choose"[52] is to deny that there can ever be an 'original' voluntary choice. While this criticism seems to have logical force, it appears to contradict the psychological facts of one's own life and to negate the phenomenological character of the choice situation. In the first place, as Aristotle said in his *Nicomachean Ethics*, choices to do seem to be *voluntary* acts that involve a subjective sense of effort or will in the individuals making them. If choices were not, in some sense, voluntary, it is difficult to know how one could attribute responsibility for a choice (*adiaphoric* or morally significant) to an agent or an individual who is said to be the 'cause' of the choice. To be sure, it is not 'volition' that chooses but the particular psychophysical individual at a particular stage of his development. In order to account for the phenomenological sense of intentionality it is surely not absurd to refer to a voluntary choice. If choices are not voluntary, then how is it possible to account for the transition from the subjective sense of intention to an overt (or covert) action? In his chapter on "The Will," Ryle himself uses the word 'choice' in reference to possible moves in a game of chess; and one may ask: what is the meaning of the word 'choice' in Ryle's own illustration? If it does not have reference to a voluntary or intentional act (which can only be subjectively verified and not intersubjectively verified insofar as it refers to the *intention* to do something) then its meaning is obscure in the context of Ryle's discussion. If a choice, in such an instance, is not a voluntary act

at all, how can one say, for example: "He *chose* to move the
pawn"? I cannot attribute the choice to *anyone*. How do I know
whether this individual did not move the chess piece accidentally
(or unconsciously) or involuntarily? There must be a psychological basis for the voluntary overt action—a prior state of consciousness of the agent that accounts for *this* particular action
or behavior. It will not do to say that such an individual is
"minding" or "heeding" various possible choices since this obviously entails no overt action whatsoever insofar as it refers to
"attending" to something. Surely there must be some way in
which we can refer to the preceeding intentional decision to
choose to act in this way or that way that preserves the subjective *nisus* or *conatus* of the individual, his sense of effort or of
striving to do this or that. I believe that Kierkegaard's analysis
of the dialectic of choice (even though it is concerned with
"momentous," absolute, or significant choice and not with what
he describes in *Either/Or* as "aesthetic choices") is in many respects more faithful to, and does more justice to, the psychological facts of one's immediate experience in significant-choice
situations.

Whether it is possible to 'say' that one chooses to choose without implicitly involving oneself in an infinite regress is a logical
question that may be valid, but the possibility of choosing to
choose does seem to have meaning in relation to the concrete
immediacy of human experience. Surely it makes sense to say
that all possibilities of action (i.e., intentional or voluntary action that is, strictly speaking, the only paradigm for action) are,
previously, possibilities of choice. To take Gilbert Ryle's notion
of "heeding" or "attending" (which, incidentally, seems to do all
the work, as analytical philosophers are wont to say, of the *consciousness* of "the philosophers"), we may ask, is it possible on
any occasion to choose to heed something or to choose not to
heed that something? If there are these possibilities of choice,
does it not make sense to say that an individual can choose to
choose to heed something or to refrain from heeding that something? To take another example, one that is closer, I believe, to
what Kierkegaard had in mind, one may say that at a particular
stage of his life an individual (who, let us assume, had been in-

terested in religious questions for some time) is offered the choice of becoming a convert to a particular religious organization or sect. Let us assume that he chooses not to do so. Nor does he choose to accept any other commitment in regard to religious questions (i.e., he does not choose to be an agnostic or an atheist). Could we not say of such a person that (in regard to what we assume is a serious question for his life) he is irresolute, that he was unable *to make* a choice? Now, it seems to me that the expression "to make a choice"—an expression that is a rather common one—gives the show away, for "to make" something surely requires an activity. But what kind of activity can this be? Is it a decisive activity? But surely if one *decides* to choose, this has, *mutatus mutandis,* the same meaning as "to choose" to choose. if, in Aristotle's language, it is possible for one to choose—if one has the capacity for choice—then it must be possible for one not to choose. But if it *is* possible for one to choose or not to choose, then something must be decisive in the situation, namely, choice itself. To be sure, Kierkegaard implicitly agreed with Aristotle that "a man is the originator of his actions."[53] It is not a "volition" that causes a choice even though, of course, Kierkegaard does assume that man is a being capable of volition. Certainly "absolute" choice is a voluntary, self-conscious, intentional, cognitive-emotive act that is, in general terms, a *spiritual* act of a specific temporal-historical individual.

For Kierkegaard (as for the Heidegger of *Sein und Zeit*), there are ontic possibilities that have already been realized by an individual or that have been realized for him; but these possibilities were not realized by virtue of resolute, self-conscious choice. If an individual has been irresolute, then he has not yet made an 'absolute' choice since he has not decided to choose. Surely we can say of an individual who is confronted with a significant choice at a crucial stage of his life that he may refrain from making such a choice or that he can be resolved to make it. From the perspective of an individual's personal development it is clear that one can put off decisiveness in regard to one's life. In procrastination an individual does not choose, is not decisive, is unable or unwilling to decide to choose. To return to the illustration of a game of chess, we may say that a player is confronted with a number of possible moves and, hence, a number of possible choices; if he chooses to make one move rather than any other possible move, he may be said to have made *this* choice as the possiblility he would realize. Could we not hold that this selection is itself a choice? It would seem that the prior decision to make this or that choice is itself a choice. Now, if we abandon a description of choice in terms of intentional volition (bearing in mind that this, too, is an act of a complex psycho-physical individual), it is difficult to know how *voluntary* action is possible, and it is also difficult to distinguish voluntary from involuntary 'action' or behavior. To answer the question "Who did this act?" or "How did this action come about?" by simply saying "He did it" is surely not a solution of a philosophical problem but rather the emergence of one.

It may be noted *en passant* that it is somewhat ironical that Ryle's analysis of choice and the origin of human action is dependent to a great extent upon some aspects of Aristotle's *Nicomachean Ethics*. This is ironical because when Ryle argues that "volitions" cannot bring about action since it is "a man" who does this or that he is clearly bearing in mind Aristotle's assertion that "a man is the origin of his actions" (*anthropos einai arche ton praxeon*).[54] But despite the influence of Aristotle on his analyses, Ryle seems wary of attempting to do what Aristotle did in his *Ethics*. That is, he does not want to trace the process of the initiation of action back beyond the particular man himself, does not want to get back to the question of *how* or by what means "a man" does this or that. In his zeal to avoid "mentalism" Ryle has left a serious lacuna in his account of intentional behavior. Without at least postulating something like volitional activity, how can we comprehend the transition from an understanding of possibilities of choice and possibiliites of action to the actualization of one of these possibilities? Even if it is admitted, as Ryle puts it, that "most voluntary actions do not issue out of conditions of indecision and are not . . . results of settlements of indecisions,"[55] it is not the case that voluntary actions imply that one is merely "minding what he is doing." One can appeal to Aristotle's view that choice is a voluntary act; but not all voluntary actions issue from choices. If we attempt to illuminate the subjective *nisus* of the individual in intentional action (including, for example, an act of believing this or that) we seem to blur the distinction between voluntary action and involuntary 'action'. Of course, a voluntary action is "done on purpose" or is intended; but surely this means that an individual has chosen to do it. For Kierkegaard, at any rate, the 'absolute' either/or he refers to is related to questions of indecisiveness. In Heidegger's terms, what is required for an authentic being-one's-self is a "making up for not choosing" (*Nachholen einer Wahl*) that "signifies *choosing to make this choice.*"[56] That for the sake of which one chooses to choose is, for Kierkegaard, one's self. Phenomenologically, the decisive act of making an "absolute" choice is itself considered to be a volitional choice. If one chooses to choose (what Kierkegaard refers to as the "reality" of the act of choice), there seems to be no need to account for this specific choice in terms of an immediately prior choice even though, of course, previous 'choices' in one's life history (which, for Kierkegaard, would be aesthetic choices, for the most part) will affect one's present capacity for resolute choice. To be sure, Kierkegaard implicitly agrees with Aristotle that "a man" is the origin of his action (and, hence, of his choices); but he also holds that it is by virtue of an act of will or volition that a choice is made. To my mind, it may be impossible to *know* what the original or ultimate basis of choice is; but we can attempt to describe how the subjective act of choice is brought about 'from within' in terms of an explication that would resemble Kierkegaard's phenomenology of choice. That it has been shown that individuals can initiate movements of electrically controlled artificial limbs by virtue of what seems to be rather precise deliberate intentions does not, of course, demonstrate that there are volitions or acts of will, but it does suggest that both from an empirical and a philosophical standpoint, the question of the *initiation* of decision, choice, or action is one for which we do not as yet have an apodictic answer. To say that an "I" chooses or that "a man" chooses this or that raises the questions of what the 'I' is, or what a man is, and *how* a man or the 'I' does in fact choose.

An act of "absolute" choice is the act of an individual who already 'had' the potentiality-for becoming a self and is, hence, the realization of a possibility that had been implicitly present for this individual insofar as he had the potentiality for subjective, concernful consciousness. A subjective concern for the actualization of a spiritual possibility through choice already has an ethical significance, according to Kierkegaard, since this subjective concern for the self-being of one's own "reality" is the hallmark of the ethical sphere of existence. To exist in persistent striving, in subjective inwardness, to strive to become a self is, as we shall see, Kierkegaard's prescription for an ethical mode of being. Needless to say, the activity of existing, as Kierkegaard describes it, is as difficult to attain as to sustain throughout a lifetime. To become an authentic person or self is as difficult, in Kierkegaard's terms, as it is to become a Christian. Nevertheless, the means by which one initiates this *nisus* towards selfhood is clear in Kierkegaard's analysis of the dialectic of choice: it is the decision to make an "absolute" choice that intensifies subjective consciousness and consolidates the self by virtue of the individuating character of resolute, "absolute" choice. Insofar as the individual asserts his own unique individuality in making a significant choice (as opposed to an "indifferent" aesthetic choice) he has made an "absolute" choice of himself.

While it is true, as James Collins has observed, that Kierkegaard's central conception of "choosing oneself" is occasionally presented "in very hazy, metaphorical language" and in the language of German idealism,[57] the notion is more subtle and complicated than Collins has indicated. The expression "choose oneself" means the unconditioned choice of oneself as absolute (or, in Kierkegaard's hyperbolic phrase, the self in its "eternal" validity). It is the choice of the self as guilty and as in despair. However, Kierkegaard also relates choosing oneself to Socrates' "know thyself" insofar as it involves an active search for self-knowledge. Only in resolute, absolute choice has an individual "assumed himself" or, as Kierkegaard expresses it,

> so totally penetrated himself that every moment is attended by the consciousness of a responsibility for himself, only then has he chosen himself ethically, only then has he repented himself, only then is he concrete, only then is he in his total isolation in absolute continuity with the reality to which he belongs.[58]

In the second sense of choosing oneself, then, Kierkegaard has in mind a wholehearted acceptance of responsibility for what one has been and for what one is now and for what one is becoming. This choice is itself 'absolute' in the sense that it is not conditional or charaterized by the relativity of aesthetic 'choice'. This kind of analysis is, of course, no longer expressed in the idiom of Aristotle's ethics, but it is, rather, a modification of Hegelian notions and is, as we shall see, an echo of Spinoza's dictum, "freedom is the recognition of necessity."

To choose oneself as *in* despair is a significant movement in the dialectic of self-becoming since it is, first of all, a spiritual state—a state that is, as Kierkegaard says in his journals, "a self-accusation." The choice of despair indicates that an individual has taken responsibility for his spiritual state of being. Despair (like choice, anxiety, etc.) is individuating and hence it recalls one back to one's own existential possibility to become a self. First in his journals, and then in *The Sickness unto Death,* Kierkegaard describes the curious circle of the choice of despair. In despair over oneself one reveals a *prior* hope, a possibility that appears to have been lost. But this despair over oneself is a despair in the face of not willing to be oneself (i.e., not choosing oneself) that is traceable to a despair that is undergone in the will to be oneself. An absolute choice of oneself requires that one recognize that one has been and is in despair.[59] Although I cannot begin to deal with Kierkegaard's complex phenomenology of the forms of despair, there is one such form that is clearly relevant to his conception of ethical existence.

The notion that in choosing myself absolutely "I choose despair" is ambiguous insofar as it may refer either to the formerly irresolute individual's self-conscious acceptance of his prior state of despair (which had been "unconscious" or repressed) or to the despair that Kierkegaard suggests is an ineluctable ingredient of of an ethical existence. Since the "ideal" self that it is the task of the ethical individual to seek to become can never be fully realized, there is an inevitable asymptotic relationship between what one is and what one ought to be (and what one wills to be). For this reason, despair underlies ethical existence since, insofar as the self does not become what it ought to be, it is in despair. It is this despair that intensifies the dialectical tension of the persistent striving of an ethical existence. In his *Concluding Unscientific Postscript* Kierkegaard (through the pseudonym of Johannes Climacus) remarks that "the ethicist has *despaired* . . . in this despair he has *chosen himself*; in and by this choice he *reveals* himself."[60] By persisting in this despair and transforming it through ethical determination the individual can "at last [win] himself." Curiously enough, the "defiant despair" or despair of strength described in *The Sickness unto Death,* although it is criticized in some respects under the pseudonym of Anti-Climacus, closely resembles the state of being of the subjective ethical individual. For the conscious, willful despair of one who wills to become himself, an intense despair held in *Indesluttethed*—"close reserve" (or, as Walter Lowrie translates it, "introversion")—is certainly characteristic of what I believe to be Kierkegaard's existential ethics. This is clear when it is said that "the self despairingly wills . . . to create itself, to make itself the self it wills to be, distinguishing in the concrete self what it will and what it will not accept."[61] Again, this type of despairing self "is content with regarding itself, and by that it is supposed to bestow upon its undertakings infinite interest and importance." As I will attempt to suggest, this description of a form of despair that is characteristic of an individual who wills "as tirelessly as Tantalus" to be himself is quite similar to some of the characteristics of one who persistently pursues an ethical goal (*Maal*).

While the notion of choosing oneself absolutely can be understood as either a complete, unconditional choice of oneself as one has been (or is) or a complete, unconditional choice of oneself as one has been, is, and is becoming, it is not too clear what Kierkegaard means by the choice of the "eternal validity" of the self (if this is meant to be something other than a rhetorical flourish). It is clear, for one thing, that the actual self (as a dynamic synthesis of necessity and possibility) cannot *exist* in an eternal realm insofar as "movement" is, as Kierkegaard says both in his journals and *Concluding Unscientific Postscript*, impossible in eternity.[62] Moreover, the eternal, from the finite perspective of an individual, can only be an 'object' of faith (*Troen*) since it is, from the standpoint of knowledge, an objective uncertainty. That the self is eternal (*den Evige*) is a possibility. In point of fact, Kierkegaard sometimes suggested that the "Socratic faith" (which is an ethical faith, not a religious faith) was "faith in the wide sense." That is, as Cornelio Fabro expresses it in his "Faith and Reason in Kierkegaard's Dialectic," "one may even speak of faith in the sphere of pure nature," for example, the instance of "Socrates' unshakable faith in the immorality of the soul, even when he goes to death, does not arise from a logical necessity but from the inwardness of his being."[63]

One may describe the "eternal validity" of the self or, rather, the choice of it, as an expression of what James Collins calls "ethical faith," a faith that I would describe as being related to the goal of an ethical existence and to the 'eternal' validity of an authentic ethical existence in itself—that is, the unexpungeable, intrinsic value of the ethical existence of an individual. To choose oneself as absolute, then, may be understood as interpreting one's self as having absolute value or significance—in Kantian language, to treat oneself as an end in itself. While these notions may be aspects of what Kierkegaard means by an absolute choice of oneself as absolute, they are dialectical phases of a complex process. It is a process, one may assume, because Kierkegaard refers in *Either/Or* to the dialectical *movements* of choice or the initial phases of ethical subjectivity.

Choosing oneself implies, aside from an understanding of oneself as having been and being in despair, choosing to have a conscience and choosing that "alteration of the subject within the subject" which he calls guilt. Kierkegaard plays upon the relationship between "conscience" and "consciousness," indicating that an intensification of subjective, concernful consciousness entails the emergence of conscience. In a concernful deliberation about one's own unique spiritual possibilities there is an ineluctable anguished conscience that arises by virtue of the ironical recognition of the asymmetry between one's own imperfect actuality and what one believes or knows it is possible for one to be. Even if conscience is understood, in Freudian terms, as the "result" of the introjection of moral or ethical values conveyed to an individual by significant others, a point is reached in the development of a reflective individual when he critically analyzes this 'conscience'. But in this self-reflective understanding of oneself as having a conscience (what was called in Middle English *inwit,* "knowledge within") it is possible for one to choose to appropriate this conscience as one's own or flee from it. Conscience does not only mean, as Gilbert Ryle casually remarks in *The Concept of Mind,* that one has the inclination to provide "refresher lessons to [oneself] in . . . magisterial tones of voice."[64] In Heideggerian language, conscience is a call that recalls the individual to his potentiality-for-becoming-a-self. A rational, self-conscious individual *can* choose to have a conscience—can choose to be conscientious about his own choices, decisions, and actions. If one is to choose to be thoroughly responsible for what one is and is becoming, one must, *a fortiori,* choose to 'have' a conscience. More often than not it is not the case, as Shakespeare's Hamlet says, that "conscience doth make cowards of us all"; rather, it is consciencelessness that usually does so.

Since, for Kierkegaard, man has a freedom for the possibility of conscience, the self-conscious acquisition of conscience is something that may or may not be chosen. Conscience is not, as Kant avers in his *Lectures on Ethics,* "an instinct to pass judgment on ourselves according to moral laws."[65] For, in choosing oneself as having a conscience, one is not accepting a critical understanding of one's own spiritual condition in relation to either universal moral laws or an absolute *telos* or God; rather, one chooses to have a conscience because one recognizes an obligation that one has to oneself to become a self. Kierkegaard's assertion that "God's power is in the conscience" is an appropriate view for a "man of faith" who is already subjectively certain of the 'actuality' of God (an 'actuality' that is, from the rational standpoint, a conceptual-imaginative ideality), but it is by no means entailed by his conception of ethical existence. Although Kierkegaard admits, in *Concluding Unscientific Postscript,* that he (or, more accurately, Judge Wilhelm) tended to infuse *Either/Or* with a religious orientation that is misleading, he makes it clear, in his comments upon ethical existence in *Concluding Unscientific Postscript,* that an authentic ethical existence is possible "outside Christianity" and, for that matter, outside any religious faith. It was Kierkegaard , and not (as is commonly supposed) Heidegger, who first applied Christian notions (e.g., conscience and guilt) to states of being of man that have a purely existential significance and are not necessarily related to a religious mode of existence.

In his journals Kierkegaard relates conscience (*Samvittighed*) to a person's knowledge of his actions and the motives for them and describes the anguished conscience of ethical existence as an intensified awareness of the tension between what one is and what one ought to be.[66] We can see, then, that conscience is related to concernful subjective consciousness and critical self-reflection. One may say that one of the outcomes of an examined life is the realization of the possibility of conscience. While it is true that one may relate conscience to consciousness of duty (as Fahrenbach does, in his *Kierkegaards existenzdialektische Ethik*, in his discussion of "absolute self-choice" in terms of conscience and "duty consciousness"),[67] it must be borne in mind that this duty is for Kierkegaard fundamentally a duty toward oneself to become an authentic person. The universal (as I shall have occasion to mention in another context) is related to the individual not in the sense that one acts out of respect for a principle of duty but insofar as it is realized concretely in the concrete existence of an individual. The "secret of conscience," Kierkegaard remarks in *Either/Or*, is the recognition that an individual life can be at one and the same time a manifestation of "the universal."[68] While this may seem obscure, I hope to be able to clarify this statement in terms of a later discussion of the relationship between universality and subjectivity in Kierkegaard's practical ethics. Nevertheless, choosing oneself as having a conscience intensifies I-consciousness and discloses the actual, imperfect self as alienated from its possibility for self-being. For Kierkegaard, conscience is an important existential state of being because it "constitutes a personality." The choice to have a conscience entails, of course, a choice of oneself as guilty.

In the choice of conscience is disclosed the acknowledgement of the self as guilty. The guilt that Kierkegaard analyzes as a phenomenon of existential concern is not a neurotic, obsessive feeling of guilt about specific imagined or actually performed acts that are seen as morally repulsive. To be sure, Kierkegaard

himself was no stranger to intense feelings of guilt about his own
behavior; thus, there is an obscure reference to "the extraordinary
way in which something long forgotten suddenly bursts into consciousness . . . for example, the recollection of something wrong,
of which one was hardly conscious at the moment of acting."[69]
Deep personal feelings of guilt are precisely those feelings that
most human beings would dearly love to forget. The curious
thing about a guilt that one would desire to repress is that its
sudden recollection can shock an individual into a recognition
that he has indeed forgotten what he had thought he could never
forget; this can often generate a feeling of anxiety about oneself
insofar as one has apparently forgotten one's self or has forgotten
what one has been. Unfortunately, a neurotic feeling of guilt
(which is often cultivated with a kind of masochistic vengence)
is often ennervating, debilitating, and crippling to one's self-
concept. Perhaps, Kierkegaard might have said, it is because an
individual has not chosen himself as guilty, as completely responsible to himself for what he has been and is, that neurotic
guilt can often undermine the self-confidence that seems to be
required for resoluteness, for the choice of what we know to be
right in a particular situation. Neurotic guilt may be seen as a
kind of self-torturing fascination with one's own immorality. In a
deliberate choice of oneself as guilty, as "essentially and uncon-
ditionally guilty," one does not assume that one is only momen-
tarily guilty but accepts guilt as a pervasive aspect of one's existence. In some of his journal entries Kierkegaard compares guilt
to the debt that an individual owes to what is best in himself.
Or, one is in guilt because one has failed to take risks, has failed
to endeavor to become an integral self, or has been irresolute in
regard to what ought to have been a matter of subjective concern.
One may say that guilt may be encountered as a negativity 'in'
the self, a subjective sense of unrealized potentialities. Psychologically, it seems to be true that we often feel guilty about what
we have not done with our lives as often as we feel guilt over a
specific event in our lives that offends our moral consciousness.
What Kierkegaard says about despair—that it is the doubt of
personality—could with equal justice be said of guilt. In choosing
ourselves as guilty we put in question what we have been and

what we are now; but this understanding of ourselves as guilty
is transformed, in a manner of speaking, insofar as we have freely
chosen to take up responsibility for what we have been (and are)
and, by doing so, we have implicitly assumed responsibility for
what we will become. Responsibility for one's choices, decisions,
and action is a *responsum*, a response to the choice of ourselves
as guilty. Although Kierkegaard would, in a sense, have agreed
with Heidegger that "in the idea of 'Guilty' there lies the character of the 'not',"[70] he would have denied that this sense of "lack"
or negativity is not related to the notion of the "ought" (*Sollen*).
For the concept of guilt is inseparable from the conception of
"the ought" or, in Kierkegaard's language, the "oughtness-capability" that he assumes is immanently present in the being of rational, self-reflective, self-conscious human beings.

Choice and Self-Knowledge

In Kierkegaard's phenomenology of the ethical becoming of a
self, choosing oneself is related to knowing oneself. "When," he
writes, "the individual knows himself and has chosen himself he
is about to realize himself, but as he has to realize himself
freely he must know what it is he would realize." The individual
must endeavor to know himself, in all of his specificity, as he has
been and is, and he must attempt to discern the "ideal self" that
is potentially present in himself. In terms of *The Sickness unto
Death*, the individual must understand himself as a synthesis of
necessity and possibility.

The act of choosing oneself is not only individuating. It is an
act whereby the individual brings to fruition the possibility of
freedom. To choose oneself means to choose oneself as responsible for being what one is, what one has been, and what one is
becoming; it is an *aufgeheben* of the necessity that has determined one's life. The individual who chooses himself ethically
chooses himself as the concrete individual who is in being here
and now and who has been shaped by causal factors over which
he has had little or no control. "The individual," that is,

> becomes conscious of himself as this definite individual, with
> these talents, these dispositions, these instincts, these passions,

influenced by these definite surroundings, as this definite product of a definite environment. But being conscious of himself in this way, he assumes responsibility for all this.[71]

By virtue of this free choice of what has been imposed upon him the individual accepts what he has been and takes upon himself the burden of responsibility for what he does with these inherited dispositions and traits. Kierkegaard remarks that the individual who would become a person must "at some point take over his entire being"—must, that is, "choose himself." While it certainly is paradoxical that one is required to take responsibility for aspects of one's self that were shaped by causative factors outside one's control, I believe that what Kierkegaard means is that such an appropriation of one's past is a precondition for a clarification of one's present state of being and, hence, enables one to have at least sufficient self-knowledge for a rational choice of one's own unique spiritual possibilities. It may be said that freedom (for authentic possibilities) is not, as it was for Spinoza, the recognition of necessity; rather it is the appropriation of necessity *and* possibility in one's own being. Kierkegaard certainly did not hold that by knowing (so far as this is possible) the "necessity" in one's being one thereby negated it or transcended it. One cannot alter the "facts" of what one has been or has done, though an individual may repress certain memories or interpret these facticities in different ways at different stages of his life. Through a resolute choice of one's own being, however, the individual transforms or transfigures his own past and mitigates the necessity that governs a life in which resoluteness in regard to one's own existence has been postponed or avoided. What Kierkegaard seems to mean by this understanding of this apparent necessity in one's personality is quite similar to Stuart Hampshire's analysis of a similar (though, of course, not identical) phenomenon. In his *Thought and Action*, Hampshire points out that the notion that "freedom is the recognition of necessity" is a "misstatement of a truth." For an understanding of why I behave in a specific way or why I have a disposition to behave in this way or that does not mean, ipso facto, that I am independent of causal laws or that, as Hampshire puts it, I am "an exception to the causal law." Rather,

knowledge of the factors that have been influencing my conduct
without my knowledge does in itself open to me new possibilities of action. . . . I can think of the causal factors explaining my
past behavior as something that I may at least try in some way
to circumvent or to some degree counteract in future. . . . I have
brought to the forefront, and within my range of vision, something that I could not even attempt either to combat or to promote, because it was working its effects in the dark. . . . recognition of a causal uniformity [affecting one's behavior] at least is
a first step towards finding the means of evading its effects by
trying to alter . . . the boundary conditions, upon which its
operation depends.[72]

Although Heidegger's notion that *Dasein* is its possibility
(*Dasein ist je seine Möglichkeit. . . . Dasein wesenhaft je seine
Möglichkeit*) is clearly derived from Kierkegaard's philosophical
anthropology, it is not faithful to Kierkegaard's conception of the
self. For Kierkegaard maintains that 'man' has possibility in his
being in the sense that man is a contingent being, one that may
or may not be, or 'has' possibilities insofar as he has possibilities
for various modes of being, for freedom, absolute choice, for
authentic existence, etc. In addition, he is capable of understanding or reflecting upon a variety of possible occurrences in
the future and of encountering the "nothingness of possibility"—
hence the experience of anxiety in the face of the openness of
possibility.[73] In reflective self-knowledge, then, the individual attempts to arrive at an understanding of the necessity in his being
and the possibility in his being. The possibility that is said to be
"in" man is not independent of man's consciousness of possibility
either in imagination, conceptualization, or in the self-reflective
awareness of spiritual possibilities. An actual individual, then,
is a synthesis of necessity and possibility. This is an interpretation
of man's being that can be found in *Either/Or, Concluding Unscientific Postscript*, and *The Sickness unto Death*. The reason
I mention this is to indicate that there is a reasonable amount of
internal consistency in Kierkegaard's intrepretations of both the
self and the process of ethical self-realization.

The phase of an absolute choice of oneself is a kind of individuating isolation. As Kierkegaard describes it:

The first form which the choice takes is complete isolation. For
in choosing myself I detach myself from the entire world. . . .
The individual in having chosen himself in terms of his freedom,
is *eo ipse* active. His action, however, has no relation to any
surrounding world, for the individual has reduced this to
naught and exists only for himself.[74]

This process (which resembles Sartre's analysis of the *néanti-
sation* or nihilation performed by the *pour-soi*) contributes to the
consolidation of personality by virtue of a subjective intensification of individuation. In this concernful reflection upon himself the individual knows himself in terms of the actual self
that he has been and is and in terms of the possible, ideal self
that he can be. When Heidegger avers that *Dasein* is more than
what it is factually, since it has a possibility for being what it is
not yet, a possibility recognized in and through an implicit
knowledge of the self (*Sebsterkenntnis*), he is speaking in the
idiom of Kierkegaard. Since Heidegger equates self-knowledge
with the "transparency" of the self, we are reminded of Kierkegaard's view that in this isolating choice of oneself "the ethical
individual is transparent to himself."[75] While it is questionable
whether the self can be completely "transparent" to itself in
terms of Kierkegaard's interpretation of the self, it is curious to
note how often Heidegger adopts quite specific characteristics
of ethical self-being (as described by Kierkegaard) and changes
their meanings in the context of his fundamental ontology. One
particular assertion about the being of *Dasein* could be translated, with little difficulty, into Kierkegaard's conception of an
understanding of oneself as a synthesis of necessity and possibility. That is, the statement that "*Dasein* is never more than it facti-
cally is, for to its facticity its potentiality-for-Being belongs essentially."[76] If self-knowledge (which is tantamount to "choosing
oneself") reveals that one's potentiality-for-being (an amplification of Kierkegaard's notion of potentiality-for or *kunnen*) is im-
picitly present in one's "facticity," could we not say that, for
Heidegger, *Dasein* is a synthesis of "facticity" (*Faktizität*) and
"possibility" (*Möglichkeit*)? Kierkegaard, at any rate, conceives
of this isolating act of self-knowledge or choice of oneself as a
knowledge of "the actual self"—the necessary characteristics of

the self—and of "the ideal self" or the authentic self that is possible. In the inwardness of choice of oneself the individual discloses his particularity as well as the subjective end that can guide his ethical self-determinism. As Kierkegaard expresses it in *Either/Or*:

> He who has ethically chosen and found himself possesses himself as he is determined in his whole concretion. He has himself, then, as an individual who has these talents, these passions, these inclinations, these habits, who is under these influences, who in this direction is affected thus, in another thus. Here, then, he has himself as a task, in such a sort that the task is principally to order, cultivate, temper, enkindle, repress, in short, to bring about proportionality . . . a harmony [in himself].[77]

The purpose of the endeavor to understand what Kierkegaard calls the necessity in the self is to become "so radically conscious of himself that no adventitious trait escapes him," to understand oneself in order to acquire at least some degree of self-mastery. That one should choose to be responsible for what one could not have been responsible for (e.g., the family into which one was born, the hereditary traits one acquired, the nation into which one was born, the historical period in which one came into being, etc.) is of course a paradoxical requirement. But it is based upon Kierkegaard's belief that the authenticity of future choices requires at least some knowledge of the factors that have shaped one's being up to the present. Freedom is not the recognition of necessity; but it is manifested simultaneously in choosing oneself and is possible, *in futuro*, insofar as one has appropriated and wholly accepted the "necessity" in one's actuality. However, it is a mistake to assume that Kierkegaard holds that this necessity is ever annulled entirely.

There is a relationship of similarity between Kierkegaard's account of the self in *Either/Or* and his remarks about the self in *The Sickness unto Death*. As a conscious synthesis, the self is capable of understanding itself in terms of a dialectical relationship between the limited and the unlimited, the necessary and the possible, in itself. The intensification of I-consciousness in concernful self-reflection is related to a choice of oneself insofar as it involves an understanding of the oppositions between necessity and possibility, the actual self and the "ideal" self or the relationship between actuality and ideality in regard to one's own self-existence. Subjective thought requires, for Kierkegaard, an interrelationship among feeling, knowledge, and will under the dominance of imagination. Although Kierkegaard often refers to *conceived* possibility, his typical view is that, for the most part, the modality of possibility (*Mulighed*) is intimately related to the activity of imagination. In his journals he explicitly claims that "imagination is the medium of ideality." This obviously is related to the notion of an ideal self, the "ideality"[78] of resoluteness, and the subjective positing of an ethical *telos*. Indeed, in this regard Kierkegaard tended to accept J. G. Fichte's notion that the productive imagination (*Einbildungskraft*) is the fundamental origin of the categories.[79]

The ethical becoming of the self is related to imagination since it is by virtue of imagination that possibility is apprehended. However, the endeavor to become a self requires an understanding of oneself as characterized by necessity and possibility. Whereas Hegel held that necessity is a unity of possibility and actuality, Kierkegaard held that, in regard to human existence, actuality is a unity of possibility and necessity. In order to realize one's own spiritual possibilities it is first necessary to understand what one has been (or to understand the causal factors that have "shaped" one's present being) or, as Kierkegaard puts it, "to submit to the necessary in oneself, to what may be called one's limit."[80] The will (*ville*) to become what one ought to be (e.g., a self or a person) requires a retrospective understanding of what one has been and a prospective anticipation of what it is possible for one to be. At every moment or stage in an individual's becoming there is a dialectical relationship between necessity and possibility in the actual self that is sustained by the relational activity of a subjective, concernful consciousness. The choice to choose oneself is an individuating, existential transformation that was, *kata dunamin*, already present, as possibility, in the actual, imperfect being of an individual. To put it simply, Kierkegaard (following Socrates, as he understood him) maintained that in order to become an authentic self the individual must engage in an ironical, critical examination of himself and endeavor to attain sufficient self-knowledge for rational choice to be possible. Although what Kierkegaard calls the "necessity" in the self may have been contingently acquired, it is now a persistently determining characteristic of the self that ought to be analyzed so that one's actions can be relatively free from the unconscious or inaccessible causal factors that have affected what one has been.

In this regard, there is an analogy between Kierkegaard's analysis of what is required in order for an individual to strive for ethical self-realization and some psychoanalytical interpretations of human development. Ideally, the individual in therapy attempts to discover or uncover the causal factors (usually psychic factors that are conditioning present behavior) that are presently inhibiting his self-control and his capacity for self-determination, that promote compulsive behavior, that inhibit decisiveness, and that generally undermine the individual's subjective *nisus* towards self-existence or realization of self. Although Freud is referring to a possible (and paradoxical) acquaintance with the "unconscious" drives or impulses that affect our behavior, the following passage from his essay on "A Difficulty in the Path of Psychoanalysis" is, *mutatis mutandis*, illustrative of the analogy I am suggesting. Freud remarks that the conscious ego assumes that it is familiar with all that goes on in the mind—that our ordinary consciousness is apprised of our states of being, our dispositions, and our proclivities. But a great deal more is occurring in our minds, Freud avers, than we are ordinarily aware of in what may be described as our casual consciousness of ourselves. "Come," Freud counsels,

> let yourself be taught something on this one point! . . . You behave like an absolute ruler who is content with the information supplied him by his highest officials and never goes among the people to hear their voice. Turn your eyes inward, look into your own depths, learn first to know yourself! Then you will understand why you . . . fall ill; and perhaps you will avoid falling ill in future.[81]

While Kierkegaard, too, was aware that if an individual postpones a significant choice in regard to a "life problem" then it is possible that "the personality choses unconsciously, or the choice is made by obscure powers within it,"[82] his requirement for self-knowledge is, if anything, more stringent than that of Freud. For Kierkegaard advocates a complete analysis of all the relevant factors that comprise what he sometimes calls the "natural self," the historical factors that have impinged upon one's development in one's immediate domestic environment as well as the impulses, inclinations, and dispositions that have become significant aspects of the self. In addition, of course, the kind of self-knowledge that Kierkegaard refers to includes a disclosure of one's primal potentiality-for, one's "oughtness-capability," and those spiritual possibilities that can be realized only through repetitious resoluteness. For Kierkegaard, one never entirely transcends the "necessity" in one's being; rather, it is appropriated self-consciously and transformed by an individual's understanding of himself. In choosing himself the individual has chosen himself as a task, has chosen the realization of personal existence as "the absolute," as its own end and purpose.[83]

In my explication of the meaning of Kierkegaard's conception of "choosing oneself" it may be said that I have left out an essential ingredient of the ethical "movements" of the self, namely, the acceptance of oneself as sinful or 'in' sin. My reason for doing so is because the category of sin is fundamentally characteristic of the religious sphere of existence. From the standpoint of the man of faith, of course, an individual must accept himself as in sin in relation to the absolute *telos* or God; before God, all men are in sin. However, Kierkegaard explicitly denies that sin is necessarily relevant to his conception of ethical existence. As he writes in *Concluding Unscientific Postscript,* "sin is a decisive expression for the religious mode of existence." Even though, as he admits, the ethicist in *Either/Or* had given the ethical category of "choosing oneself" a "religious color," this is not, strictly speaking, accurate.[84] The concept of sin has meaning only within the context of a subjective faith in a being before whom one is necessarily sinful. Even the notion of the teleological suspension of the ethical (which led Brand Blanchard to charge Kierkegaard with moral nihilism)[85] does not mean that the individual is "beyond good and evil." For, as Kierkegaard puts it in *Concluding Unscientific Postscript*, "the terrible emancipation from the requirement of realizing the ethical [e.g., in the case of Abraham's spiritual trial in relation to the sacrifice of his son, a trial in which "the ethical is present every moment" even though "the individual cannot realize it" since it is not a question of an individual who is related to his task "as possibility to actuality, but as impossibility"]; the heterogeneity of the individual with the ethical, this suspension from the ethical, is *Sin*, considered as the state in which a human being is."[86] The possibility of sin is the basis for the dialectical tension of religious existence. It cannot be so for an ethical existence that may be lived outside a theistic framework. Insofar as there is a repentance in the self-becoming of an individual who has chosen to make the ethical movement, it is a self-reproachful attitude toward what one has done or has not done, a regret or dissatisfaction over what one has allowed oneself to become, as well as a feeling of regret or dissatisfaction over the fact that one had not chosen oneself before, had not taken responsibility for one's life, had not attempted to realize one's spiritual capacity to become an authentic self. To put it simply, in ethical self-consciousness one repents over the fact that one had not chosen to *exist*.

A final remark concerning the "movements" of ethical existence must be made before I turn to a consideration of Kierkegaard's concept of the self (and its relation to ethical existence), as well as to a consideration of the paradoxical view that the ethically existing individual endeavors to become the universal or paradigmatic man—that is, the question of the relationship between repetition and ethical existence.

While I have suggested that the notion that in the subjective teleology of ethical becoming there is a repetitious renewal of choice and resoluteness that seems to be somewhat related to Aristotle's notion of the moral development of the individual, there is a sense in which Kierkegaard's conception of ethical repetition is unique. To be sure, one may interpret Aristotle's account of ethical self-development in terms of a repetitious *eupraxia* by which an individual acquires dispositions and habits that will affect future choices. However, Kierkegaard seems to

hold that on each fresh occasion of significant choice the individual must decisively choose again, in resolute repetition, no
matter what he may have chosen before or on other occasions.

In *Repetition* Kierkegaard had tried to show that an aesthetic
repetition—the repetition of an enjoyable experience in the past—
is not possible. It is clear, however, that he thought of repetition
as central to the becoming of the individual in ethical existence.
In thinking about what has been, i.e., the past, one is concerned
primarily with recollection; but when one is concerned with the
actualization of possibilities *in futuro* one is concerned with
repetition. Repetition always involves a "movement" characterized by transcendence. For Kierkegaard, the existential category
of repetition (*Gentagelse*) is related to the Greek notion of
kinesis or movement insofar as it implies a renewed transition to
something that has already been. In *Johannes Climacus* Kierkegaard had said that there is no true repetition in the natural
world or in actuality as such. Rather, repetition becomes possible
only when ideality is brought into relationship (in the relational
activity of consciousness) to actuality. In a realm in which all is
necessary, repetition would not be possible since there could be
no change, no movement, no becoming. The same would be true
in a realm in which everything is merely possible because there
is no *actual* being that can 'move', change, or become. Furthermore, there can be no repetition "in the moment" of the actuality
of the self, since this would be characterized by unique (unre-
peatable) specificity. Nor, on the other hand, can there be repetition in ideality (since ideality comprises imagined or conceivable possibility or the immutable self-identity of conceptual
unity). Hence, as Kierkegaard argues, there is repetition only
when ideality and actuality are related in subjective, concernful
consciousness.[87] The only authentic repetition is a repetition *in*
consciousness, in the projective activity of an individual capable
of making resolute movements from possibility to actuality.

In the ethical development of an individual repetition "signifies freedom itself" as manifested in the interested existence of
an individual. In the "motion" or "movement" of spiritual purposiveness there is a radical differentiation from logical development insofar as there is a transition that is a genuine *becoming*.

Repetition emerges by virtue of the activity of relating in subjective consciousness possibility and actuality; it entails a movement of the self as a transcendence towards the actualization of
a possibility. In discussing this question in his journals Kierkegaard relies once more on his appropriation of Aristotelian notions. Thus he remarks that "when . . . Aristotle said that the
transition from possibility and actuality is a *kinesis* he was not
talking about logical possibility and actuality, but about the
possibility and actuality of freedom, and therefore he quite
rightly posits motion."[88] In regard to the "ideal" self as the goal
of ethical becoming one can see that the 'spiritual' movements
of the actual self (at any stage of its development) require a
repetition of a commitment to seek again (*re-petere*) to attain
the goal that one had posited in terms of one's own possibility
of becoming a self. While one may be able to acquire the habit
of resoluteness, one cannot acquire the 'habit' of resolving again
to pursue this particular goal each day of one's life.

   In his discussion of the ethical task of becoming subjective
(i.e., that of becoming a person or a self) in *Concluding Unscientific Postscript*, Kierkegaard, under the pseudonym of Johannes
Climacus, avers that "the ethical is not merely a knowing; it is also
a doing that is related to a knowing . . . a doing such that the
repetition may in more than one way be more difficult than the
first doing."[89] The transcendence of the self toward its ethical
possibilities requires repetition, a renewal of a commitment one
had made before, a reassertion of the self in decisiveness. The
goal of movement for an "existing individual" is to arrive at a
decision, and to renew it in repetition. In a repeated decisiveness
to become what one ought to be is found the continuity that is
characteristic of ethical existence.

   Repetition, is, as Heidegger expresses it, "a resolute projection
of oneself." The relationship between resoluteness and repetition
that is explicit in Kierkegaard's writings is preserved in Heidegger's view that "the resoluteness which comes back to itself
and hands itself down . . . becomes the *repetition* of a possibility
of existence that has come down to us."[90] Although Kierkegaard
would have agreed with Heidegger that "by repetition, *Dasein*
first has its own history made manifest," he would not have

related this "resoluteness which hands itself down" to *Dasein* to
the way in which *Dasein* exists as "fate" (*Schicksal*).[91] For there
is no 'fate' that permeates the existence of man or that is manifested in a repeated resoluteness to realize possibilities that have
already been there. To be sure, it may be said that if the fate of
Dasein is revealed in its simplicity in terms of a recognition of
its finitude and its being-unto-death, then Kierkegaard would
have found this acceptable insofar as it is the "objective possibility" of one's own death that is the background against which
one must place his description of the ethical becoming of an
individual. However, there is no 'fate' in the sense of a disposition
given over to man that manifests itself in the resolute repetition
of ethical becoming. If *Schicksal* is understood as destiny, then
the only destiny that an individual who has chosen an ethical
existence has is the one he creates for himself through his repeated choices, decisions, and action. For Heidegger, *Dasein*
takes over its history through repetition, whereas for Kierkegaard,
it is through repetition that man acquires a history for himself
even though, we have seen, he does take into account the "historical" context into which man is born in terms of the "necessity" that is part of his being. What we may expect in Heidegger's
account of the role of repetition in authentic existence is his
assumption that "everything is haunted by the enigma of Being,"
that it is being (*das Sein*) that has been disclosed in a preliminary way in his phenomenological existential analysis of the
being of *Dasein*. In Kierkegaard's Hegelian phenomenology of
the spheres of existence there is an existential analysis of the
various modalities of being open to man that attempts to disclose man's being in order to recall man to the "primitive impression of existence." It is curious to see how Heidegger wholly
appropriates Kierkegaard's existential category of repetition and
describes it in terms directly derived from his writings and then
gives it a slightly different and distorted meaning in his fundamental ontology. Heidegger makes three references to Kierkegaard in the footnotes to *Sein und Zeit*; he ought to have made
at least a hundred!

Although the description of the dialectic of choice is presented
in dramatic terms and in an edifying form that seems to offend

some contemporary philosophers, it is a penetrating analysis of the complexity of crucial choices that have pervasive effects upon the subsequent development of individuals. The central notion of choosing oneself (which is often repeated in commentaries on Kierkegaard or is characterized as obscure) has a meaning that can be clarified and related to other aspects of his conception of the "becoming" of individuals. If Kierkegaard seems to exaggerate the entire phenomenon of an individual's choice of himself, it is because he believes that too many choices in men's lives are made casually or with a lack of seriousness that is the hallmark of aestheticism or nihilism. It is against the trivialization of individual existence that he is fighting. He desired to make ethical consciousness "the aim and measure of human existence," to preserve the meaningfulness of personal existence. While the self is central to his conception of ethical existence, he did not intend to cultivate a kind of psychological egoism. For, as he remarks, "we forget that egotism [Egoisme] is one thing and I-ness or subjectivity [Egoitet] is another."[92] An ethics of subjectivity requires that we be objective toward ourselves and subjective toward others, that we endeavor by virtue of repetitious resoluteness, to become the self that we ought to become. Since the notion of the self is central to Kierkegaard's existential ethics, I shall attempt to relate his conception of the self to ethical existence and to explicate what I believe to be the essential meaning of the assertion that an ethical individual is a synthesis of the universal and the particular.

4

The Self and
Ethical Existence

The real subject is not the cognitive subject
. . . the real subject is the ethically existing
subject—S. K., *Concluding Unscientific Postscript.*

When the question "What ought I to do?" is raised one immediately thinks of a more fundamental question: "What can I do?"
And both questions tend to lead to the problem of the self, since I
cannot know what I can do unless I have at least a rudimentary
knowledge of what I am. The primitive question for Kierkegaard,
the one that underlies his philosophical anthropology, is, "What
am I?" or, "What is the self?" He quite often makes reference to
Socrates' comment in Plato's *Phaedrus:* "I must first know myself.
. . . Am I a creature more complicated and swollen with passions
than the serpent Typho, or a creature of gentler and simpler sort,
to whom nature has given a diviner and quieter destiny?"[1] The
search for self-knowledge, as we have seen, is an integral aspect
of Kierkegaard's description of the act of "choosing oneself." In
one sense, of course, man is thrown into being and is determined
by countless factors over which he has no control. And in this
sense he is but one other form of natural being conditioned by
its natural environment—conditioned by circumstances that, to
some extent, determine what he is. But what Kierkegaard sometimes calls one's "natural self" can be transformed by virtue of
resolute choice, decision, and action. The finite freedom of man
is circumscribed only by the limits of what it is within his power
to do—by the limited number of possibilities he has the capacity
to realize. Man is, to be sure, a part of history and is carried
forward by its momentum. And yet, even though "history is more
than the product of the free actions of free individuals"[2] an indi-

vidual can create a continuity for his life, can affect the development of his own life history. The individual (*Individ*) is neither
impotent nor omnipotent. Insofar as each individual can, within
a limited sphere, take up responsibility for what he is becoming,
he can appropriate the characteristics he has inherited or acquired independent of choice and determine what he will be.
For Kierkegaard, it would seem, the ambiguity of the self is
precisely related to its synthetic form as a dynamic unity of
necessity and possibility. The deliberate choice of responsibility
for the necessity in one's being is a necessary condition for the
possibility of freedom of choice in the future. In order to make
a self-conscious choice in the face of alternative possibilities I
must have already accepted the facticity of my past being—I
must accept myself in terms of those aspects of myself that I have
acquired independent of choice. Once an individual has chosen
to appropriate these accumulated characteristics he is capable of
endeavoring to realize himself in terms of the actualization of
possibilities that lead to the development of the self. Obviously,
Kierkegaard realized that each individual is already physiolo-
gically individuated. (Indeed, because of his own deformity he
probably realized this more acutely than those of us who have
been spared such an affliction.) But this form of biological individuation is passively acquired by an individual and is certainly
nothing to which blame or praise could be applied. To be sure,
Kierkegaard held that the body is of course an aspect of the self
and, therefore, that its physiological individuation is by no means
irrevelant to a consideration of the nature of the self. However,
it is in the spiritual becoming of an individual that the self of an
individual is paradigmatically revealed.

The Nature of the Self

Although Kierkegaard makes numerous references to the self
in his writings, it is difficult to determine with precision what his
fundamental conception of the self is. Some of his attempts to
describe the nature of the self are unfortunately obscure. Thus,
for example, when generalizing about man's nature he remarks
that, although man's being is rooted in nature and animality, man

is essentially spirit. At times, he avers that "spirit" is the self and, furthermore, that the self understood qua spirit is self-consciousness. While it is true that self-consciousness requires a relationship to actuality in its concrete immediacy, Kierkegaard held that self-consciousness "attains its satisfaction" in a critical, ironical relationship to a self that it is the task of the individual to become, and thus he could not agree with Hegel's dictum that "self-consciousness attains its satisfaction only in another self-consciousness."[3] The self in concernful reflexivity is "spiritual"— is that synthesis of necessity and possibility which is characterized by a paradoxical, dialectical relationship between passion (*Lidenskab*) and concrete thought (*conret Taenkning*). While there are echoes of Hegel's terminology in Kierkegaard's conception of the self as spirit, there are significant differences between his notion of the 'spiritual' character of the self and that of Hegel. First of all, spirit is never equated with reason (*Vernunft*) as it is, on occasion, by Hegel in his *Phenomenology of Spirit*. Secondly, 'spirit' is not substance and not "unbending righteous self-sameness, self-identity." However, Hegel's notion that 'spirit' is "concrete ethical actuality" or *Wirklichkeit* comes close to Kierkegaard's understanding of the self, except that a 'spiritual' *telos* of realizing "concrete ethical actuality" in oneself is the ethical goal that an individual ought repeatedly to strive to attain. Insofar as an individual chooses to undergo individuating 'spiritual' states of being he approximates the self he ought to become. Although Kierkegaard would tend to agree with Hegel that "spirit analyzes itself, distinguishes its moments, and halts at each individual mode in turn," that "such moments presuppose spirit itself and requires spirit for its subsistence . . . this isolation of modes [of consciousness] only exists within spirit, which is existence," he would have denied vehemently that "spirit is . . . consciousness in general."[4] For Kierkegaard, "spiritual" states of being (e.g., despair, guilt, anxiety, concern, etc.) are always individuating states of being and the self qua spirit is always an individuated, actual self.

Concernful self-reflexivity is the fundamental condition for the possibility of self-knowldege as well as ethical self-existence. Both in his journals and under the pseudonym Anti-Climacus

Kierkegaard described the self as "a relation which relates itself to its own self, or is that in the relation that the relation relates itself to its own self." While this description of the self seems to out-Hegel Hegel, it is one that is related to certain aspects of his conception of consciousness as set forth in his unpublished work *Johannes Climacus or, De Omnibus Dubitandum Est*. For consciousness, as we have seen, was conceived of as that which relates ideality (imagination, conceptualization and/or language) and actuality (concrete immediacy), or as that relationship itself. At one point in *Johannes Climacus* consciousness is equated with spirit and is described as that which *is* in the process of relating opposites or antinomies and which is affected by subjective concern.[5] The intensification of consciousness, Kierkegaard remarks in *The Sickness unto Death*, intensifies the actuality of the self. Although consciousness is *real*, it is not actual in the sense that what is encountered in immediacy is actual. Immediacy, for Kierkegaard, seems to mean concrete experience (a paradigm for which would be sensation) as it is undergone prior to classification, organization, or description in terms of concepts or language. If consciousness is not an actuality, it is also not an ideality. That is, it is not an imagined or conceived possibility, but that which intends imaginative or conceptual "idealities." Consciousness cannot be an 'object' for itself since it is that which is the condition for the possibility for comprehending anything as object. It is, as Kierkegaard puts it, that which is "in-between" actuality and ideality. Or, it is the "energizing force" that relates the relata of actuality and ideality, concrete immediacy, and imaginative-conceptual possibility.

In *Johannes Climacus* Kierkegaard distinguishes between reflection and consciousness by maintaining that reflection is disinterested (or objective thought) while consciousness (*Bevisthed*) is a relational activity in which there is subjective concern (or subjective thought).[6] For Kierkegaard the paradigmatic form of consciousness is not, as it is for Husserl and Sartre, impersonal, but is always personal, concernful consciousness. Consciousness, as spirit, is that relational activity by which the psychophysical synthesis of individual being is brought about. Spirit is self-consciousness or that cognitive-affective activity which is capable of synthesizing the various aspects of the 'self' in such a way that one's existence has a semblance of continuity. Borrowing a Kantian expression, one may say that subjective consciousness is, for Kierkegaard, the "I am" that accompanies all my existential concerns or states of being. Spiritual consciousness is, by its very nature, enigmatic and paradoxical. Although it may be said that we have an intuitive acquaintance with ourselves in I-consciousness, when we attempt to describe this self in language we tend to talk about it as if it were a determinate entity, an objective entity and not a dynamic *activity*. Most descriptions of subjective consciousness tend to objectify it and to bracket its relational character. Kierkegaard's ostensible definition of the self is designed, I believe, to indicate the complexity of the self as well as its dynamic, paradoxical, and dialectical nature. One thing is clear, however, in Kierkegaard's analysis of subjective consciousness: the self that is revealed in the approximation-process of self-consciousness is not an impersonal consciousness, not a universal consciousness-in-general. As Kierkegaard expresses it in *The Concept of Dread*, "self-consciousness is not contemplation . . . for [he who is engaged in the activity of self-consciousness] sees that he himself is meanwhile in the process of becoming and so cannot be a finished product as the object of contemplation."[7]

Although Kierkegaard intended to preserve the notion that consciousness is invariably I-consciousness (with the proviso that this consciousness has emerged in the development of an individual in the actualization of a possibility and is characterized as a consciousness of dialectical opposition), he has not entirely avoided the problem of attributing personal being to this consciousness. Whereas Hegel held that spirit is consciousness in general, and assumed that when consciousness understands that the "reality" objective to itself is nothing but the objectification of its own self-existent being, it ought properly to be termed self-consciousness, Kierkegaard desired to equate the self, as spirit, with the existing individual who is a synthesis of actuality and possibility. Now, if a consciousness of this self is possible (as Kierkegaard suggests), how can that which is conscious of the self be itself that which it is conscious of in this process? If consciousness is intentional, as Husserl has held, then how is it possible that the intended phenomenon of consciousness (the self) is itself the consciousness for which it is an ostensible phenomenon? To be sure, Kierkegaard would deny that the self is ever an *object* of consciousness. Nevertheless, it would seem that once it is assumed that consciousness is the central characteristic of 'individual' being, we seem to be led to assume that there is an impersonal, transcendental consciousness that can know the self or ego, but that cannot itself be the individual, personal self that it knows. The presupposition of what Husserl described as a "primordial dator consciousness" as the ultimate reference of all experience and thought invariably leads to the view that the personal self or the actual self is constituted by, or constructed by, a deindividuated consciousness. Despite the fact that Kierkegaard held that self-consciousness emerges in terms of the consciousness of relationships of opposition, he did not maintain that the self *is* consciousness.

For Kierkegaard, the Cartesian formula *Cogito, ergo sum* is a play on words, since the "I am" logically signifies nothing other than "I am thinking" or "I think."[8] In relation to his conception of consciousness this seems to mean that the emergence of consciousness (or what he sometimes calls the actualization of consciousness) is simultaneous with the emergence of I-consciousness. As he puts it in *The Sickness unto Death*, consciousness of self "is the decisive criterion of the self"; "the more consciousness, the more self."[9] Subjective consciousness is inevitably interrelated with will, intellect, imagination, and emotion. In the temporal actuality of an individual the self is potentially 'present' as possibility. The emergence of the self requires an intensification of consciousness of self by virtue of radically individuating activities or states of being (e.g., absolute choice, anxiety, etc.). Self-consciousness is not a process brought about by an activity of an impersonal consciousness. And the self is not the "philosophical self" (*das philosophische Ich*) that (as Wittgenstein averred in *Tractatus Logico-Philosophicus*) is the "metaphysical subject" (*metaphysische Subjekt*) that is "the limit, not a part, of the world" (*die Grenze—nicht ein Teil—der Welt*).[10] If there were such a self, it could never change or become—could never strive to be what it ought to be. The actual, temporal, human self—the only self that can *exist*—cannot attain a vantage point from which it may view things *sub specie aeterni*—cannot transcend the world that Kierkegaard describes in his journals as "the medium in which we exist."[11] Rather, the self is a dynamic interrelationship between the psychic, the physical, and the spiritual, which is never finished or complete (so long as it lives) in temporality since its existence is manifested in the actuality of becoming (*Vorden*). The self is a spiritual synthesis, "a relation which relates itself to itself" in subjective consciousness. The existing individual is revealed to himself in the activity of existing, in those individuating experiences which intensify an immediate, intuitive sense of one's own self-being, in subjective dread (*Angst*) in the face of one's own unique possibilities or in the face of the 'openness' of possibility, in moments of absolute choice, in the anticipation of the possibility of one's own death, in concern for one's own being—in all the various modalities of "inwardness" (*Inderligheden*) wherein one's existential actuality is experienced in concrete immediacy.

The self as spirit is that which relates subjective consciousness or *subjektive Reflexion* and sensory psychological experience in a dynamic, integral being. In self-reflective consciousness, in individuating acts or states of being, the individual is aware of himself as an actual, particular self characterized by necessity and possibility. In an ethical mode of existence (which is paradigmatic of consciousness of self), however, an ideal, possible self is discovered and posited as the *telos* toward which an individual ought to strive. This "ideal" self must be, as it were, potentially present in the actual, imperfect self insofar as it is the individual, and he alone, who assumes the project of striving to become that self. The project of attempting to realize one's own highest ethical possibilities or those unique spiritual possibilities that enhance individuation is posited by the actual self (which is not an 'object' for consciousness, but a lived actuality) and is repeatedly sought as a goal by the individual at particular stages of his life. The pursuit of an ethical teleology projected by the actual self can only be sustained by virtue of repetitious resolution. While Kierkegaard holds that the endeavor to become a person or a self is itself individuating and, hence, approximates Socratic subjectivity, he also maintains that the ethicist aims to become the paradigmatic man, to exemplify what is universal in man. The underlying paradox of Kierkegaard's phenomenology of practical ethics is this notion that the truly existent ethical individual manifests an accentuated subjectivity and also is an expression of, or approximation to, the "universal man." The projective, relational being of the self is the basis for the constant process of striving for the sake of an end characteristic of ethical existence and is the focus of the synthetic process of relating the various aspects of the self, of the subjective *nisus* that gives continuity, meaning, and history to the self-becoming of the individual.

By choosing an ethical mode of being the individual gives to his life a history and a continuity. In this regard, he may be said to have begun to "create" himself; but this creation is not *ex nihilo,* since it is the act of imperfect actual being who has acquired numerous characteristics in his "immediacy"—the act of a self-reflective individual who discovers in himself possibilities that are as much a part of his being as are the dispositions, tendencies, abilities, preferences, and habits that characterize his present individuality. In metaphorical language it may be said that the self, for Kierkegaard, is that relational activity which is "in-between" necessity and possibility—that intermediate "reality" which relates these aspects of itself to itself. The necessity in the self is the limiting factor of the self; the possibility of the self is the unlimited factor of the self. The dialectical tension between necessity and possibility is sustained by the self as spirit or subjective self-consciousness. The "movement" of the self is toward the future, toward what is not yet, toward what is possible. Thus, in *The Sickness unto Death*, Kierkegaard avers that "the self *kata dunamis* is just as possible as it is necessary; for though it is itself [in its immediacy], it has to become itself. Inasmuch as it is itself, it is the necessary; and inasmuch as it has to become itself, it is a possibility."[12] The possibility the ethical individual strives to realize is the possibility of being an authentic, individuated self in whom an ethical "ideality" has become concrete. The dynamic, dialectical teleology of striving to become a self is that repetitious, decisive activity which is *existence*. And for each man the ethical goal of his life is *to exist*. That in doing so he implicitly discloses what all men "were meant to be" essentially is a typical Kierkegaardian paradox that reveals the central meaning of his conception of the ethical sphere of existence.

The notion that the ethical task of the individual is to become a person, to intensify his own subjectivity, to "become subjective," is modeled upon what Kierkegaard understands as the implicit ethical prescription of Socrates. In his last journal entries Kierkegaard refers once more to what he understood Socrates' basic concern to be. "Socrates," he writes, "concerned himself with the problem, what it means to be a man. . . . Socrates doubted whether we are men at birth; one does not so easily get the chance to become a man or to know what it is to be a man."[13] According to Kierkegaard, in *The Concept of Irony*, Socrates sought to make actual (*virkelig*) the ethical possibility of being an ethically self-conscious individual, an integrated, self-sufficient person. In the simplest terms, the ethicist, for Kierkegaard, is one who proclaims only that "I have sought to be myself" (*jeg har søgt at vaere selv*). Kierkegaard, perhaps optimistically, thought that the self-conscious endeavor to become a self enabled one to become an integrated individual with character (following Aristotle's view in the *Nicomachean Ethics*, Kierkegaard conceived of character as being one thing—the immoralist is a chaotic multiplicity: Aristotle quotes with approval a verse proclaiming that "goodness is simple, badness manifold," *esthloi men gar aplos, pantodapōs de kakoi*).[14] Most human beings, Kierkegaard seemed to believe, are disunified for the most part, characterized by unresolved conflicts among various aspects of the self. To be sure, the dialectical tension among the various aspects of the self may never be overcome entirely; nevertheless, the subjective *nisus* toward a kind of 'spiritual' homeostatis is essential to ethical self-existence.

Kierkegaard seemed to hold, by implication, that the subjective teleology to become a person or a self entailed the moral transformation of the individual. He seemed to believe that a heightened sense of one's own self-being, of self-knowledge, would tend to lead to the inhibition of vicious impulses, to a

greater self-mastery and self-control that would, in turn, strength-
en one's resolution to become a moral being. It is as if he assumed that the choice of a life-project of becoming an authentic
self precluded the development of dispositions to act in an unjust
or immoral way. That is, striving to become the self one ought to
become is correlated to letting others be themselves in their own
self-being (which, as one might expect, corresponds to Heidegger's conception of authentic *Mitdasein* in *Sein und Zeit*). Thus,
it is said (in *Concluding Unscientific Postscript*) that "the highest
degree of resignation that a human being can reach is to acknowledge the given independence in every man, and after the
measure of his ability do all that can in truth be done to help
someone preserve it."[15] This, incidentally, is one of the functions
of Socratic irony (as Kierkegaard understands it): to bring another, through indirection, to a realization of his ignorance of
himself, of what he is not, to lead him to live an examined life
by means of the suggestion of an ethical possibility that it is
within an individual's power to realize. The ethical task of each
individual is one that he alone can realize existentially, namely,
to strive to become a self, to become subjective. It is a "struggle"
and a "victory" over one's propensity for aesthetic self-dissolu-
tion, irresolution, and the "thoughtlessness" that Kierkegaard
(and later Heidegger) equates with "forgetfulness of birth and
death." The concern (*interesse*) that characterizes subjective
consciousness is intensified by virtue of an understanding of
oneself as being "in between" birth and death. As Heidegger
expresses it:

> Factical *Dasein* exists as born; and as born, it is already dying,
> in the sense of being-towards-death. As long as *Dasein* facti-
> cally exists, both the 'ends' and their 'between' *are*, and they
> are in the only way which is possible on the basis of Dasein's
> being as *care*. Thrownness and that being-unto-death in which
> one either flees it or anticipates it, form a unity; and in this
> birth and death are 'connected' in a manner characteristic of
> *Dasein*. As care, *Dasein* is the 'between'.[16]

As an illustration of how one can become subjective, the individual's thought about his own death is a dramatic case in point.

Kierkegaard does not recommend a persistent reflection upon the possibility of one's own death because he wants to cultivate a morbid introspectionism. Rather, the individual's thought about his own death is itself an individuating "deed" that recalls him from forgetfulness and thoughtlessness—from the casual attitude of mind that enables an individual to postpone any commitment to anything, to live with the illusion that everything will go on as before, and to suppose that there is nothing that one ought to be serious about. In regard to the choice of becoming subjective, "we wish to know," as Kierkegaard puts it in *Concluding Unscientific Postscript,* "how the conception of death will transform a man's entire life, when in order to think its uncertainty he has to think it in every moment, so as to prepare himself for it." When one has chosen to become a self or to become subjective

> then the thought of death is not, for the individual subject, something in general, but is verily a deed. For the development of the subject consists precisely in his active interpenetration of himself by reflection concerning his own existence, so that he really thinks what he thinks through making a reality of it.[17]

While the persistent reflection upon one's own death can be negating insofar as it seems to rob one of one's confidence or hope and accentuate one's sense of the transitory nature of actuality, it can also engender a sense of the significance and meaningfulness of the temporal actuality of one's own life and thus can force one to ask oneself the question (a question that, for Kierkegaard, already has *ethical* significance): What am I doing with my life? An anxiety in the face of the possibility of death is aggravated by a more profound anxiety concerning what one has been, is, and is becoming. The meaningfulness of one's life is not a *datum,* a gift freely given to man; it is something to be won, a task to be accomplished, a goal toward which the individual must repeatedly strive in subjective self-consciousness.

The important emphasis in Kierkegaard's conception of the becoming of the self is on *how* the individual comports himself to himself and others, *how* he relates himself to the task of becoming subjective. For Kierkegaard the moral value of a choice or an action does not lie in its consequences but in its purpose— in that for the sake of which it is done. We can never know when we ought to evaluate the 'consequences' of a choice or an action; nor can we know with any certainty *what* the consequences of our action will be in the long run (no matter how good our intentions). The conception of ethical development that Kierkegaard propounds is neither an ethics of consequences nor an ethics of duty (except in the sense that one has a 'duty' to become a self); it is an ethics of self-realization. The goal of the ethical individual is to "strive to develop himself with the utmost exertion of his powers. . . . He would . . . *choose* to remain in ignorance of what he had accomplished [in the world] in order that his striving might not be retarded by a preoccupation with the external."[18] This emphasis (as expressed in *Concluding Unscientific Postscript*) clearly distinguishes Kierkegaard's conception of practical ethics from all forms of utilitarianism and from what F. H. Bradley characterized as "duty for duty's sake" or "the morality of pure duty."

One of the dominant forms that Kierkegaard's conception of ethical existence takes is that of an ethics of self-actualization or self-realization. He does not proclaim an ethics of duty toward universal and universalizable moral laws, nor does he present an ethics of self-renunciation. In *Concluding Unscientific Postscript* we can discern the relationship between the prescription (in *Either/Or*) to endeavor to realize one's "ideal self" and what may be called an ethics of subjectivity. For it is said (under the pseudonym of Johannes Climacus) that existence constitutes the highest interest of the existing individual and that his interest in his existence constitutes his *reality*—that *ethical self-existence is the only true reality.*[19] What this assertion indicates is Kierkegaard's underlying skepticism concerning objective truth and empirical knowledge of what Heidegger calls "innerworldly beings" or nonhuman actualities. This skepticism halts only before the self-certainty of the ethically existing individual. Ironically, this general skepticism concerning the reliability of objective knowledge (*objektive Reflexion*) combined with a certainty concerning one's own actuality and one's capacity for self-realization is paralleled in the writings of a philosopher who is often considered as a kind of anti-Kierkegaard, Nietzsche. For this philosopher also attacks the notion of objective truth and emphasizes the intrinsic value of the self-consciously existing individual. Although skeptical about knowledge of the world or of "reality," Nietzsche is rarely skeptical about the energetic existence of an individual who strives for self-assertive existence and creative self-realization in the "river of becoming."

Even Nietzsche's view that we must transform and transfigure our *physis* has its parallel in Kierkegaard's admonition to attempt to appropriate our "natural being" and to transform ourselves. Despite his occasional hymns in praise of natural drives, Nietzsche also held that every morality is "a bit of tyranny against 'nature' . . . but that is no objection against it." Self-mastery is as much a part of Kierkegaard's existential ethics as it is of Nietzsche's. And when Nietzsche writes that "the essential thing in heaven and earth is," as he says in *Beyond Good and Evil*, "that there be long, continued obedience in a specific direction," that "something always comes of this in the end, on account of which it repays one to live in this world—something glorifying or purifying,"[20] he seems close to Kierkegaard's stress upon the positing of a strenuous process in terms of the realization of an "ideal" self as a primary ethical requirement. Even Nietzsche's central prescription for man, that one should strive for *Selbstüberwindung*, is consonant with the spirit of Kierkegaard's practical ethics. Given the significant differences between Nietzsche's and Kierkegaard's conceptions of man's being (especially in regard to the ambiguous relationship between the individual and the impersonal *Wille zur Macht* that manifests itself in so many different ways), it is significant, in the light of the usual interpretations of Kierkegaard's ethical sphere of existence, that there are indeed similarities between Nietzsche's conception of "becoming oneself" and that of Kierkegaard's ethics of subjectivity. Nietzsche's assertions about what one "ought" to be are clearly compatible with the admonitions of Kierkegaard. In *Joyful Wisdom* Nietzsche remarks that conscience (*Gewissen*) proclaims: "Thou shalt become what thou art."[21] When Nietzsche maintains that each individual should become who he is (*Du sollst der werden, der du bist*), he means, *mutatis mutandis*, what Kierkegaard means by "becoming subjective," becoming the "true self" that Nietzsche avers is "immeasurably high above you, or at least above what you usually take for your ego." What has been said in regard to Nietzsche's ethics could, with equal justice, be said of Kierkegaard's existential ethics: "Individuality, worth, and dignity are—to recall Kant's play on words—not *gegeben,* i.e., given to us as data by nature, but *aufgegeben,* i.e., given or assigned to us as a task which we ourselves must solve."[22]

An ethics of subjectivity requires a persistent striving (*Straeben*) for self-realization and a repeated choice of those states of consciousness or states of being that accentuate individuation. The "how" of this subjectivity is, of course, subject to a temporal dialectic and is, hence, never a permanent possession but rather a continuous striving towards a goal, a repeated renewal of resoluteness. The goal of "movement" for an existing individual is, as it is expressed in *Concluding Unscientific Postscript,* to arrive at a decision concerning a *telos* construed as a good, and to renew it. An ethical existence is one in which an individual is transformed in "inwardness," an activity that is ascribed to the paradigm of an ethical individual, Socrates. The ethical pathos, the pathos of resolve, is not an intentional act of an impersonal consciousness but an act on the part of a finite, temporal, existing individual who is the focal synthesis of reflection and action, passion and thought, the is and the ought, of necessity and possibility. The self of an ethically self-conscious individual is not a consciousness-in-general, not a metaphysical self, but a subjectively reflective particular being whose existence is fundamentally paradoxical insofar as he is the locus or the dynamic 'center' of the awareness of oppositions, conflicting tendencies, and possibilities. The restlessness of man's spiritual existence (which is reminiscent of Hegel's conception of subjective spirit as spirit being for itself) is manifested in the dynamic, projective *nisus* of the individual toward his own unique, subjective reality, which is formed by virtue of the attempt to realize his own authentic possibilities in accordance with a movement, in inwardness, towards a repeatedly reaffirmed *telos* that infuses his life with purpose and meaning. From an ethical point of view, then, man is 'spirit' in the sense that he is passionately engaged in the decisive inwardness of striving persistently to become the integrated, self-sufficient self he ought to be. The true subject, as Kierkegaard puts it, is not a cognitive, knowing subject (even though man, of course, can be such a subject), but the ethically existing individual. In heightened self-consciousness the individual relates himself to himself in a way in which he can never be related, in objective reflection, to other actualities.

This is not to suggest that Kierkegaard held that nonhuman beings or actualities are "unreal." What he did hold was that a knowledge of these beings is necessarily mediated by human consciousness and that an objective conceptualization of actuality (*Virkeligheden*) involves the transformation of that actuality, as actuality, into possibility. Every actuality other than one's own is either (a) encountered in preconceptual, prelinguistic immediate experience or (b) is a conceived 'actuality' that, since it is necessarily conceived of or expressed in terms of "ideality," is understood as possibility. When I think about a state of affairs in "the world" I think about a *possible* state of affairs. Again, if I understand an empirical proposition I think about the *possible* state of affairs that I would have to encounter in order to judge whether the proposition is true. If I conceive of something (e.g., a thousand-sided figure) I necessarily conceive of it as possible— as logically possible. The ethical reality of the individual, Kierkegaard argues, is the only reality that does not become a possibility in being known. It is for this reason that, in understanding another, one can never understand the other in his immediate actuality but can understand him only in terms of conceived 'reality', which is, strictly speaking, possibility. Because he holds this view, he can claim, without falling into solipsism, that the only 'reality' that we know by means of subjective reflection is the existing self in its ethical or individuated actuality.[23]

In his conception of the reality of the self as the "in-between" that relates its states of being and states of consciousness to itself, Kierkegaard had borne in mind Schelling's Berlin lectures of 1841/42. Schelling had provided an analysis of the inability of speculative reason (*reine Vernunft*) to comprehend fully immediate actuality, and he had said: "If reason seeks actual being,

if it seeks the actuality of any object realized from out of itself
in the concept, and accordingly as something merely possible, it
must subject itself to the authority of the senses . . . because we
recognize through them . . . present existence."[24] If it is granted
to Hegel that "pure thought" apprehends necessity (*Notwendigkeit*), Schelling avers: "Of a decision, an action, or even of a
deed, pure thought in which everything develops through necessity knows nothing."[25] Objective thought is appropriate to logic,
mathematics, or science in general; but one cannot comprehend
concrete existence by such means, since objective thought knows
only the universal, transforms a particular actuality into a possibility, and thematizes or objectifies the phenomena it attends to
in its activity. As Kierkegaard expresses it in his journals, "existence corresponds to the individual; as Aristotle has already
taught the individual lies outside of and is not absorbed in the
concept. For a particular [being] . . . is certainly not concept-
existence."[26] Hence, an actual individual cannot be known by
means of objective thought. Only in the temporal existence of
the self-being of an individual who chooses to exist as an ethical
being can "ideal being" (*ideel Vaeren*) and "actual being" (*ac-
tuelle Vaeren*) be related in concrete reality. Kierkegaard understood quite well the paradoxical nature of what he was trying to
express in his existential philosophy, and he understood, moreover, that the kind of philosophy of the concrete that he was endeavoring to create could only be an approximation-process, since
there is an ineluctable asymptotic relationship between conceptualization (and/or linguistic expression) and the actuality
that it ostensibly describes. The important thing for him was at
least to recognize the distinction between conceptual 'existence'
and existence as lived and manifested in the actuality of the
dialectic of authentic existence. "What confuses the whole idea of
'essence' in logic," he wrote in his journals,

> is that attention is not given to the fact that one continually func-
> tions with the "concept" existence. But the *concept*, existence,
> is an ideality, and the difficulty is precisely whether existence is
> absorbed in the concept. Then Spinoza may be right, *essentia
> involvit existentiam*, namely, the concept-existence, i.e., exis-
> tence in ideality. From another point of view, Kant is right in

saying, "Existence brings no new predicate to a concept." "Obviously, Kant . . . thinks of existence as not being absorbed into the concept empirical existence. In all the relationships of ideality it holds true that *essentia* is *existentia*. . . . Nothing is added to a concept whether is has existence or not; it is a matter of complete indifference; it indeed has existence, i.e., concept-existence, ideal existence.[27]

If we synthesize all the various aspects of Kierkegaard's ethics of subjectivity, we will find that much of Heidegger's conception of *eigentlich Existenz* (if we bear in mind the distinction between Heidegger's ontologism and Kierkegaard's existentialism, Heidegger's central concern with *das Sein* or Being and Kierkegaard's consistent concern with individual existence) bears a remarkable resemblance to it. This is especially the case in regard to the central ingredient of Kierkegaard's existential ethics: inwardness. Although it may be assumed that the notion of inwardness is, in Kierkegaard's writings, vague, barren, and empty of content, this is clearly false. Admittedly, Kierkegaard does tend to overuse the term without always making explicit what he means by it in various contexts. However, in its most general sense inwardness means a 'spiritual' turning-in upon oneself—a kind of serious, concernful introspection. It entails the cultivation of seriousness in regard to one's life, a concern for what one has been, is, and is becoming. The aesthete and nihilist refuse to take responsibility for their lives, refuse to take their own spiritual condition seriously, and refuse to open themselves to radically individuating experiences that would intensify their sense of their own actuality.

The loss of the dynamic, dialectical tension of personal existence or its absence signifies the loss of, or the absence of, the meaningfulness of individual existence or the subjective sense of the reality of one's own actuality. The sense of the undeniable actuality of one's own temporal, particular existence is paradigmatic of all states of inwardness (*Inderligheden*). Meditation on the possibility of one's own death (which Kierkegaard, like Epictetus, suggested that one must do every day) generates a state of inwardness. Choosing to have a conscience, choosing to put one's own existence under scrutiny, is an instance of the experience of inwardness. Inwardness is characterized by individuating cogni-tive-emotive states of being in which one's own self is a matter of concern, states in which te self of the individual relates itself to itself in heightened self-consciousness. Simpy put, inwardness is the subjective intensification of personal existence (*personlige Existents*). Inwardness is not a state of being, alas, that reveals identifiable behavioral criteria. Someone may know that I am vain because I reveal this character trait in my overt (if unself-conscious) behavior. But can one tell whether an individual has despaired over his unwillingness to become a self? One may know that I am angry by observing the behavioral criteria from which this state of consciousness or emotion may be inferred. But can one easily discover the anxiety I experience in the face of the possibility of my death? One may know that I have a dispo-sition to be generous by observing my behavior in relevant con-texts. But can another truly know my own deepest aspirations— aspirations that pervade my *entire* existence—by donning the guise of the behaviorist? Did Kierkegaard's friends know that the young man who was so jovial and witty at their *soirée* went home and thought only of suicide? The self is, to some extent, revealed to others in overt behavior; but it is revealed to itself in an inti-mate way that Kierkegaard called the state of being of inward-ness. The 'spiritual' aspects of the self (which are central to its existence) are not transparent to others at all. We may not have privileged access to many of our states of being, but we do have such access to those states of being that ofen matter the most to us. Although I believe that Kierkegaard is mistaken in holding that the self, in inwardness, is "transparent" to itself (for it would seem that self-knowledge involves an activity of the self as interpreter of itself or of its states of consciousness), he is certainly correct in assuming that we have, in self-knowl-edge, access to profound aspects of the self that need never mani-fest any clearly identifiable behavioral criteria.

One of the central paradigms of subjective inwardness, for Kierkegaard, is the dialectical experience of subjective dread. This is the vertigo that one can experience in the face of sheer possibility—a sense of what may be called (after Berdyaev) meonic freedom.[28] Subjective dread, as a response to the understanding of possibility, is an encounter with nothingness, since it is "the nothing," as Kierkegaard puts it in *The Concept of Dread,* "which is the object of dread." The subjective awareness of the "nothingness of possibility" is simultaneously an awareness of freedom as well as a dread of this possibility, this freedom. By succumbing to this dread or anxiety, by living through it, the individual is inevitably turned back upon himself, upon his own possibilities, upon his own finite situation in the world. Subjective anxiety is egotistic, since only the particular individual, only an I, can encounter it. This dread is an anxiety concerning what I might become, what I could become, or what could happen to me. Kierkegaard's analysis of subjective dread is always couched in the language of possibility and is ultimately an anxiety in the face of existence, or the possibilities of existence, itself. From an ethical point of view, dread is encountered in terms of one's own possibility for good or for evil. In addition, of course, anxiety is also that state of being or mood in which one truly realizes the meaning of the contingency and finitude of one's existence. In this regard, Heidegger, in *Sein und Zeit,* stressed only one aspect of Kierkegaard's conception of anxiety, namely, the anxiety that one endures in the face of the *possibility* of one's own death, an anxiety that is without any object as such, an irrelative condition in which one anticipates the possibility of one's own impossibility.

As a mode of inwardness, anxiety reveals the individual as individual and as concerned with his own being and his possibilities. In an ethical mode of being anxiety may be experienced in terms of one's responsibility for one's own possibilities. Precisely because of the nonnecessity of one's own ethical self-realization in subjectivity, one chooses oneself and chooses to become a self in "anxious freedom." The radical individuation that is characterstic of the mood of anxiety recalls the individual to a serious concern for his own existence. This subjective concern is of course tinged with egoistic interest; but it is also a sense of how much one is responsible for in one's life and how much depends upon our own resoluteness. The inwardness of anxiety is revealed in a heightened sense of existence as a risk—as, in Dewey's phrase, an "aleatory affair" pervaded by dialectical tension. In Heidegger's classical expression, "Anxiety individuates *Dasein* and . . .

discloses it as *solus ipse*."[29] And, for Kierkegaard, all states of inwardness disclose the individual as *solus ipse*, unprotected by the social veils that tend to subdue or negate authentic experiences—as isolated from the conventional world of social actuality, the world of conventional, ordinary practical concern.

In contemplative, aesthetic, or disinterested reflection the experience of inwardness is precluded. Only in concernful reflection or subjective reflection is the state of being of inwardness possible. In the face of his own subjectively apprehended potentiality-for (good or evil) the ethically existing individual lives through an anxious freedom that is yet another mode of inwardness. In general, inwardness, since it is a state of being deliberately chosen by the individual and not merely a mood that comes upon him or that "happens" to him, is an *activity* characterized by a heightened sense of self-consciousness, self-concern, or self-being. In such a state or condition the individual experiences an intensification of the paradoxical nature of his being and existence, the paradoxical relationship between thought and passion. In regard to the notion that inwardness (or subjectivity) is characterized by the process of relating the universal to one's own particular actuality, we may fill in a lacuna in Kierkegaard's analysis of subjectivity by providing an illustration that he himself does not use. First of all, however, we must turn to Kierkegaard's distinction between objective and subjective thought.

In objective thought or disinterested reflection the individual is indifferent to himself as an existing subject and the interest of the individual is focused upon the *result* of this activity (e.g., the logician attempting to solve a particular puzzle). In subjective thinking there is a concentration on the dialectical process of thought itself in relation to one's own actuality. Since the existing individual is "constantly in process of coming to be" his subjective reflection is itself a contribution to this process and is *in* this process. The paradoxical nature of inwardness in subjective thought is precisely the attempt to relate relata that are in opposition one to the other. In a formulation in *Concluding Unscientific Postscript* Kierkegaard remarks: "The reflection of inwardness gives to the subjective thinker a double reflection. In thinking, he thinks the universal; but as existing in this thought and as as-

similating it in his inwardness, he becomes more and more subjectively isolated."[30] In objective thinking there is no opposition
between the act of thinking and the 'objects' that are thought or
that are related in thought. Since, as Wittgenstein suggested,
one cannot think what is illogical (*Unlogisches*) or what is logically impossible and, therefore, "what is thinkable . . . is possible" (*Was denkbar ist . . . möglich*),[31] there is a correspondence
between objective thinking and the concepts or propositions that
are the intended 'objects' of such thinking. In this regard, Kierkegaard held that in objective thinking there is an identity relationship between thought and being (i.e., *entia rationis*). But this
is not the case in what he describes as subjective thinking.

We can illustrate specifically an instance of inwardness in the
case of the choice to be resolute in regard to one's own life. Prior
to making this choice, I know that it is *possible* to be decisive or
indecisive, resolute or irresolute, in regard to my own development. In thinking objectively about the *concepts* of resolution or
irresolution I am not personally involved; indeed, I can go so far
as to write a book entitled "The Concept of Resolution" and yet
be utterly indifferent to the relationship between this concept
and my own immediate existence. One can, of course, engage in
any number of intellectualistic or aesthetic enterprises in which
the furthest thing from one's mind is the actual relationship between what is thought (or written) and one's own actuality.
But to choose to relate the concept of resolution (e.g., the universal as conceived 'reality' or possibility) to one's own self is a
paradoxical process insofar as an "ideality" is being related to an
"actuality." Reason or objective thought cannot sustain this relationship because one is inevitably tempted to think about an
ideality in an abstract way, to resolve the subjectively experienced dialectical tension by converting a question that is related
to the *pathos* of one's existence into an objective, theoretical
question. In subjective thinking the individual relates an "ideality" to his own actuality by means of a subjective *appropriation*
of that "ideality." In choosing to be resolute one intensifies one's
own subjective existence since by so choosing one becomes involved in a process in which there is a dialectical interrelationship
between passion and thought. This mode of subjective knowl-

edge is, as Kierkegaard puts it in *Concluding Unscientific Postscript,* the only knowledge that may not transform itself at the last moment into a hypothesis.[32] Inwardness requires "the self-activity of personal appropriation," which is not communicated directly to another, and the existential synthesis of thought and actuality. If the ethical task or goal is to become a self or a person, then the individual who becomes subjective in the activity of inwardness has at least approximated the attainment of that goal or, to put it another way, is engaged in the activity of existing. Kierkegaard would agree with those who say that 'existence' is not a predicate; rather, existence is an *activity* in which one is engaged in the persistent striving to become an authentic self.

Inwardness may be described as the passionate sense of the subjective specificity of one's own existence, a specificity that eludes abstract categorization or objective thought. Although Kierkegaard mentions that inwardness is sometimes considered as a *consequence* of objective reflection, he himself disagrees with this view. As he puts it, in the sphere of reality or existential actuality, immediacy is the immediacy of inwardness. Although *pathos,* too, is an immediacy, it would be insignificant and unintelligible if it were not interpenetrated by thought—if it were not related to an "ideality" that is subjectively appropriated. While it is "impossible to exist without passion," the existential reality of an individual is characterized by the self-consciously sustained relationship between thought and passion. Inwardness is, indeed, a mode of understanding, but it is a form of concrete understanding. The more concrete the content of consciousness, the more concrete is the understanding of this content. The most concrete kind of consciousness possible is not pure self-consciousness (i.e., the Hegelian conception of consciousness) but rather a self-consciousness having such specificity that it cannot, strictly speaking, be described objectively. This subjective I-consciousness cannot be conceptualized since it can only be encountered in lived actuality and cannot be understood in terms of the "ideality" of conceptualization or the linguistic expression of concepts. This analysis of inwardness is obviously related to our earlier discussion of the self as a dynamic, relational being. For it is clear, despite Kierkegaard's use of Hegelian terminology in his description of the self, that he desired to distinguish his conception of the self from that of Hegel. Even the *concept* of "self" itself signifies the implicit contradiction of attempting to posit the general as the particular. Thus it is argued in *The Concept of Dread* that

> no science can state what the self is, without stating it in perfectly general terms. The general *is* only by the fact that it is thought or can be thought . . . and is *as* that which can be thought. [The point in the particular is its negative, its repellent relationship to the general; but as soon as this is thought away, individuality is annulled, and as soon as it is thought it is transformed in such a way that either one does not think it but only imagines one is thinking it, or does think it and only imagines that it is included in the process of thought.] . . . every man who gives heed to himself knows what no science knows, since he knows what he himself is . . . this is the profundity of the Greek saying, *gnothi seauton* (know thyself), which so long has been understood in the German [or Hegelian] way as pure self-consciousness.[33]

The conceptualization of the individual self is a paradoxical and ultimately self-negating enterprise. One cannot be said to 'know' the self objectively at all. We do not know the self in the way in which we may be said to know a mathematical or an empirical proposition. In the process of attempting to describe the self one universalizes what is particular by virtue of the use of universal categories. Since the individual engaged in the activity of becoming, of existing, cannot be an *object* of consciousness at all, the I-consciousness that characterizes inwardness for Kierkegaard is neither a species of objective knowledge nor a contemplative self-consciousness (*à la* Hegel). Since the self is an actuality that initiates change or undergoes change, that is constantly in the process of becoming, that is a radically contingent being, it is necessarily a temporal being; hence there can be no question, for Kierkegaard, of there being a "transcendental consciousness" for which the empirical ego can be a phenomenon. The only transcendental subjectivity that Kierkegaard might recognize would be the transcendence of the actual self toward the realization of possibilities or toward the openness of the future. As soon as one begins to think of the ego or empirical self as an "object" or "phenomenon" *for* consciousness or as an intentional object *of* consciousness one becomes entangled in the question of postulating a transcendental ego that knows the empirical ego as object.

For Kierkegaard self-consciousness or I-consciousness is an activity, a deed that is inwardness and is an intensified consciousness of a self that already *is* in the actuality of becoming. Although such self-reflective consciousness is itself a manifestation of inwardness, it may be said that subjective knowledge or subjective self-consciousness is a paradoxical process that affects the relational being it would know and can only be what Kierkegaard would call an approximation-process. One cannot have apodictic self-knowledge because in the very process by which one is endeavoring to attain such knowedge the self is being transformed by virtue of this 'activity'. Kierkegaard seems to assume that we have an immediate, direct, intuitive understanding of, or acquaintance with, ourselves as we exist (especially in individuating states of being), an understanding that is obscured, not clarified, by our attempt to express this understanding in terms of objective knowledge. We may say, then, that subjective reflection is an act of an existing individual involved in the process of existing and that it bears a reciprocal dialectical relationship to that process. Hence, subjective reflection cannot be an activity of an absolute, atemporal, transcendental consciousness; it is rather the activity of a complex, dynamic psychophysical individual who exists in dialectical tension (as "in-between" or *interesse* ideality and actuality, possibly, and necessity) in a temporally conditioned projective *nisus* toward the future. The 'spiritual' self must be this finite, particular self-consciousness, this intermediate being that relates itself to itself in a dynamic, 'moving' synthesis that is never finished or complete in time. The paradigm for subjective self-existence is that inwardness or overlapping (*übergreifende*) subjectivity in which an individual relates himself to himself in seriousness. The activity of inwardness is the paradigm of subjective individuation, the means by which there is an accentuation of personal existence. Becoming sub-

jective means endeavoring to become a self—striving to become
the "ideal" self that one ought to be—by means of a repetitious
choice of the various possibilities for inwardness. It is this persistent striving to exist in inwardness (Kierkegaard relates the
two when he avers that *Existentsen selv . . . er Straeben*—"existence itself is striving"—and *Det Ethiske er Inderligheden* since
the ethical task is to exist) that is central to Kierkegaard's conception of the ethical sphere of existence.

There remains one final question that must be dealt with in regard to an explication of Kierkegaard's ethics of subjectivity
namely: What is the relationship between this conception of the
self-conscious development of subjectivity as the ethical goal for
man and the notion that the individual who chooses to live in
the ethical sphere of existence ought to endeavor to 'become' a
universal man, a paradigmatic man? While Kierkegaard, in some
of his earliest journal entries, often tended to link the ethical
mode of being with the Christian (referring, for example, to the
ethico-religious standpoint), he gradually began to separate the
ethical sphere of existence and the religious. However, he continued to insist upon the necessity of the development of ethical
self-consciousness and, hence, ethical subjectivity in order to
attain realization of self. He avers in his journals that "ethical
reflection and going through the universal involved in it first
makes each human existence a truly authentic existence."[34] If, in
the teleological dialectic of life, a truly ethical existence is one involving a persistent striving and resolution to realize one's potentiality for individuating, spiritual states of being, to accentuate
one's subjective existence, what role does the universal play in
this conception? Surely it is paradoxical to say that by intensifying subjectivity one also "becomes universal" or manifests
"the universal" in one's existence.

Subjectivity and Universality in Ethical Existence

When Kierkegaard asks himself, in his journals, "What is humanness [*Menneskelighed*]?" and then answers, "It is human
equality [*Menneske-Lighed*],"[35] he is surely not merely making
a casual play on words. However, it is hard to determine precisely what he does mean by this remark. Has he not emphasized

that only a subjective existence, one characterized by inwardness and a repeated resoluteness to strive to attain a subjectivity positel ethical *telos,* is central to ethical existence? Has he not practically equated an ethical mode of existence with one that is chiefly characterized by individuating states of being (i.e., by various forms of inwardness: anxiety, subjective concern, conscience, guilt, self-knowledge, resolution, irony, etc.) that, by their very nature, are isolating and not universal? Finally, what is this "human equality" to which he refers in this statement?

The answers to these questions are found in two pervasive notions that Kierkegaard placed at the center of his philosophical anthropology. First, as we have mentioned before, he assumes that each rational, self-reflective individual possesses what he calls a primitive "oughtness-capability" that is the potentiality-for that must be discovered by each individual and that is the basis for the possibility of an existence characterized by the pursuit of authentic selfhood. Since each individual who is capable of self-understanding can discover his own potentiality-for-becoming-a-self, he can discover the ethical possibility in himself and assume that it is present in others. Secondly, the ultimate aim of ethical existence as the development of subjectivity requires that an individual submit himself to universal requirements that can be posited by other individuals as well. In *Fear and Trembling* he notes that "the ethical as such is the universal" and "it applies to everyone."[36] Like all ethicists, Kierkegaard assumes that ethical principles must be universal or universalizable. The paradoxical nature of what he conceives of as the universal is that it can only be realized existentially in the concrete existence of an individual. That is, the universal ethical requirement is to "become oneself" (i.e., to strive to become what he and F. H. Bradley call the "ideal self" that one ought to endeavor to realize), to "become subjective." If the ethical "task" of each individual is to become himself, to become subjective, then what is meant by this universal (or "humanness"), which presumably is made manifest in the individual's existence? Since, as Kierkegaard remarks in *Concluding Unscientific Postscript,* everyone is already something of a subject, is it not odd to prescribe that "one [ought to] become what one already is" and then to claim that by doing so one *be-*

comes the universal man? What does it mean to say, as he does
in *Either/Or,* that the ethical individual "expresses the universal
in his life"? Clearly the human equality he refers to can only mean
the presumed equality of each man (capable of reasoning and
self-reflection) insofar as he has the potentiality-for ethical existence or the potentiality-for-becoming-a-self. But how can anything *universal* be "expressed" in the intensified specificity and
subjectivity of one's own particular actuality?

While it may be asserted that the central notions of the ethical
mode of existence that are presented in *Either/Or, Concluding
Unscientific Postscript,* and elsewhere can only legitimately be
attributed to the pseudonyms under which these works were
written and thus do not comprise any clearly delineated practical
ethics that can be attributed to Kierkegaard himself, such a view
is fundamentally false. There is a consistency between Kierkegaard's notations in his journals concerning ethical existence and
many of the more elaborate descriptions of ethical existence
in his so-called "aesthetic" writings. Kierkegaard himself holds
that an intensification of personal, subjective existence is precisely the means by which one becomes a self and that this ought
to be the ethical goal of each individual. The ethical (*ethisk*) is a
"being-able, an exercising, an existing, an existential transformation of the self," an intensification of the "voice [*per + sonare*]
of the individual."[37] The key to his conception of the relationship between the individual and universal, between authentic
subjective existence and what he calls "the essential" is found in
what he describes as his report to the public and to history, *The
Point of View for My Work as an Author.* Commenting on his
concept of "the individual," he states:

> In every one of the pseudonymous works this theme of 'the
> individual' comes to evidence in one way or another; but there
> the individual is predominantly the pre-eminent individual in
> the aesthetic sense. . . . In every one of my edifying works the
> theme of 'the individual' comes to evidence . . . but there the
> individual is what every man is or can be. The starting point of
> the pseudonyms is the difference between man and man . . . the
> starting-point of the edifying works is the edifying thought of the
> universal human. But this double meaning is precisely the dialec-

tic of 'the single individual.' The 'single individual' can mean the
one and only, and the 'single individual' can mean every man. . . .
The pride in the one thought incites some, the humility in the
second thought deters others, but the confusion involved in the
double meaning provides attention dialectically; and, as I have
said, this double meaning is precisely the thought of 'the individual'.[38]

In his journals Kierkegaard notes that "the aesthetic emphasizes the differences amongst men; the ethical emphasizes the
similarities among men."[39] Since the endeavor to attain subjective, personal existence is a possibility for all reflective men, it is
(or can be) a universal ethical requirement. If there is anything
like a categorical imperative in Kierkegaard's writings, it is: Become an authentic self. He assumes that by undergoing an intensification of one's own unique individual existence in the
various modes of inwardness one realizes or "expresses" what is
essential in human existence as such. It is misleading to say that
"each man exists, and each man exists as subject. . . . He must exist as a self."[40] For, while Kierkegaard does admit that each man
is more or less subjective in some respects, he prescribes as the
ultimate ethical task for man to become subjective, to choose to
realize the "ideal self" for which he has a potentiality-for by virtue of repeated choices of individuating 'spiritual' states of being.
Hence existence, *sensu strictissimo*, means, for Kierkegaard, that
activity in and through which an individual endeavors to intensify his sense of subjective being so as to become a self. To exist
is an ethical *telos*—a life-long task that is ended only by death and
is that activity through which the individual expresses "whatever
is essentially human." Kierkegaard held that "whatever is great
in the sphere of the universally human must . . . not be communicated as a subject for admiration, but as an ethical *requirement*. In the form of a possibility it becomes a requirement. . . .
the good should be presented in the form of a possibility."[41] But
what is the central "good" that Kierkegaard postulates as the ethical goal of human life? It is to *exist*, to become subjective, to become a self. The persistent striving that is characteristic of
ethical existence is a "movement" towards a *telos* that must be
repeatedly renewed. As Kierkegaard puts it in *Either/Or*, "The

individual has his teleology in himself, has inner teleology, is himself his teleology. His self is . . . the goal towards which he strives."[42] In an authentic ethical existence the individual 'becomes' the universal or paradigmatic man insofar as he expresses, manifests, or reveals in his existence the essence of man. Before Unamuno or Heidegger, Kierkegaard implicitly maintained that *the essence of man lies in existence.*

To exist in subjectivity, in the intensity and seriousness of inwardness, to strive persistently to become the "ideal self" we ought to be, is to express the essence of man in temporal actuality, to make manifest what man ought to be. What Heidegger has separated from a purely ethical context (and placed in an ontological context) was already described by Kierkegaard in his phenomenology of ethical existence. In remarkable detail, Kierkegaard provided Heidegger with the schema for his conception of *eigentlich Existenz.* Insofar as Kierkegaard held that the "essence" of man is expressed in the authentic existence of a subjective individual he did not entirely renounce essentialism. However, this notion is not fundamentally derived from the philosophy of Hegel but is one that was suggested to Kierkegaard by his reading of Aristotle. The general notion of a striving for an end or goal in terms of the *movements* from potentiality to actuality underlies Kierkegaard's understanding of man's self-becoming. While Aristotle describes all of nature as dynamic, as being pervaded by a *nisus* toward a realization of potentialities, man is, in a sense, an anomalous being in this 'world'. For, man has rational capacities, has a capacity for deliberate choice and action (in point of fact, Aristotle holds that only man can act), that enables him to make transitions from potentiality to actuality in terms of a subjectively posited *telos.* This raises a question about the "essence" of man. In one sense, the essence of anything, for Aristotle, is its *to ti en einai,* its "what is was to be." Now, the "what it is" of any entity is, in Hegelian language, only a moment in the unfolding of its "what it was to be" or its essential nature. The complete realization (*entelecheia*) toward which entities move (or, in the case of nonhuman beings, are moved) is the realization of their essence. In regard to man's endeavor (*conatus*) to become what he was to be, to attain self-realization, this teleology must be appropriated by man himself. If we superimpose aspects of Aristotle's metaphysics over his *Nicomachean Ethics,* we can see how Kierkegaard may have come to understand the *entelechia* of man in terms of the endeavor to become what one ought to be. In the moral development of man the *entelecheia* that is pursued is one that must be voluntarily pursued in choice, decision, and action. For Kierkegaard, at any rate, it is in the activity of existence (as he understands it) that the essence of man is realized insofar as it can be realized in temporality. In ethical self-existence both goal and activity are in the agent since it is the consciousness of the *entelecheia* (*en,* "in"; *telos,* "end"; and *echein,* "to have") that is the teleological factor pervading an ethical existence. The ethical goal of man, then, is to realize in his existence the essence of man insofar as this is possible. It is in this sense that the ethical individual is a synthesis of universality and individuality, the universal and the particular, a particular existing human being and a paradigmatic man. The primary duty of man is to realize the universally human existentially.

If only some aspects of *Either/Or* are attended to it might be assumed that Kierkegaard put forward a practical ethics modeled upon Kantian ethics. But, while it is true that Kierkegaard's understanding of man was informed by various aspects of Kant's ethics (e.g., his phenomenology of man's oughtness-capability and the notion of a primal potentiality-for is an amplification of Kant's view that the thought of "ought" implies the thought of the freedom of "can"),[43] it was certainly devoid of the aprioristic purism of Kant's conception of man as self-legislator. To be sure, Kierkegaard does say in *Either/Or* (through the character of Judge Wilhelm) that the ethical individual acts in accordance with a universal principle of duty. However, a view such as that of James Collins, which proclaims that in Kierkegaard's descriptive ethics "every aspect of an individual's being [must be brought] into conformity with the universal law, so that what is essentially human may be expressed in the individual instance,"[44] is misleading. As I have indicated, the universal to which an individual ought to conform is not a universal moral law as posited by pure practical reason but the universal in man as such. That is, one's primary duty is to become a person or a self. A principle of duty has meaning only in relation to how I (or any other individual) reveal the universal in my own choices, decisions, and actions. In doing *my* particular duty, Kierkegaard seems to say, I manifest what is universal in man. The relationship between the universal and the particular individual is a paradoxical one. It is paradoxical insofar as the universal can only be realized in and through the actuality of a particular being. Kierkegaard assumes that "this universal can very well coexist with and in the particular without consuming it."[45] Furthermore, for Kierkegaard, the realization of a principle of duty in one's own existence requires passion (*eros*), since the individual is not required to act out of a *pure respect* (which is a paradoxical *feeling* that is somehow unrelated to the empirical actuality of the individual) for a principle of duty. If one wants to say that the imperatives "become subjective" or "become a self" could be construed as principles of duty when the analogy to Kant breaks down immediately insofar as such "principles" are not posited by man as a purely rational being but are *chosen* with passion and energy by a particular, actual being who is concerned (*interesse*) with his own actual existence. Certainly it was not Kierkegaard's intention (although it was Kant's) "to construct a pure moral philosophy" that, as Kant says in his *Fundamental Principles of the Metaphysic of Morals,* would be "perfectly cleared of everything which is only empirical and which belongs to [practical] anthropology."[46]

Ironically, it is in Kant's popular *Lectures on Ethics* that we can find certain assertions that seem to be in the spirit of Kierkegaard's practical ethics. Thus, for example, in discussing "Duties to Oneself," Kant avers that "The duties we owe to ourselves do not depend on the relation of the action to the ends of happiness. . . . The basis of such obligation is not to be found in the advantages we reap from doing our duty towards ourselves, but in the worth or value of manhood." For a moment, Kant comes within a hair's breath of describing what might be called the existential basis of morality. Thus, he says that

Our duties towards ourselves constitute the supreme condition

and the principle of all morality; for moral worth is the worth of
the person as such. . . . Only if our worth as human beings is
intact can we perform our other duties; for it is the foundation
stone of all other duties.[47]

There are other aspects of Kant's ethics that do seem to reappear in Kierkegaard's description of ethical existence. Thus, for
example, the emphasis upon the purpose or intention of a choice
or a decision, as opposed to a concern with possible or probable
consequences, is expressed in almost precise Kantian terms.
Kierkegaard's notion of the "*valore intrinseco* of inwardness"
seems parallel to Kant's conception of the intrinsic value of a
pure good will. Again, Kant's notion that rational beings are *persons* and that the "*subjective* principle of human action," as he
expresses it in *The Fundamental Principles of the Metaphysic of
Morals,* is that each man conceives of his existence as an end in
itself seems to underlie Kierkegaard's view that one must choose
oneself as absolute in an ethical commitment. However, there
are so many dissimiliarities between Kant's ethics and the practical ethics of Kierkegaard that any attempt to establish a direct
analogy between the two is doomed to failure. We must remind
ourselves that Kant held that "all moral conceptions have their
seat and origin completely *a priori* in reason," whereas Kierkegaard suggests that such conceptions have their 'origin' in man's
being, in his primitive potentiality-for (*kunnen*), in his potentiality-for-becoming-a-self, in his capacity for critical self-reflection.
In the ethical "turn" it is the cognitive-affective act of choice that
is decisive, not *a priori* reasoning: the motivation for becoming
an ethical being must come "from within," from the *eros* or
pathos that Kierkegaard regarded as the "material" of moral
virtue. In this regard, he quotes with approval Plutarch's assertion, in *De virtute morali,* that "ethical virtue has the passions
for its material, and reason as its form."[48] Despite the occasional echoes of Kantian sentiments in Kierkegaard's writings
(especially in *Either/Or*), the bifurcation between his ethics
of self-becoming and Kant's formalistic, metempirical ethics is,
mutatis mutandis, complete. A detailed analysis of the distinctions between Kantian ethics and Kierkegaard's ethics of sub-

jectivity or existential ethics would require another monograph.

For Kierkegaard, the relationship between the universal requirement of ethics is, as I have said, fundamentally paradoxical: duty or, rather, a principle of duty is of course universal; and yet all that an individual can do is the particular. Kierkegaard holds, contra Kant, that an ethical existence does *not* demand that I act out of "respect" for the universal as such, as if it and it alone had absolute validity. No, the ethical individual must appropriate the universal in his own existence, must actualize it, as it were, in his own particularity. As Kierkegaard puts it in *Either/Or*:

> There is [a] scepticism . . . which applies to all duty, namely, the consideration that I am utterly unable to do duty. . . . language itself emhasizes this scepticism. I never say of a man that he does duty or duties, but I say that he does *his* duty, I say, "I am doing *my* duty, do *yours*." This indicates that the individual is at once the universal and the particular. Duty is the universal which is required of me. . . . my duty is the particular, something for me alone, and yet it is duty and hence the universal. Here personality is displayed . . . for . . . personality reveals itself as the unity of the universal and the particular.[49]

Kierkegaard understood that one can do "duty" and yet not do his own duty—one can act in accordance with a universal principle of duty and yet not do one's own duty. Personality is the unity of the universal and particular insofar as the individual relates the universal to his own actuality as a possibility that he must attempt to realize *in concreto*. It is for this reason that Kierkegaard insists that ethical existence must be characterized by subjective intensification, by a dialectical tension between "ideality" and actuality, rational understanding and passion.

Certainly, for Kierkegaard, there is no "duty for duty's sake." Indeed, he maintained that the ethically existing individual has himself as his central interest or concern. "Existence," he says, "constitutes the highest interest of the existing individual, and his interest in his existence constitutes his reality."[50] The *reality* of the individual who exists in ethical self-consciousness is "an *interesse*," an "intermediate being" between "ideality" (e.g., a principle of duty) and actuality (the actual being he has been or is). The moment the question is raised concerning how an individual can, for example, do *his* duty or can relate the universal to the particularity of his own existence, we are asking a question concerning the ethical reality of the individual. Ultimately, as I have already indicated, the primary obligation of the individual is to become a self (in *Either/Or* Kierkegaard remarks that the "movement" of the individual in ethical existence is "from himself through the world to himself")[51] or, as he expresses it in *Concluding Unscientific Postscript,* the claim that the *ethisk* makes upon an individual is "that he should exist." Before Heidegger, Kierkegaard had insisted that only man *can* exist. He anticipates Heidegger when he avers that "God does not exist, He is eternal. Man thinks and exists,"[52] or, more properly, man has a potentiality-for existence that may or may not be realized in temporality, which is to say in the only realm in which spiritual "movement" is possible. Insofar as an individual strives to become subjective or to become a person (with all that Kierkegaard understands by this) he exists as a reality in actuality. But in doing so he reveals, manifests, or expresses the essence of man or what man was meant to be. In order to live in the ethical sphere of existence, then, the individual must appropriate and transform the ethical "universal" in his own existence and thereby bring about a transformation of the self in actuality.

What Kierkegaard did in what I have called his philosophical anthropology is, in one sense, a radical departure from traditional Western conceptions of the relationship between existence and essence; that is, he proclaimed that the essence of man has an exclusive ethical meaning and lies in the very activity of existence, an activity comprising a complex of individuating states of being, of inwardness, of a persistent striving in a teleological, dialectical tension that most men, for the most part, would avoid so far as possible. The essence of man, then, is conceived of as an *ideal telos* that may in fact never be fully realized in finite existence by any existing individual. However, it is this strenuous endeavor to live an authentic (and hence, for Kierkegaard, ethical) existence that gives purpose and meaning to human life since, by virtue of this repetitious striving, the individual intensifies his existence and thus brings meaning and purpose into human life generally. Whereas a religious mode of existence in faith requires a subjective, paradoxical commitment to an objective uncertainty, to an absolute *telos* that one believes transcends temporality (a *telos* before which one has an ethico-religious obligation), it is obvious that ethical existence does not demand religious faith, nor does it require that one act in conformity with any universal moral laws that are understood to have the "necessity" of universal natural laws. Kierkegaard explicitly states, in *Concluding Unscientific Postscript*, that an ethical existence is possible outside Christianity. To be sure, an authentic ethical existence is compatible with, and capable of being incorporated into, a religious existence. An ethical existence, at any rate, is one in which an individual can become that "reality" which can be apprehended in its subjective actuality. In his existential ethics Kierkegaard raises the question whether it is possible that an intrinsic good, an intrinsic value, can become manifest in the world in the ethical reality of an individual human being who truly exists. Or to express it another way, is it not possible that in the authentic, subjective existence of an individual "truth" has come to be in finite temporality?

Kierkegaard's answer to such questions is, of course, affirmative. The often misrepresented notion that "truth is subjectivity" or "subjectivity is truth" does *not* mean, as some critics of Kierkegaard and existentialism have maintained, that *all* truth is subjective or that the only truth that man can *know* is subjective truth. Kierkegaard is not the converse of the logical positivist who avers that the only "truths" are either logical truths or verified (or, more humbly, "confirmed") empirical assertions. On the contrary, he agrees with the logician that tautologies or analytic statements are of course true, and that objective reflection does indeed apprehend 'real' objective truths. He also agrees with the empiricists that empirical truths are approximations or probable truths. Indeed, in his journals he expresses the sophisticated notion (for his time) that we learn nothing from experience as such except "statistical knowledge."[53] Kierkegaard's sensitivity to the empirical was in the spirit of William James. Thus, he remarks, ironically, that in "an age of empiricism" no one seems concerned with "Christian experience" or even with "the existential" (*det Existentielle*).⁵⁴ Kierkegaard, before James, attempted to engage in a radical empiricism that would take into account the subjective perspective that, once again, is under attack from so many quarters. His emphasis upon "subjective truth"—the *manifestation* of truth in the authentic existence of an individual—is, as he puts it, a "corrective" to the tendency (which, alas, has been exacerbated by time) to deny the validity of the subjective perspective or to relegate it to fantasy, reverie, or an inconsequential, irrelevant domain. Kierkegaard's view is not that truth *is* subjective. Rather, it is a more radical notion: in the intensification of subjectivity in an authentic ethical existence, he believed that truth becomes or is revealed in temporality. That the individual can exist 'in' truth is an echo of a Hegelian notion that the way to truth is not only an epistemological process but a historical process as well. Although Hegel would not have followed Kierkegaard to the ostensible anthropocentric 'extreme' that he defended, Hegel did maintain, as Marcuse has observed in his *Reason and Revolution,* that "there is, in the last analysis, no truth that does not *essentially concern* the living subject and that is not the subject's truth."⁵⁵ The Heideggerian notion that *Dasein* can be 'in' truth is a notion that is a Hegelian one as seen through the prism of Kierkegaard's conception of the 'truth', which is expressed in an authentic human existence. Such a truth is not, of course, an *object* of knowledge; rather, it is a "lived truth" that attests to the "absolute validity" of an ethical existence that is lived intensely. To paraphrase Heidegger, one may say that so long as man lives there is the possibility of truth and, so long as man can *exist* it is possible for there to be a truth that is other than propositional truth—other than tautological or analytical truth. In his radical subjectivity and inwardness Socrates, the paradigmatic existential thinker, existing in truth, had attempted to live an authentic or "true" existence in the uncertainty of finite existence, in an "inwardness" that accentuated his subjectivity and attested to his intensified sense of his own reality. As Kierkegaard remarks in *Concluding Unscientific Postscript*:

The infinite merit of the Socratic position was precisely to accentuate the fact that the knower is an existing individual, and that the task of existing is his essential task. . . . Socratically speaking, subjectivity is untruth if it refuses to understand that subjectivity is truth, but, for example, desires to become objective. Here, on the other hand, subjectivity in beginning upon the task of becoming the truth through a subjectifying process, is in the difficulty that it is already untruth. Thus, the labor of the task is thrust backward . . . in inwardness. So far is it from being the case that the way tends in the direction of objectivity, that the beginning merely lies deeper in subjectivity.[56]

In the ethical sphere of existence, becoming subjective is the means by which an individual realizes truth (or what Kierkegaard regards as the most significant mode of truth) in his own existence and strives to become what each man ought to be. Insofar as an individual is able to realize the essential characteristics of man in his own individual existence, he has also brought to realization in time the "truth" of human existence. Of course, Kierkegaard regards his "doctrine" that "subjectivity is truth" as a "thought-experiment" and we are free, therefore, to regard it as yet another hypothetical possibility—or we are free to accept it as a truth "for us."

Since radical individuation, specificity, inwardness, and the development of subjectivity are central to Kierkegaard's existential ethics, it is clear that, essentially, the spirit and intention of his practical ethics is divorced from the formalism of Kant. Kant places duty "above" the sentiments, the feelings, the *pathos* of the individual and his own subjective existence. In addition, he assumes that his ethical prescription is universally applicable to every individual insofar as the individual is a "rational being" or insofar as he participates in a realm of intelligibility. It is precisely what is not personal, existential, or individual in man (i.e., "reason," *Vernunft*) that is subject to the discipline of ethical prescription. In these respects, as well as in many others, Kant's formalistic, aprioristic, rationalistic ethics of duty is not the dominant influence on Kierkegaard's ethics of subjectivity. The conception of ethical existence as a life lived in accordance with, or out of respect for, a universal principle of duty is not, as has so often been suggested, the central basis of Kierkegaard's conception of ethical existence. For Kierkegaard the primary "duty" of each individual is the duty "to become himself," to become subjective, to become the "ideal" self that he, and he alone, knows he can become.

One's own ethical possibility is not subject to doubt: it must either be chosen or not chosen. The temporal existence of man was conceived of by Kierkegaard as a "time of test" (*Prøvens Tid*) in which decisiveness in regard to what one wants to do with one's life is essential, is something which cannot be put off indefinitely since we are, as Heidegger reminded us, "Being-unto-death" (*Sein zum Tode*). In reading Kierkegaard, I am reminded of the Buddhist tale of the man who was shot with an arrow. Agitated and excited, he asked his companions from which direction they thought the arrow was fired, from what angle it was fired, the character of the individual who fired it—his family, background, his nature, his name, etc. What he *ought* to have done was to pull the arrow from his back decisively. If one puts off decisiveness in regard to one's life, will it be possible to be decisive later? In the final analysis, Kierkegaard believed that we cannot entirely escape our subjective sense of our own ethical potentiality-for, our self-knowledge of what we ought to be, but are not yet. Like Socrates, as he understood him, Kierkegaard seemed to believe that our most pressing obligation is to ourselves, to the realization of our own unique, irreplaceable, individual being in terms of a constant critical examination of our lives, and a persistent striving to be all that we can be. It is neither reason nor consciousness-in-general that promulgates universal moral laws that are binding on each "rational being"; rather, it is the complex, paradoxical, dialectical, psychophysical individual who discovers in himself his own ethical possibility, who chooses it or refuses to acknowledge it, who can posit as his ethical goal the persistent striving to become a person, to become subjective, to realize the "ideal self." As F. H. Bradley expresses it,

> against this ideal self the particular person remains and must remain imperfect. The ideal self is not fully realized in us, in any way that we can see. We are aware of a ceaseless process,

it is well if we can add progress, in which the false . . . self is
constantly subdued but never disappears.[57]
Bradley, of course, would have been offended by Kierkegaard's

insistence that the "real" or "true" self is the subjectively existing
individual. But, then, he made the Hegelian assumption (perhaps justified in some cases) that there is an "objective" morality embodied in society or the state that is the ultimate morality
to which we must conform. Even in this context, however, it is an
'I' that must sustain and endeavor to promulgate "public morality," to renew its commitment, in subjectivity, to an "ideality"
that can only be realized, insofar as it ever is realized, concretely—in the existence of individuals. It is unfortunate that
philosophers, such as Hegel and Bradley, who hold that morality
is embodied in the "objective spirit" (*objektive Geist*) seem
to ignore the fact that conformity to such a "morality" does not
by any means guarantee subjective morality, that most moralists
in the Western world have put forward ethical requirements
that transcend those of a flaccid public morality. What is often
neglected in discussions of the individual's conformity to universal moral laws, to what Hegel and Bradley believed to be the
spiritual morality of the community, is the essential subjective
nisus toward the actualization of any morality. Again, even Bradley had to admit that

> this inward, this "subjective," this personal side, this knowing in
> himself by the subject [of his relation to the universal] or this
> consciousness in the . . . subject . . . is necessary for all morali-
> ty.[58]

To be sure, as Kierkegaard has said in his journals, the individual does not exist in total isolation from "the world," which is
called the "medium in which we exist," nor is the subjectivity of
ethical existence something that occurs in a vacuum: all choice,
decision, and action take place "in situation."[59] For Kierkegaard,
too, each man ought to have his "station and its duties," ought to
have, as it is put in *Either/Or*, "a duty to work," ought to have a
"calling."[60] But he assumed that only if an individual is transformed in his own being, only if he has chosen inwardness, only

if he persistently strives to become a self, can he be a moral being in the public sphere of action. In the ethically existing individual in whom is manifested the "intermediate reality" that is paradigmatic of human existence the individual undergoes a "reduplication" of his subjectivity insofar as he endeavors to become objective toward his own subjectivity.[61] By being related objectively to his own subjectivity the individual applies a "corrective" to subjective self-satisfaction: one must be ironic towards one's own authentic subjectivity. But then irony is, as Kierkegaard puts it, a "determination" of spiritual self-existence, a critical awareness of the asymmetrical relationship between one's own imperfect actuality and the ethical "ideality" that one endeavors to bring to actualization.

Kierkegaard's description of the ethical sphere of existence, his phenomenology of practical ethics, reveals it to be one that is clearly antihedonistic, nonutilitarian, and neither a form of Kantian ethics nor a form of eudaimonism. Ethical existence is a constant, self-critical activity by which one attains a deepening of subjective individuation, an approximation to selfhood, that is not motivated by the pursuit of an illusory or imaginary happiness. Although it has been said (by James Collins) that Kierkegaard's conception of ethical existence is eudaimonistic, I can find no evidence for this view. In Kierkegaard's conception of human existence contradiction, dialectical tension, and ironic tension are never mediated in consciousness. Perhaps, he avers, there is a joy or happiness in a life of faith as there is "hope" in the possibility of "the eternal" (*den Evige*), or there are moments, such as those he experienced at Gilleleie and Gilbjerg, when the meaningfulness of existence is experienced in *pathos* and not merely thought as a postulate.[62]

The *telos* that motivates the pursuit of an ethical existence is not happiness. Kierkegaard would agree with Kant that "unfortunately, the notion of happiness is so indefinite that although every man wishes to attain it, yet he never can say definitely and consistently what it is that he really wishes and wills." The uncertainty of existence, the arbitrary rewards and punishments of life, the paradoxical counterfinalities of empirical life (e.g., the negations that so often emerge out of the attainments of goods that one had previously thought would bring happiness), the senselessness of contingent events that bring misfortune to oneself or to others, the sheer greed, stupidity, and irrationality that so often create and sustain historical earthquakes that swallow up the promises and hopes of individuals—all these and more make the pursuit of happiness in this life a precarious, if not an impossible, enterprise. For Kierkegaard, at any rate, it is within the limited sphere in which one's finite freedom is effective that one ought to "express the universal-human and the individual," ought to strive to become an authentic self, to intensify personal existence in subjectivity.

In a decidedly unedifying time such as ours it is rejuvenating to hear at least someone say that it is possible *aedificare*, "to build" or "to construct" something. If the cynic asks, why ought I to exist?, Kierkegaard would probably answer: because it is never possible, so long as one lives, to obliterate the inchoate realization that you *can* exist—to deny completely your subjective knowledge of your potentiality-for-becoming-a-self.

Notes

Chapter 1

1. Søren Kierkegaard, *The Concept of Irony*, trans. by L. Capel (New York, 1965), p. 13.

2. *Søren Kierkegaard's Journals and Papers*, ed. and trans. by H. V. Hong and E. H. Hong (Bloomington and London, 1970), vol. 2, p. 221: "I feel what for me . . . is an enigmatical respect for Hegel; I have learned much from him, and I know very well that I can still learn much from him when I return to him again. . . . His philosophical knowledge, his amazing learning, the insight of his genius, and everything else good that can be said of a philosopher I am willing to acknowledge as any disciple."

3. Throughout his interesting commentary on Hegel's "Preface" to the *Phenomenology of Spirit* Kaufmann attempts to undermine Kierkegaard's originality. He suggests that Hegel provided a "critique of Kierkegaard before the latter was born" [sic!], that Kierkegaard relied heavily on the *Phenomenology*, and that the description of the self in *Sickness unto Death* is "taken straight from . . . the Phenomology." (Walter Kaufmann, *Hegel: A Reinterpretation* [New York, 1965], pp. 19, 35.) While it is certainly correct to say that Kierkegaard's philosophical language is quite often Hegelian, it is misleading to suggest that Kierkegaard did not employ Hegel's language in a unique way in order to formulate his conception of the self (which of course, is not expressed solely in *Sickness unto Death*) and his original emphasis upon the existential dimensions of human life. The basis of my objections to such undermining references to Kierkegaard is the insinuation that Hegel's thought incorporated Kierkegaard's extentialism and that Kierkegaard did not really "go beyond" Hegel in his conceptions of human existence or the dialectic of life.

4. The description of the "nihilistic standpoint" as a possibility for man at any time was first presented in the *Concept of Irony*, which was written in 1841, some thirty-one years before Nietzsche wrote his first major work, *The Birth of Tragedy*. Furthermore, the following

journal entries indicate that Kierkegaard was aware of the threat of nihilism as a general cultural phenomenon some time before Nietzsche's philosophical writings. Kierkegaard remarks that "since Christianity has been abolished . . . the whole realm of the temporal has . . . come to be muddled, with the result that it is no longer a question of a revolution once in a while, but underneath everything is a revolution which can explode at any moment. . . . It is certainly true . . . that the more meaningless we make life, the easier it is, and therefore that life in a sense has actually become easier . . . by abolishing Christianity. But . . . when a generation must live in and for merely finite ends, life becomes a whirlpool, meaninglessness, and either a despairing arrogance or a despairing disconsolateness." *Søren Kierkegaard's Journals and Papers,* trans. by H. V. Hong and E. H. Hong (Bloomington and London, 1967), I, pp. 437–38.

5. Cp. Hegel's *Philosophy of Right,* trans. by T. M. Knox (Oxford 1952), p 109: "The right of individuals to be subjectively destined to freedom is fulfilled when they belong to an . . . ethical order, because their conviction of their freedom finds its truth in such an objective order. . . ." Cp., also, the following addition to paragraph 145 of the same work: "Since the laws and institutions of the ethical order make up the concept of freedom, they are the . . . universal essence of individuals, who are thus related to them as accidents only. Whether the individual exists or not is all one to the objective ethical order. It alone is permanent and is the power regulating the life of individuals. Thus the ethical order . . . [is] in contrast with . . . the empty business of individuals [which] is only a game of see-saw."

In F. H. Bradley's *Ethical Studies* (New York, 1951), p. 109, Hegel's concept of "the universal Ethos" is appealed to in a critique of a subjective ethics. Bradley attributes to Hegel the view that an "isolated morality of one's own is futile and . . . impossible of attainment." Although this reference is presented as a translation of portions of Hegel's *Philosophy of Right,* only a few sentences in this reference correspond to anything in the original text. It could be said, however, that Bradley certainly captures the spirit of Hegel's remarks.

6. Norman Gulley, *The Philosophy of Socrates* (London, 1968), p. 63.

7. Martin Heidegger, *Sein und Zeit* (Tübingen, 1963), p. 5.

8. Immanuel Kant, *Introduction to Logic,* trans. by T. K. Abbott (New York, 1963), p. 15: "For philosophy . . . is the science of the relation of all knowledge and every use of reason to the ultimate end of human reason, to which . . . all other ends are subordinated. . . . The

field of philosophy . . . may be reduced to the following questions:

1. What can I know?
2. What ought I to do?
3. What may I hope?
4. What is man?

"The first question is answered by *Metaphysics,* the second by *Morals,* the third by *Religion,* and the fourth by *Anthropology.* In reality, however, all these might be reckoned under anthropology, since the first three questions refer to the last."

9. *The Encyclopedia of Philosophy,* ed. by Paul Edwards (New York, 1967), vol. 2, p. 386.

10. Kierkegaard, *Concluding Unscientific Postscript,* trans. by D. F. Swenson and W. Lowrie (Princeton, 1941), p. 449.

11. Kierkegaard, *The Concept of Irony,* p. 338.

12. Gulley, *The Philosophy of Socrates,* p. 83 ff. While there is a respectable tradition supporting such a straight-forward interpretation of Socratic ethics, Gulley seems to ignore the importance of self-knowledge in Socrates' thought. At only one point in his study does he allude to this aspect of Socratic ethics. Thus, he remarks on page 202 that " . . . the life dedicated to philosophy is, for Socrates, the good life. And by this he means a life dedicated to critical analysis . . . he thinks of this activity as constituting in itself the good, and not as a means to attaining goodness by establishing what the good is . . . it was Socrates' conviction that the good is sufficiently defined in terms of the . . . activity of 'examining oneself and others' by the method of critical analysis which he himself practised." The fact that such a commitment to this kind of existence is characterized as "an objective specification" indicates that Gulley has missed the centrality of self-knowledge in Socrates' thought. For Kierkegaard, at any rate, self-knowledge is central to his conception of ethical existence and the Socratic formula, "know thyself," is equated—in *Either/Or*—with an absolute choice of oneself. In his journals Kierkegaard notes: "Insofar as the ethical could be said to have a knowledge in itself, it is self-knowledge, but this is improperly regarded as a knowledge ["of an object," *objektive Videnskab*]. It is subjective knowledge." *Søren Kierkegaard's Journals and Papers,* I, p. 289.

13. Søren Kierkegaard, *The Point of View for My Work as an Author,* trans. by W. Lowrie (New York, 1962), p 41: " . . . Socrates . . . was a dialectician, he conceived everything in terms of reflection." The intimate relationship between Socratic irony and what Hegel called a "subjective form of dialectic" (*Lectures on the History of*

Philosophy [London, 1955], I, p. 398) is discussed in *The Concept of Irony*, trans. by L. Capel (New York, 1965) in a chapter on "The World Historical Validity of Irony" (pp. 276–88). Throughout *The Concept of Irony*, of course, Socrates is presented as a master of what I have called the dialectic of reflection.

14. Kierkegaard, *The Concept of Irony*, p. 340.

15. Hermann Diem, *Kierkegaard's Dialectic of Existence*, trans. by H. Knight (London, 1959), p 42.

16. *Søren Kierkegaard's Journals and Papers*, I, pp. 306–07.

17. Kierkegaard, *The Concept of Irony*, p. 117.

18. Ibid., p. 192.

19. Paul Friedländer, *Plato* (New York, 1964), p. 150.

20. Edmund Husserl, *Erste Philosophie* in *Husserliana*, VII (The Hague, 1956), pp. 7–11.

21. Kierkegaard, *The Concept of Irony*, p. 279.

22. *Søren Kierkegaard's Journals and Papers*, I, p. 307.

23. Friedrich Nietzsche, *Joyful Wisdom*, trans. by Thomas Common (New York, 1960), p 270.

24. Cf. Walter Kaufmann, *Nietzsche* (New York, 1968), chapter 13 ("Nietzsche's Admiration for Socrates"). Kaufmann refers to Nietzsche's "ambiguous" attitude towards Socrates and indicates that a distinction should be made between Nietzsche's attitude toward "Socratism" and toward Socrates the man. Reference is also made to the fact that Nietzsche, like Kierkegaard, likened himself to Socrates at times.

25. It has been argued that " . . . Wittgenstein holds a view about truth which, by its very nature, makes it impossible to account for the 'truth' of the view itself. . . . The final outcome of the *Tractatus* is *nihilism*. . . . It is a nihilism which negates the very possibility of philosophy itself." J. C. Morrison, *Meaning and Truth in Wittgenstein's 'Tractatus'* (Paris and The Hague, 1968), p. 143. For an analysis of the contrast between Heidegger's and Wittgenstein's treatment of the correspondence theory of truth, see the following: J. C. Morrison, "Heidegger's Criticism of Wittgenstein's Conception of Truth," *Man and World*, 2, 4 (1969) 551–73. Cf. also: G. J. Stack, "Heidegger's Concept of Meaning," *Philosophy Today*, XVII, (1973), pp. 255–66.

26. Martin Heidegger, *The Question of Being*, trans. by W. Kluback and J. T. Wilde (New York, 1958), pp. 89–103.

27. One of the most accessible sources in English for a statement of this theme is *The End of Philosophy*, trans. by J. Stambaugh (New York, 1973).

28. Stanley Rosen, *Nihilism* (New Haven, 1969), p. xiv.

29. Martin Heidegger, *Der Satz vom Grund* (Pfullingen, 1957), p. 158.

30. This comparison between the Śunyavāda teachings and certain aspects of Heidegger's later thought is admittedly exaggerated. There are, however, some similarities in regard to the conception of the impermanance of actuality, the negativity *in* beings and the ineffable nature of *Sūnya* ("void") as the ground and origin of the being of entities. Cf. S. Dasgupta, *Indian Idealism* (Cambridge, 1962), pp. 81, 95, 156.

What the Buddhist philosopher Nāgārjuna says about Sunyātā is similar to some of Heidegger's oracular statements about Being. It is that which is "beyond thought, that which is not produced . . . that which is beyond measure." S. Radhakrishnan, *Indian Philosophy* (London, 1948), vol. I, p. 663.

In an introduction to D. T. Suzuki's *Zen Buddhism* (New York, 1956) William Barrett claims that Heidegger confided in a German friend of his [Barrett's] who said that Heidegger saw a relationship between Suzuki's interpretation of Zen Buddhism and his own thought (p. xi). There is little doubt that there are at least some similarities between Heidegger's later philosophy and oriental thought. To pinpoint these relationships in any detail would be a difficult undertaking.

31. *Søren Kierkegaard's Journals and Papers*, I, p. 448.

32. Heidegger makes reference to this indictment of the idea of Being (expressed by Nietzsche in *The Twilight of Idols*) in *An Introduction to Metaphysics*, trans. by R. Mannheim (New Haven, 1959), p. 36.

33. Hegel describes the nature of finite beings in the following passage which, no doubt, was not far from Heidegger's mind when he sought to delineate the finiteness of *Dasein*. "When we say of things that they are finite, we mean . . . that Non-Being constitutes their nature and their Being. . . . The finite does not only change . . . it perishes; and its perishing is not merely contingent, so that it could be without perishing. It is rather the very being of finite things that they contain the seeds of perishing as their own Being-in-Self, and the hour of their birth is the hour of their death." *Science of Logic*, trans. by W. H. Johnston and L. Struthers (New York, 1929), I, p. 142.

34. S. Dasgupta characterizes the *nāstika* as a form of nihilism which proclaims that "nothing exists." Primarily the *nāstika* doctrine stressed the nonexistence of any transcendent reality or survival

after death. S. Dasgupta, *History of Indian Philosophy* (London, 1950), III, pp. 518–21.

35. George J. Stack, "Nietzsche and the Phenomenology of Value," *The Personalist* (1968), p. 84.

36. Wilhelm Dilthey, *Gesammelte Schriften* (Leipzig, 1927), I, p. 413. Cf. *Dilthey's Philosophy of Existence* (New York, 1597), p. 20.

37. Cf. George J. Stack, "Kierkegaard's Ironic Stage of Existence," *Laval Théologique et Philosophique*, XXV, pp. 193–207.

38. Rosen, *Nihilism*, p. xiii.

39. *Hegel's Philosophy of Right*, trans. by T. M. Knox (Oxford, 1952), pp. 12–13: "Philosophy . . . appears only when actuality is already there cut and dried after its process of formation has been completed. The teaching of the concept . . . is that the ideal first appears over against the real. . . . When philosophy paints its grey in grey, then has a form of life grown old. By philosophy's grey in grey it cannot be rejuvenated but only understood. The owl of Minerva spreads its wings only with the falling of dusk."

40. Søren Kierkegaard, *The Last Years, Journals 1853–1855*, trans. by R. G. Smith (New York, 1965), p. 113.

41. In Mahāyāna Buddhism it is paradoxically affirmed that *saṁsāra*—the wheel of birth and death comprising the phenomenal world —and *nirvāna* or the transcendental state of liberation from attachment and desire are ultimately one. That is, "The real and the phenomenal are not ultimately different. They are two moments of the same thing, one reality with two aspects. . . . The realm of birth and death is the manifestation of the immortal." S. Radhakrishnan, *Indian Philosophy* (London, 1948), I, pp. 595–96. A similar identity of the phenomenal realm of time and the transcendental world of eternity is expressed in D. T. Suzuki's interpretation of *Zen Buddhism* (New York, 1956), pp. 266. Cf., also: Alan Watts, *The Way of Zen* (New York, 1957), pp. 71–72: "Nirvāna is saṁsāra . . . [means] that what appears to us to be *saṁsāra* is really *nirvāna*, and what appears to be the world of form (*rupa*) is really the void (*sunya*)."

42. Kierkegaard, *Either/Or*, trans. by D. F. Swenson and L .M. Swenson (Princeton, 1959), I, p. 35.

43. William James, *Selected Papers on Philosophy* (New York, 1956), pp. 106–07.

44. Martin Heidegger, *Nietzsche* (Pfullingen, 1957), II, p. 127.

45. Heidegger, *Sein und Zeit*, p. 436.

46. *Ibid.*, pp. 227–28.

47. Martin Heidegger, *Gelassenheit* (Pfullingen, 1959), pp. 65–66.

Heidegger's supplement to this statement—i.e., that the independence of truth from man is nevertheless a "relation to man"—is unconvincing. To say that A is completely independent of B and then claim that this independence is a relation between A and B seems conceptually odd.

48. Martin Heidegger, *The Essence of Reasons*, trans. by T. Malick (Evanston, 1969), pp. 37–39.

49. Rosen, *Nihilism*, pp. 100–01.

50. Heidegger, *Sein und Zeit*, p. 287.

51. Hölderlin, *Samtliche Werke*, ed. by F. Beisser (Stuttgart, 1946), II, p. 61.

52. Rainer Marie Rilke, *Samtliche Werke* (Wiesbaden, 1955), I, p. 717. This translation of part of the "Ninth Elegy" of the *Duino Elegies* is rendered by H. F. Peters in *Rainer Marie Rilke: Masks and the Man* (New York, 1960), p. 171.

53. Heidegger, *Nietzsche*, I, p. 358.

54. The question of political nihilism as a distinctive form of nihilism is a difficult one. Aside from the rather anomalous form of attitudinal nihilism epitomized in the character of Bazarov (in Turgenev's *Fathers and Children*) and the activistic nihilism promulgated by numerous groups that use terroristic tactics against various other groups and institutions, the question of a purely political nihilism is difficult to deal with because it is ensnarled with a repulsive moral nihilism. In point of fact, it is difficult to discover any political ideology, movement, or system that is wholly nihilistic. For even if a political ideology is willing to use immoral means to attain its goals (and this applies to most extremist political ideologies of any persuasion), its spirit and intention does not entail a negation of the actual world, the negation of all values, the denial of knowledge or truth, or the assertion of the meaningless character of the totality of reality. Of course, we may be able to identify (all too easily) the moral nihilism of a particular political party or group. Thus, a specific political organization may be thoroughly unscrupulous, may not honor its treaties or agreements, and may needlessly and cruelly imprison, torture, or murder countless numbers of noncombatants on the basis of some fanatical political belief or purpose. This does not mean that such sociopolitical organizations are, in themselves, nihilistic; nor does it mean that they consciously will the negation or destruction of all sociopolitical organizations, including their own. To be sure, there is such a politically motivated negativism—e.g., Pisarev's fanatical view that the youth of the Russia of the "sixties" ought to strike out at every existing institution, inflicting destructive blows against such

institutions in order to see which can survive. The Russian nihilists did not have a meaningful political platform, did not have a practical political program or organization that would replace ostensibly "immoral," "decadent," or "outmoded" institutions or organizations. Such groups are not necessarily *theoretical* nihilists, nor are they necessarily *moral* nihilists except in the sense that their passions often lead them to immoral actions against those whom they believe to be their enemies; in this regard their moral consciences are dulled by the fanatical zeal with which they seek to realize their purely negative, destructive aims. What one must condemn in totalitarian forms of political organizations in this century is their gross moral nihilism, their shocking ability to use any means, no matter how nefarious, to achieve their ends. Generally, all political fanatics justify the means they use in terms of grandiose, if not quixotic, conceptions of the ends they seek. In the specific case of terrorists, there is a paradoxical commitment to vicious, immoral actions in the interest of social justice, peace, or revolutionary ideals. Insofar as such groups do have detailed political goals, they are not, strictly speaking, nihilistic. To my mind, the tendency towards the "politicalization" of human life in this century is not, in itself, nihilistic, but is a desperate attempt to overcome a spiritual nihilism that has become so pervasive and oppressive that only the harshest remedies are deemed sufficient to cure the disease. The extremist political movements of our time have not been nihilistic in themselves (despite the moral nihilism of their practice). The political revolutions of the left and the right, which have rocked (and continue to rock) the world, can be seen as fanatical attempts to transcend a psychological and spiritual nihilism that has apparently pervaded the consciousness of many.

A stochastic confluence of the "death" of the Judaeo-Christian *Weltanschauung*, a suspicion of reason, the erosion of the concept of truth, and a weariness with civilization was coeval with the spiritual, moral, and theoretical nihilism of which Kierkegaard and Nietzsche were sensitive enough to be aware before others. Into the spiritual vacuum of the last and present centuries has come a hydraheaded monster—the politics of power and violence—that, many seem to believe, has all the virtues and powers that were once attributed to God.

Nevertheless, a completely self-consistent political nihilism would be self-destructive, would, in fact, have willed its own self-destruction. Needless to say, this is not characteristic of sharply defined political organizations. Though political groups do have an unfortunate capacity for a willing suspension of morality, it is rare to find a political organization or ideology that has a nihilistic teleology. In this sense, what is often called "political" nihilism usually refers to the moral nihilism—the indifference to promises, treaties, or agreements, to the needs, rights, and lives of human beings—that (alas!) has been all too characteristic of the fanatical political movements of this century.

55. *Søren Kierkegaard's Journals and Papers*, I, p. 371.

56. Irving Babbitt, *Rousseau and Romanticism* (New York, 1955), p. 207.

57. *Solgers nachgelassene Schriften und Briefwechsel*, ed., L. Tieck and F. Raumer (Leipsig, 1826), II, p. 514. Cited in Kierkegaard's *The Concept of Irony*, p. 333.

58. Kierkegaard, *The Concept of Irony*, p. 341.

59. Giacomo Leopardi, *Zibaldone di pensieri* (Rome, 1955), I, pp. 1071–72.

60. John Keats (in a letter to Woodhouse, October, 1818), cited in M. Praz, *The Romantic Agony* (New York, 1956), p. xii.

61. E. R. Dodds, *The Greeks and the Irrational* (Boston, 1957), p. 184.

62. Søren Kierkegaard, *The Concept of Dread*, trans. by W. Lowrie (Princeton, 1957), p 140.

63. *Søren Kierkegaard's Journals and Papers*, I, p. 463.

64. *The Journals of Kierkegaard*, trans. by A. Dru (New York, 1959), vi (1838), p. 41.

65. G.F.W. Hegel, *The Phenomenology of Mind*, trans. by J. B. Baillie (New York, 1967), p. 249.

66. *The Journals of Kierkegaard*, p. 58.

67. To the kind of question that Nietzsche raises in *The Will to Power* Kierkegaard has a deceptively simple answer. Nietzsche remarks that "the philosophical nihilist is convinced that all that happens is meaningless and in vain; and that there ought not be anything meaningless and in vain. But whence this: there ought not to be? From where does one get this 'meaning,' *this* standard." *The Will to Power*, trans. by W. Kaufmann, (New York, 1968), 36, p. 23. Kierkegaard would probably have replied: "From one's self."

Chapter 2

1. William Barrett, *What is Existentialism?* (New York, 1964), pp. 152–54.

2. James Collins, *The Mind of Kierkegaard* (Chicago, 1953), p. 111.

3. Søren Kierkegaard, *Philosophical Fragments,* trans. by D. F. Swenson (Princeton, 1944), p. 64.

4. Hegel, *Science of Logic,* II, pp. 180–84.

5. *Søren Kierkegaard's Journals and Papers,* I, p. 111. This passage is incorporated almost verbatim in *Philosophical Fragments.*

6. Aristotle, *Metaphysics,* trans. by R. Hope, (Ann Arbor, 1960), XII, 1069b16.

7. William James, *Essays in Pragmatism,* ed. by A. Castell (New York, 1948), p. 171. The first reference is found in his journals. Cf., *Søren Kierkegaard's Journals and Papers* (Bloomington and London, 1967), I, p. 450: ". . . life must be understood backwards . . . it must be lived forwards." In his *Essays in Radical Empiricism* (London, 1922), p. 238, James refers explicitly to Kierkegaard's statement (which he discovered in an article by Höffding in the *Journal of Philosophy* in 1905) and remarks that his "Radical empiricism insists upon understanding forwards also, and refuses to substitute static concepts of the understanding for transitions in our moving life." There is also a further reference to Kierkegaard in *A Pluralistic Universe* (London, 1932, p. 244): "We live forward, we understand backward, said a Danish writer; and to understand life by concepts is to arrest its movement, cutting it up into bits . . . and immobilizing these in our logical herbarium."

8. Plato, *The Sophist,* trans. by H. N. Fowler (London, 1961), 247e.

9. Aristotle, *Posterior Analytics, Topica,* trans. by E. S. Forster (London, 1966), 126a–126b.

10. Aristotle, *Magna Moralia* (London, 1962), 1183b–84a.

11. In this regard, Nietzsche once said that it is "nature" that "divides from one another the ones predominantly intellectual, the ones predominantly strong in muscle and temperament, and those distinguished neither in the one nor in the other respect." Recently, Nietzsche's assumption that there is a "natural order . . . over which no arbitrariness . . no 'modern idea' has power" (F. Nietzsche, *Werke,* ed. by K. Schlechta [Munich, 1955] II, p. 1226) has come under attack. Despite some real hereditary deficiencies, many of the presumed "inevitable" dispositions, tendencies, or deficiencies in human beings are not necessarily determined by "nature" alone but also by socially and institutionally determined factors, by cultural deprivation, or by physiological deprivations in the earliest years of life. Whether the capacities or incapacities of individuals are ineluctably transmitted genetically, or whether man or his science can intervene to correct or

inhibit the blunders of a blind nature—this whole question of human capacities is one that is generally ignored by writers on moral philosophy. One wonders if it should be.

12. Aristotle, *Nicomachean Ethics*, trans. by H. Rachman, London, 1962, II, i, 4: "We did not acquire the faculty of sight or hearing by repeatedly seeing or repeatedly listening, but the other way about —because we had the senses we began to use them. . . . The virtues on the other hand we acquire by first having actually practised them."

13. Ibid,. II, i, 3.

14. *Søren Kierkegaard's Journals and Papers*, I, p. 107.

15. Ludwig Wittgenstein, *Philosophical Investigations*, trans. by G. E. M. Anscombe (New York, 1959), p. 48.

16. Søren Kierkegaard, *The Sickness unto Death*, trans. by W. Lowrie (1954), p. 142.

17. Gilbert Ryle, *The Concept of Mind* (London, 1949), p. 135 ff. Ryle equates care with "heeding" something and makes no reference to the emotional aspect or basis of care. Care is simply said to mean paying attention to something and implies "thinking" about what one is doing. There is not even passing reference, in Ryle's discussion of "care," to anything resembling existential concern. In *Johannes Climacus* Kierkegaard refers to the intellectualistic aspect of concern, characterizing it as a form of "objective reflection."

18. Karl Löwith, *Nature, History, and Existentialism* (Evanston, 1966), p. 102.

19. *Philosophical Writings of Peirce*, ed. by J. Buchler (New York, 1940, p. 79: "In the idea of reality, Secondness is predominant; for the real is that which insists upon forcing its way to recognition as something other than the mind's creation."

20. *Johannes Climacus* or *De Omnibus Dubitandum Est*, trans. by T. H. Croxall, (Stanford, 1948), pp. 148–51.

21. Ibid., p. 151.

22. Heidegger, *Sein und Zeit*, p. 4.

23. Moritz Schlick, *Allegemeine Erkenntnislehre* (Berlin, 1925), p. 56.

24. Søren Kierkegaard, *The Concept of Dread*, trans. by W. Lowrie (Princeton, 1957), p. 74.

25. *The Journals of Kierkegaard*, trans. by A. Dru (New York, 1959), p. 98.

26. *Søren Kierkegaard's Journals and Papers*, I, p. 111. Kierkegaard uses this journal entry in *Philosophical Fragments* and paraphrases it in *The Concept of Dread*.

27. G. W. F. Hegel, *Science of Logic*, p. 175.

28. Heidegger, *Sein und Zeit*, p. 268.

29. Aristotle, *Metaphysics*, trans. by H. Tredennick (London, 1961), IX, ii ff.

30. Ibid., IX, v, 3.

31. Aristotle, *Nicomachean Ethics*, III, ii, 2.

32. Aristotle, *Magna Moralia*, I, xi, 1: "Man has the power of producing or creating; and among other things he produces, from certain originating causes . . . his deeds or actions. . . . True action cannot be ascribed to any inanimate substance, nor to any animate being except man . . . it is man who has this power of originating actions."

33. *Søren Kierkegaard's Journals and Papers*, I, p. 307.

34. R. D. Laing, *The Divided Self* (London, 1960), pp. 100–12.

35. *Søren Kierkegaard's Journals and Papers*, I, pp. 306–07.

36. *Søren Kierkegaard's Journals and Papers*, ed. and trans. by H. V. Hong and E. H. Hong (Bloomington and London, 1970), II, p. 73: "A person can go so far that he finally loses even the capacity of being able to choose."

37. Aristotle, *Nicomachean Ethics*, III, ii, 11.

38. Kierkegaard, *Either/Or*, trans. by W. Lowrie (New York, 1959), II, p. 264.

39. Kierkegaard, *The Sickness unto Death*, p. 163.

40. Aristotle, *Nicomachean Ethics*, X, 7, 1177b26.

41. *Søren Kierkegaard's Journals and Papers*, I, p. 48.

42. Ibid., pp. 269–306.

43. Nicola Abbagnano, *Critical Existentialism*, trans. by N. Langiulli (New York, 1959), p. 106.

44. Cf. Richard Schlegel, *Completeness in Science* (New York, 1967), pp. 166–71, 218–19.

45. Heidegger, *Sein und Zeit*, p. 65. Innerworldly [*innerweltlich*] beings are the nanhuman entities that are found, as Heidegger puts it, "present-at-hand 'in' the world."

46. Abbagnano, *Critical Existentialism*, pp. 85 ff., 125.

47. Jean-Paul Sartre, *Being and Nothingness*, trans. by H. Barnes (New York, 1956), pp. 9–11. Cf., Mary Warnock, *The Philosophy of Sartre* (London, 1965), p. 27: ". . . there are objects of imagination . . . [that] are unique. But all of them have this in common, that, though they are 'stable appearances,' they are *nothing*. Thus the act of imagination is essentially this: a grasping of *nothing*, a projecting and positing of what is not, *le néant*."

48. Heidegger derives freedom (or human possibility) from the

"openness" in which *Dasein* exists. That is, "it is the being of man as an area of openness which obligates man as a being within such an area. This is why his freedom is a presupposition of all our actions . . . and why it imposes obligation . . . which always occurs within openness." W. B. Macomber. *The Anatomy of Disillusion: Martin Heidegger's Notion of Truth*, Evanston, 1967, p. 101. Cf. *Sein und Zeit*, pp. 316–23 *and Vom Wesen des Grundes* (Frankfurt a. M., 1955), pp. 19–20. The 'hidden' source of openness is characterized as "the mystery." *Vom Wesen der Wahrheit* (Frankfurt, 1954), p. 19.

49. *Das Mystiche* or "the mystical" refers to that which is "inexpressible" or to the phenomenon that there is a world at all. Ludwig Wittgenstein, *Tractatus Logico-Philosophicus*, trans. by D. F. Pears and B. F. McGuinness, (New York, 1961), pp. 149–51. What I am suggesting in this reference is that the question of the origin of possibility is analogous to the question concerning the fact that there is a world and should perhaps be relegated to "the mystical." Admittedly, I am not being precisely faithful to the rationale for which Wittgenstein postulates the concept of the mystical.

50. Abbagnano, *Critical Existentialism*, p. 107.

51. Aristotle, *Metaphysics*, III, vi, 6.

52. Ibid., IX, vii, 2.

53. Ibid., IX, viii, 16.

54. Abbagnano, *Critical Existentialism*, p. 107.

55. Ibid., pp. 119–20.

56. Cf., Aristotle, *Metaphysics*, trans. by R. Hope (Ann Arbor, 1960), and Aristotle, *Metaphysics*, trans. by H. G. Apostle (Bloomington and London, 1966).

57. Kierkegaard refers to "the approximate truth of the God-idea" or the conception of God as "a postulate." This is the abstract idea of the possibility of God or the logical possibility that God exists. It is not, of course, the "subjective way" of faith. *Concluding Unscientific Postscript*, trans. by D. F. Swenson and W. Lowrie (Princeton, 1941), p. 179.

58. Kierkegaard, *The Sickness unto Death*, p. 171: "The decisive thing is, that for God all things are possible." Kierkegaard goes on to say that a person who believes in God believes that, for God, all things are possible. This belief, however, is based upon the possibility that if there exists such a being as God, then, for such a being, it is possible that everything is possible.

59. Ibid., pp. 168–69, 173.

60. Ibid., p. 163.

61. Wittgenstein, *Tractatus Logico-Philosophicus,* p. 145: "Just as the only necessity that exists is *logical* necessity, so too the only impossibility that exists is *logical* impossibility."

62. Sartre, *Being and Nothingness,* pp. 96–102, 487–89, 551.

63. Kierkegaard, *Concluding Unscientific Postscript,* p. 302.

64. Aristotle, *Nicomachean Ethics,* III, iii, 15.

65. Heidegger, *Sein und Zeit,* pp. 143–44.

66. Bertrand de Jouvenal, *The Art of Conjecture,* trans. by N. Lary (London, 1967), p. 4.

67. John Dewey, *The Theory of the Moral Life* (New York, 1960), p. 169. Cf., Nicola Abbagnano's Kierkegaardian view that "the possible and choice are bound together and are complementary notions." *Critical Existentialism,* p. 150.

Chapter 3

1. Cf. Jeremy Walker, *To Will One Thing* (Montreal and London, 1972).

2. Torsten Bohlin, *Søren Kierkegaards etiska åskådning* (1918), p. 215. Cited in Aage Henriksen, *Methods and Results of Kierkegaard Studies in Scandinavia* (Copenhagen, 1951), pp. 146–48. Bohlin is quite correct, of course, in seeing a strong relationship between Judge Wilhelm's ethics (in *Either/Or*) and Kierkegaard's own views. However, he assumes that Kierkegaard was perhaps more concerned with the development of a "social and civic man" which would accommodate the ethical individual to the "common man" than is entirely compatible with Kierkegaard's ethics of subjectivity. To be sure, Bohlin is not quite mistaken in attributing to Kierkegaard the view that the ethical individual must also fulfill his daily tasks and responsibilities as he seeks to intensify his subjectivity.

3. In this regard, it is quite accurate to point out that "The ethical reality of the individual, freedom tensed between its own passion and its own decision, is isolated not only from the reality of the world, but also from the reality of God." Louis Mackey, "The Loss of the World in Kierkegaard's Ethics," in *Kierkegaard: A Collection of Critical Essays,* ed. by J. Thompson (New York, 1972), p. 282.

4. James Collins, The Mind of Kierkegaard, p. 81.

5. Cf. Viktor Frankl, *Man's Search for Meaning* (Boston, 1962).

6. *Søren Kierkegaard's Journals and Papers,* I, p. 76.

7. Ludwig Wittgenstein, *Philosophical Investigations,* p. 181.

8. Søren Kierkegaard, *Johannes Climacus,* p. 149.

9. *Søren Kierkegaard's Journals and Papers,* I, p. 399.

10. Ibid., p. 258.

11. Heidegger, *Sein und Zeit,* p. 184.

12. Søren Kierkegaard, *Philosophical Fragments,* trans, D. F. Swenson and H. V. Hong, Princeton, 1962, p. 102. T. H. Croxall claims that the word *metriopathein* is not the correct term for refusal of consent. Cf., *Kierkegaard Commentary,* New York, 1956, p. 184.

13. William James, *Essays in Pragmatism,* p. 89.

14. Kierkegaard, *Johannes Climacus,* pp. 151–52.

15. Aristotle, *Nicomachean Ethics,* III, iii, 16.

16. Ibid., III, iii, 3–7.

17. *Søren Kierkegaard's Journals and Papers,* I, p. 399.

18. Ibid., p. 306: "If we reflect upon an object, we have knowledge [*Videns*]. If there is no object, but the communication itself is reflected upon, then we have the communication of capability [*kunnen*]."

19. Kierkegaard, *Either/Or,* II, p. 180.

20. Ibid., p. 171: "The aesthetic choice is either entirely immediate and to that extent no choice, or it loses itself in the multifarious."

21. Aristotle, *Nicomachean Ethics,* III, v, 2.

22. *Søren Kierkegaard's Journals and Papers,* I, p. 440.

23. Kierkegaard, *Either/Or,* II, p. 168.

24. Kierkegaard, *The Sickness unto Death,* p. 173.

25. Aristotle, *Nicomachean Ethics,* III, ii, 1.

26. Kierkegaard, *Either/Or,* II, p. 173.

27. Aristotle, *Nicomachean Ethics,* III, ii, 11.

28. Kierkegaard, *Johannes Climacus,* p. 151, n. 1.

29. Kierkegaard, *Either/Or,* II, p. 168.

30. Aristotle, *Nicomachean Ethics,* III, ii, 17.

31. *Søren Kierkegaard's Journals and Papers,* I, p. 48.

32. Kierkegaard, *Concluding Unscientific Postscript,* p. 350.

33. Aristotle, *Nicomachean Ethics,* VI, ii, 5.

34. *The Journals of Kierkegaard,* trans. by A. Dru (New York, 1959), p. 90.

35. *Edifying Discourses,* trans. by D. F. Swenson and L. Swenson (Minneapolis, 1943), IV, p. 23.

36. Aristotle, *Nicomachean Ethics,* VI, ii, 4.

37. Cf., J. J. Walsh, *Aristotle's Conception of Moral Weakness* (New York, 1963), p. 174.

38. St. Thomas Aquinas, *Summa Theologiae,* I–II, qu. 13, art. 1.

39. Louis Dupré, *Kierkegaard as Theologian* (New York, 1963),

pp. 54–56. Thorsten Bohlin has remarked that "In the doctrine of original sin of older orthodox dogma [Kierkegaard] sees a theory which, though it is the strongest possible expression of the gravity of sin, in fact weakens and paralyzes man's struggle against sin, because it accepts the occurrence of a radical change in human nature as a result of sin." *Kierkegaards dogmatische Anschauung*, p. 213. Cited in L. Dupré, *Kierkegaard as Theologian*, p. 50.

40. Aristotle, *Topica*, trans. by E. S. Forster (London, 1966), 126b5. Though direct influence on Kierkegaard's emphasis upon the relationship between potentiality and choice in this regard cannot be established, one wonders if this reference to the "category of potentiality" as applied to choice and action may not have caught Kierkegaard's eye. Certainly, the existential category of possibility (or potentiality) was central to his philosophical anthropology.

41. Aristotle, *Nicomachean Ethics*, III, v, 14.

42. Søren Kierkegaard, *Stages on Life's Way*, trans., W. Lowrie, New York, 1967, p. 113.

43. *Søren Kierkegaard's Journals and Papers*, I, p. 419.

44. Heidegger, *Sein und Zeit*, p. 297.

45. *Kierkegaard, Either/Or*, II, p. 171.

46. Stuart Hamshire, *Thought and Action*, New York, 1959, p. 177.

47. Aristotle, *Nicomachean Ethics*, VI, ii, 5.

48. Collins, *The Mind of Kierkegaard*, p. 75.

49. *Søren Kierkegaard's Journals and Papers*, I, p. 19.

50. Kierkegaard, *Philosophical Fragments*, pp. 90–91. Cp., *Søren Kierkegaard's Journals and Papers*, I, p. 111.

51. Kierkegaard, *Either/Or*, II, p. 182.

52. Ryle, *The Concept of Mind*, p. 68.

53. Aristotle, *Nicomachean Ethics*, III, iii, 15.

54. Ibid.

55. Ryle, *The Concept of Mind*, p. 68.

56. Heidegger, *Sein und Zeit*, p. 268.

57. Collins, *The Mind of Kierkegaard*, p. 80.

58. Kierkegaard, *Either/Or*, II, p. 252.

59. Kierkegaard, *The Sickness unto Death*, pp. 163–207.

60. Kierkegaard, *Concluding Unscientific Postscript*, p. 227.

61. Kierkegaard, *The Sickness unto Death*, p. 227.

62. Kierkegaard, *Concluding Unscientific Postscript*, pp. 273, 277. Cp. *Søren Kierkegaard's Journals and Papers*, I, p. 259: ". . . motion is inconceivable in the eternal."

63. Cornelio Fabro, "Faith and Reason in Kierkegaard's Dialectic,"

in *A Kierkegaard Critique*, ed. by H. Johnson and N. Thulstrup (Chicago, 1967), p. 165.

64. Ryle, *The Concept of Mind*, p. 135.

65. Immanuel Kant, *Lectures on Ethics*, trans. by L. Infield (New York, 1963), p. 69. Kant describes conscience as a *forum internum*, a description that undoubtedly would have appealed to Kierkegaard.

66. *Søren Kierkegaard's Journals and Papers*, I, p. 328.

67. Helmut Fahrenbach, *Kierkegaards existenzdialektische Ethik* (Frankfurt, 1968), p. 75ff.

68. Kierkegaard, *Either/Or*, II, p. 260.

69. *Papirer*, I (A), 254. Cited in L. Dupré, *Kierkegaard as Theologian*, p. 10.

70. Heidegger, *Sein und Zeit*, p. 283.

71. Kierkegaard, *Either/Or*, II, p. 255.

72. Hampshire, *Thought and Action*, p. 190.

73. Kierkegaard, *The Concept of Dread*, p. 69.

74. Kierkegaard, *Either/Or*, II, p. 244.

75. Kierkegaard, *Either/Or*, II, p. 262.

76. Heidegger, *Sein und Zeit*, p. 145.

77. Kierkegaard, *Either/Or*, II, pp. 266–67.

78. *Søren Kierkegaard's Journals and Papers*, I, p. 458.

79. Kierkegaard, *The Sickness unto Death*, p. 164.

80. Ibid., p. 169.

81. Sigmund Freud, "A difficulty in the path of Psychoanalysis," *Gesammelte Werke* (London, 1940), XII, pp. 3–12. Cited in Paul Ricoeur's *Freud and Philosophy* (New Haven and London, 1970), p. 427.

82. Kierkegaard, *Either/Or*, II, p. 168.

83. Ibid., pp. 228, 263.

84. Kierkegaard, *Concluding Unscientific Postscript*, p. 239.

85. Brand Blanchard, "Kierkegaard on Faith," *The Personalist* (1968), pp. 5–23.

86. Kierkegaard, *Concluding Unscientific Postscript*, pp. 238–39.

87. Kierkegaard, *Johannes Climacus*, p. 149.

88. Søren Kierkegaard, *Papirer*, ed. by P. A. Heiberg and V. Kuhr, and E. Torsting (Copenhagen, 1909–48), IV (B), p. 117, 288ff. Cited in Walter Lowrie's "Introduction" to *Repetition*, trans. by W. Lowrie, (New York, 1964), pp. 20–21.

89. Kierkegaard, *Concluding Unscientific Postscript*, p. 143.

90. Heidegger, *Sein und Zeit*, p. 385.

91. Ibid, p. 391.

92. *Søren Kierkegaard's Journals and Papers*, I, p. 215.

Chapter 4

1. Plato, *Phaedrus*, trans. by H. N. Fowler (London, 1966), 230,

2. Kierkegaard, *Either/Or*, II, p. 178. In this regard, Kierkegaard seems submissive to Hegelian thought to the detriment of his own interpretation of the contingency of individual history. For, his own analysis of historical becoming in the life of the individual should be applicable to human history as well. That he seems to capitulate to Hegel's conception of world history is clear from his statement that "The spheres with which philosophy properly deals . . . are the spheres [of] logic, nature, and history. Here necessity rules, and mediation is valid. . . . The individual indeed acts, but his action passes into the order of things which sustains the whole of existence. . . . But this higher order of things . . . digests, so to speak, the free actions and weaves them into its universal law . . . and this necessity is the dynamic of world history." [Ibid.] If this truly reflects Kierkegaard's idea of history, then there is a tension in his thought between the necessity in human history and the freedom in the life-histories of individuals.

3. Hegel, *The Phenomenology of Mind*, p. 229.   4. Ibid., p. 459.

5. Kierkegaard, *Johannes Climacus*, pp. 148–53.

6. Ibid., pp. 150–51.

7. Kierkegaard, *The Concept of Dread*, p. 128.

8. *Søren Kierkegaard's Journals and Papers*, I, p. 451. Cp. *Concluding Unscientific Postscript*, p. 281.

9. Kierkegaard, *The Sickness unto Death*, p. 162.

10. Wittgenstein, *Tractatus Logico-Philosophicus*, p. 117.

11. *Søren Kierkegaard's Journals and Papers*, I, p. 456.

12. Kierkegaard, *The Sickness unto Death*, p. 162.

13. *The Last Years, Journals 1853–1855*, pp. 282–83.

14. Aristotle, *Nicomachean Ethics*, II, vi, 14. Cp. *Søren Kierkegaard's Journals and Papers*, I, p. 437: " 'Character' is simply to be only 'one thing.' "

15. Kierkegaard, *Concluding Unscientific Postscript*, pp. 232–33.

16. Heidegger, *Sein und Zeit*, p. 374.

17. Kierkegaard, *Concluding Unscientific Postscript*, p. 151.

18. Ibid., p. 121.

19. Ibid., p. 280. Concerning the reality of an "intermediate being" such as man, Kierkegaard maintains that reality is an *interesse* ("to be between," "to be concerned") insofar as the existential reality of the individual is a "dialectical moment" in the relationship between

thought and being. This view is consistent with the conception of subjective or concernful consciousness in *Johannes Climacus* insofar as this consciousness emerges out of the opposing relationship between ideality and actuality.

In regard to every other reality external to the individual it can only be known through "thinking it." In effect, every reality other than the self is known through the conceptual medium of possibility. Hence, Kierkegaard argues, the only reality to which we have access in a "real relationship" which is not purely a "cognitive" one is our own "lived" reality. The ethically existing individual resolutely relates ideality to actuality in his own lived actuality as "in-between." It is for this reason that Kierkegaard insists that the only "real subject" is the ethically existing subject who, repetitiously, actively relates ideality to actuality in his own existential reality. This process is recognized as paradoxical and as the basis of the dialectical tension of existence. The authentic reality of the self is the only reality to which we have *direct* access and is, hence, the primary reality for us.

20. Friedrich Nietzsche, *Beyond Good and Evil*, trans. by W. Kaufmann (New York, 1966), pp. 100–101.

21. Friedrich Nietzsche, *Joyful Wisdom*, trans. by Thomas Common (New York, 1960), p. 209.

22. Kaufmann, *Nietzsche*, pp. 137–38. The analogy between Nietzsche's conception of created truth in lived-actuality is mentioned but not fully developed in Bernard Bueb's *Nietzsches Kritik der praktischen Vernunft* (Stuttgart, 1970), p. 207, n. 20. Cf. My review of Bueb's work in *Journal of the History of Philosophy*, XII (April, 1974), pp. 274–77.

23. Although Louis Mackey has accurately pointed out that Kierkegaard's assertion of the ethically existing individual as an exclusive reality means that "the only reality which the individual can grasp . . . *as reality*—by *being* it—is his own," he argues that Kierkegaard's "individual is existentially . . . acosmic." Furthermore, it said that the existing person is "infinitely free." Louis Mackey, "The Loss of the World in Kierkegaard's Ethics," in *Kierkegaard: A Collection of Critical Essays*, ed. by J. Thompson (New York, 1972), pp. 274–85. First of all, the subjectively existing individual goes on through a stage of isolating withdrawal from the world, but turns his own objectivity ironically back upon his subjective reality. Acosmism is, in a sense, a moment in the dialectic of ethical existence; it is not the culmination of it. Secondly, Kierkegaard does not (as I've tried to argue) assert a notion of 'absolute' freedom insofar as he sees the person as a syn-

thesis of necessity and possibility. Finally, Kierkegaard nowhere denies the actuality of other persons or other nonhuman entities. That we come to know other beings through the 'medium' of possibility does not mean that they are, in some senses, unreal. I do not believe, as Mackey does, that Kierkegaard contradicts himself on this point, even though there is a tension in his thought between the intensification of subjective individuation and the reality of the world. Kierkegaard admits that "to make the ethical reality of the subject the only reality might seem to be acosmism." *Concluding Unscientific Postscript*, p. 305. That this view seems to be acosmism is correct. However, what Kierkegaard is defending is the notion that we have subjective access to our own reality which is different from the cognitive understanding we have of other actualities. In Kierkegaard's terms, we know every other being by means of "idealities" (concepts of words) and, hence, we know them by means of "possibility." This does not mean that actuality as "immediacy" is negated. We encounter the immediacy of other actualities, but in the expression of our knowledge of them we annul, in Kierkegaard's terms, their "immediacy" by means of conceptual judgment or linguistic expression. In this sense, actuality is known "mediately"—through thought and language (neither of which is an immediate actuality). Cf. *Johannes Climacus,* pp. 148–49.

24. F. W. J. Schelling, "Berlin Lectures, 1841–42," in *The Search for Being*, ed. and trans. by J. T. Wilde and W. Kimmel (New York, 1962), p. 46.

25. Ibid., p. 47.

26. *Søren Kierkegaard's Journals and Papers,* I, p. 460.

27. Ibid.

28. Berdyaev refers to man's irrational or meonic freedom as derived from the *Ungrund* or "uncreated nothingness." This basic freedom of man is said to be neither determined to good nor to evil and it is construed as even independent of God. Nicholai Berdyaev, *Freedom of the Spirit* (New York, 1939), p. 131.

29. Heidegger, *Sein und Zeit*, p. 188.

30. Kierkegaard, *Concluding Unscientific Postscript*, p. 68.

31. Wittgenstein, *Tractatus Logico-Philosophicus*, p. 19.

32. Kierkegaard, *Concluding Unscientific Postscript*, pp. 280, 284–85.

33. Kierkegaard, *The Concept of Dread*, pp. 70–71.

34. *Søren Kierkegaard's Journals and Papers,* I, p. 408. Since Kierkegaard avers in *The Concept of Irony* that an authentic existence is not possible without irony, it has been suggested that irony is not only a signification of an ethical "turn" but continues to pervade ethical

existence. Insofar as it is a "determination of subjectivity," irony is an existential category applied to an ethical existence.

35. Ibid., p. 24.

36. Kierkegaard, *Fear and Trembling*, trans. by W. Lowrie (New York, 1954), p. 91.

37. *Søren Kierkegaard's Journals and Papers*, I, pp. 278, 463.

38. Kierkegaard, *The Point of View for My Work as an Author*, trans. by W. Lowrie (New York, 1962), p. 124.

39. *Søren Kierkegaard's Journals and Papers*, I, p. 426.

40. F. E. Wilde, *Kierkegaards Verstandnis der Existenz* (Copenhagen, 1969), p. 80. Wilde seems to miss the point of Kierkegaard's emphasis upon "becoming subjective," striving to realize the "ideal self," etc. Existence, in its true or authentic form is a subjective teleological activity for man, an activity characterized by dialectical tension and an intensification of subjectivity. Wilde is not alone in overlooking the distinction between mere being and existence as a goal and purpose for human life. It has recently been said that by 'existence' Kierkegaard means the "non-inferential, non-cognitive movement of choice." In illustrating this point reference is made to the assertion in *Concluding Unscientific Postscript* that "*Gud taenker ikke, han skaber; Gud existerer ikke, han er evig. Mennseket taenker og existerer.*" ["God does not think, he creates; God does not exist, He is eternal. Man thinks and exists."] The point of this statement is that only man can exist, can resolutely, repetitiously strive for self-existence. And although choice is an individuating act, it is only one aspect of existence as Kierkegaard understands it. Cf. F. A. Olafson, *Principles and Persons* (Baltimore, 1967), p. 29.

41. Kierkegaard *Concluding Unscientific Postscript*, pp. 320–21.

42. Kierkegaard, *Either/Or*, II, pp. 278–79.

43. The usual formula, "thou canst because thou shouldst," is not found in this precise form in Kant's writings. Cf. L. W. Beck, *A Commentary on Kant's Critique of Practical Reason* (Chicago, 1960), p. 200, n. 74.

44. Collins, *The Mind of Kierkegaard*, p. 74.

45. Kierkegaard, *Either/Or*, II, p. 266.

46. Immanuel Kant, *Fundamental Principles of the Metaphysics of Morals*, trans. by T. K. Abbott (New York, 1949), p. 5. A Further distinction between Kant's concept of ethics and that of Kierkegaard is obvious in the following remark by Kant: " . . . the basis of obligation must not be sought in the nature of man . . . but *a priori* simply in the conceptions of pure reason . . . all moral philosophy

rests wholly on its pure part. When applied to man, it does not borrow the least thing from the knowledge of man himself (anthropology), but gives laws *a priori* to him as a rational being." (Ibid.)

Kant's conception of moral philosophy positively prohibits the development of an existential ethics or an ethics of subjectivity. The key role that passion, resoluteness, repetition, absolute choice, and self-knowledge play in Kierkegaard's practical ethics is basically foreign to Kant's thought, especially when one contrasts Kierkegaard's conception of the motivational basis of right action to Kant's emphasis upon a "pure will" which is divorced from subjective concern. For Kierkegaard there is no action without pathos-filled interest; but, for Kant, it is precisely this subjective concern or interest which should be bracketed or overcome in morally relevant action.

47. Kant, *Lectures on Ethics*, p. 121.

48. Kierkegaard, *Concluding Unscientific Postscript*, p. 144.

49. Kierkegaard, *Either/Or*, II, p. 268. This stress upon the dialectical relationship between duty as universal and my own duty is the point of departure for an attempt to show any direct appropriation of Kantian ethics on the part of Kierkegaard. For, Kierkegaard avers that if the individual is to "perform the universal," he must 'become' the universal at the same time as he is a particular individual. The dialectic of duty is within the existing individual. One does not act, as in Kantian ethics, out of respect for a principle of duty that is apprehended as objective. Nor does Kierkegaard eschew what Kant calls "anthropological" consideration. For Kierkegaard, it is the subjective intensity of the feeling of a duty to become a self which is the motivational basis of right action, not a purely rational universal principle that one acts in accordance with in terms of an ostensible "pure" will.

Ironically, Kant approaches an existential basis of morality in his *Lectures on Ethics* when he remarks that "practical philosophy (the science of how man ought to behave) and anthropology (the science of man's actual behavior) are closely connected and the former cannot subsist without the latter. For, we cannot tell whether the subject to which our consideration applies is capable of what is demanded of him unless we have knowledge of that subject. . . . We therefore have to make at least some study of man" (pp. 2–3). Needless to say, this is not a notion Kant retains in his considered moral philosophy.

50. Kierkegaard, *Concluding Unscientific Postscript*, p. 279.

51. Kierkegaard, *Either/Or*, II, p. 279. This 'movement' of the self is characterized as the "immanent teleology" of ethical existence.

52. Kierkegaard, *Concluding Unscientific Postscript,* p. 296. Cf. Martin Heidegger, "The Way Back into the Ground of Metaphysics," in *Existentialism from Dostoevsky to Sartre,* ed. by W. Kaufmann (New York, 1965), p. 214: "The Being that exists is man. Man alone exists. Rocks are, but they do not exist. Trees are, but they do not exist. Horses are, but they do not exist. Angels are, but they do not exist. God is, but he does not exist."

53. *Søren Kierkegaard's Journals and Papers,* I, p. 469.

54. Ibid., p. 470.

55. Herbert Marcuse, *Reason and Revolution* (Boston, 1960), p. 113.

56. Kierkegaard, *Concluding Unscientific Postscript,* pp. 185–86.

57. F. H. Bradley, "My Station and Its Duties," in *Ethical Studies,* p. 140.

58. Ibid., p. 114. Presumably, Kierkegaard would have agreed with Bradley that "moral institutions are carcasses without personal morality" even though he would have to defend himself against Bradley's attack upon individuality and an ethics of subjectivity. To be sure, as I've tried to indicate, Kierkegaard's existential ethics does not exclude work, public life, or social existence despite the obvious fact that the accent in his writings pertaining to the ethical sphere of existence is on "becoming subjective." Bradley, insofar as he is under the influence of Hegel, tends to subvert personal, subjective morality in relation to institutional morality or the social moral totality of which the individual is a part. Kierkegaard seemed to think that there is nothing so unreliable or variable as a conventionally accepted public morality, a 'morality' which must be transvalued or rejuvenated by ethical individuals. Needless to say, I do not agree with commentators on Kierkegaard who proclaim that in ethical existence the individual becomes a "common man" or that "The ethicist is . . . simultaneously himself and his social fundament." In addition, I think that it is misleading to suggest that the Kierkegaardian ethicist "attaches himself to his social environment and to his past history." Adi Shmuëli, *Kierkegaard and Consciousness* (Princeton, 1971), pp. 37, 47. Such emphases tend to obscure the demanding nature of Kierkegaard's prescription for an authentic existence.

59. *Søren Kierkegaard's Journals and Papers,* I, p. 427.

60. Kierkegaard, *Either/Or,* II, pp. 286–87, 292, 296–97. The fact that Kierkegaard says that through work man "expresses at once the universal-human and the individual" indicates a compatibility

between "becoming subjective" and expressing one's existence in social life.

61. *The Last Years, Journals 1853–1855*, trans., R. G. Smith, New York, 1965, pp. 235–36: "[T]o be related objectively to one's own subjectivity is the real task . . . this . . . is only a reduplication of [one's] subjectivity . . . being related objectively to one's own subjectivity is . . . a corrective. [However] a man can neither surpass himself in such a way as to be related completely objectively to himself, nor can he be so subjective as completely to fulfill what he has understood about himself in objective [understanding.]"

62. Kierkegaard's journal entries for July 29th and August 1st, 1835 have a tone of tranquility and inner resolve that is rare in his journals. The first entry (written in Gilbjerg) expresses a mood of reconciliation: "as I stood there alone and forsaken, and the power of the sea and the battle of the elements reminded me of my own nothingness . . . then all at once I felt how great and how small I was; then did those two mighty forces, pride and humility, happily unite in friendship. Lucky is the man to whom *that* is possible at every moment of his life. . . . He has found . . . that archimedean point from which he could lift the whole world, the point which for that very reason must lie outside the world, outside the limitations of time and space." The second journal entry (written in Gilleleie) marks a turning-point in Kierkegaard's life in which he seeks "the idea for which I can live and die." He resolves to live beyond the "imperative of understanding" and seek self-knowledge. Kierkegaard pictures himself as standing "once again at the point where I must begin my life in a different way." "I shall," he writes, "now try to fix a calm gaze upon myself and begin to act in earnest; for only thus shall I be able . . . to call myself 'I'." *The Journals of Kierkegaard*, pp. 42–47.

Bibliography

I. Søren Kierkegaard's Works in English Translation

Armed Neutrality and *An Open Letter*. Edited and translated by H. V. and E. H. Hong, translated by W. Lowrie. Bloomington, 1968.

Attack Upon Christendom. Translated by W. Lowrie. Princeton, 1946.

Christian Discourses. Translated by W. Lowrie. London, 1940.

Concluding Unscientific Postscript. Translated by D. F. Swenson and W. Lowrie. Princeton, 1941.

Crisis in the Life of an Actress and Other Essays on Drama. Translated by S. D. Crites. New York, 1967.

Edifying Discourses. Translated by D. F. Swenson and L. Swenson. Minneapolis, 1943.

Either/Or. Translated by D. F. Swenson. 2 vols. New York, 1959.

Fear and Trembling and *The Sickness Unto Death*. Translated by W. Lowrie. New York, 1954.

For Self-Examination and Judge for Yourselves!. Translated by W. Lowrie. London, 1944.

Johannes Climacus or, De Omnibus Dubitandum Est and *A Sermon*. Translated by T. H. Croxall. Stanford, 1958.

On Authority and Revelation. Translated by W. Lowrie. Princeton, 1955.

Philosophical Fragments. Translated by D. F. Swenson and H. V. Hong. Princeton, 1967.

Purity of Heart. Translated by D. V. Steere. New York, 1968.

Repetition. Translated by W. Lowrie. Princeton, 1946.

Søren Kierkegaard's Journals and Papers. Edited and Translated by H. V. and E. H. Hong. 2 vols. Bloomington, 1967–70.

Stages on Life's Way. Translated by W. Lowrie. Princeton, 1945.

The Concept of Dread. Translated by W. Lowrie. Princeton, 1944.

The Concept of Irony. Translated by L. Capel. New York, 1965.

The Gospel of Suffering and the Lilies of the Field. Translated by

D. F. and L. M. Swenson. Minneapolis, 1948.

The Journals of Søren Kierkegaard. Edited and Translated by A. Dru. London, 1938.

The Last Years: Journals 1853–1855. Edited and Translated by R. G. Smith. New York, 1965.

The Point of View of My Work as an Author. Translated by W. Lowrie. New York, 1962.

The Present Age. Translated by A. Dru and W. Lowrie. London, 1940.

Thoughts on Crucial Situations in Human Life. Translated by D. F. Swenson, Minneapolis, 1941.

Training in Christianity. Translated by W. Lowrie, Princeton, 1944.

Works of Love. Translated by H. V. and E. H. Hong. New York, 1962.

II. Books About Kierkegaard

Allen, E. L. *Kierkegaard, His Life and Thought*. London, 1935. A reasonably accurate, competent work, which has been superseded by a number of more recent synoptic introductory studies.

Arbaugh, G. B., and G. E. Arbaugh. *Kierkegaard's Authorship*. Rock Island, Ill., 1967. A very useful guide to most of Kierkegaard's works that includes accurate summaries of the essential content of these works. The running commentary is often interesting, though colored by a strong religious perspective.

Channing-Pearce, M. *Søren Kierkegaard*. London, 1945. A popular, well-written essay dealing with Kierkegaard's life and thought that is useful as a general introduction to the subject.

———. *The Terrible Chrystal: Kierkegaard and Modern Christianity*. London, 1949. A general overview of Kierkegaard's impact upon modern Christianity and a clear presentation of Kierkegaard's own conception of Christianity. This is a sympathetic, uncritical essay, which is useful as a propaedeutic to a serious study of Kierkegaard.

Cole, J. P. *The Problematic Self in Kierkegaard and Freud*. New Haven and London, 1971. An interesting attempt to indicate the contrast between Freud's and Kierkegaard's interpretations of the self. In the delineation of Kierkegaard's description of authentic selfhood there is an overemphasis on the religious sphere of existence, which leads to the neglect of central aspects of ethical existence that are directly related to some elements in Freud's theory of the self.

Collins, James. *The Mind of Kierkegaard*. Chicago, 1953. A fine study of the central themes in Kierkegaard's thought that is sprinkled with insights into some of the philosophical bases of Kierkegaard's existentialism. A scholarly and reliable work, and still a very good general introduction to Kierkegaard.

Crites, Stephen S. *In the Twilight of Christendom: Hegel versus Kierkegaard on Faith and History*. Chambersburg, 1972. A scholarly, penetrating study of the relationship between Kierkegaard and Hegel that emphasizes cultural differentiations and does not always grapple with purely philosophical distinctions between the two. Because of its tracing of the internal consistency in Kierkegaard's thought and the clear presentation of Hegel's and Kierkegaard's understanding of faith and history this is a valuable contribution to a neglected area of Kierkegaard studies in English.

Croxall, Thomas H. *Kierkegaard Commentary*. London, 1956. A scholarly account of the various dimensions of Kierkegaard's works that is reasonably accurate but tends to play upon the surface of Kierkegaard's purely philosophical concerns and fails to do full justice to the ethical sphere of existence.

———. *Kierkegaard Studies*. London, 1948. Includes fairly detailed studies of Kierkegaard's concept of dread, his comments on music, the doctrine of the Trinity, and the possibility of philosophical inquiry.

Diem, Hermann. *Kierkegaard's Dialectic of Existence*. Translated by H. Knight. London, 1959. An excellent internal analysis of the development of Kierkegaard's existential categories that is especially valuable for its treatment of the classical Greek influences on Kierkegaard's existential conception of man and his development.

Dupré, L. K. *Kierkegaard as Theologian*. London, 1963. A sympathetic study of Kierkegaard's interpretation of the fundamental articles of Christian belief. Probably one of the finest inquiries dealing with the placing of Kierkegaard's understanding of Christianity in theological perspective.

Fahrenbach, H. *Kierkegaards existenzdialektische Ethik*. Frankfurt-am-Main, 1968. A good interpretation of the conception of ethical existence that accurately interrelates Kierkegaard's notion of the dialectic of existence (the self-becoming of the individual) and the ideal of ethical existence. Includes a brief, but useful, bibliography of German studies of Kierkegaard.

Garelick, H. M. *The Anti-Christianity of Kierkegaard*. The Hague, 1965. A brief, intelligent analysis of certain aspects of *Concluding Unscientific Postscript* which is sensitive to the dialectical approach to Christianity presented by Kierkegaard's pseudonym ("Climacus"), and which includes good discussions of the paradoxes of Christian faith. The "anti-Christianity" in the title refers to Climacus' failure to understand Christianity properly and his truncated movement towards Christian faith.

Geismar, Edward. *Lectures on the Religious Thoughts of Søren Kierkegaard*. Minneapolis, 1937. Provides a rather general description of Kierkegaard's philosophy of religion.

George, A. G. *The First Sphere*. London, 1965. A short essay which touches upon both Kierkegaard's aesthetic views and the aesthetic sphere of life. It includes an inchoate discussion of the relationship between Kierkegaard and romanticism.

Grimsley, R. *Kierkegaard* New York, 1973. Provides a useful overview of Kierkegaard's life and works, as well as an excellent presentation of his literary relationships. The literary aspects of Kierkegaard's works receive strong emphasis and the biographical details are reliable.

Haecker, Theodor. *Kierkegaard the Cripple*. Translated by C. V. O. Bruyn. New York, 1959. An account of Kierkegaard's physical condition and its presumed relationship to his psychological traits and his understanding of religious questions.

———. *Søren Kierkegaard*. Translated by A. Dru. New York, 1937. A series of speculations concerning Kierkegaard's role in relation to European civilization and the value of his thought for philosophy, theology, and literary interpretation.

Henriksen, Aage. *Methods and Results of Kierkegaard Studies in Scandinavia*. Copenhagen, 1951. A useful, scholarly presentation of summaries of the central themes of numerous Scandinavian commentators on Kierkegaard. Aside from detailed reports of early and recent studies of Kierkegaard (primarily in Sweden and Denmark), this expository work deals with autobiographical, psychological, and literary accounts of Kierkegaard as a person and as a pseudonymous author.

Johnson, H. A. and K. Thulstrup, eds. *A Kierkegaard Critique*. New York, 1962. No doubt one of the best collections of essays dealing with a variety of aspects of Kierkegaard's variegated writings. Almost all the selections are of high quality. This work includes an excellent, subtle interpretation of "Faith and Reason in Kierkegaard's Dialectic" by Cornelio Fabro.

Johnson, R. H. *The Concept of Existence in the Concluding Unscientific Postscript*. The Hague, 1972. An interpretation of the notion of existence that emphasizes the radical separation of Kierkegaard and his pseudonym for the author of *Concluding Unscientific Post-script*. Apparently influenced by the "unscientific" of the title, this essay refers to the distinction between the existing individual and the "scientific community" (which is charged with forgetfulness of the meaning of individual existence). An interesting study, though side-tracked by a somewhat questionable model for interpreting Kierkegaard.

Jolivet, Regis. *Introduction to Kierkegaard*. Translated by W. H. Barber. New York, n.d. A lucid, scholarly introduction to the dominant themes in Kierkegaard's existential philosophy. This fine introductory study sketches the "spiritual life" of Kierkegaard and provides very clear expositions of the stages of life. Although this essay is neither a critical study nor an interpretation of details in the Kierkegaardian corpus, it is probably the best synoptic introductory study of Kierkegaard available.

Lawson, Lewis A., ed. *Kierkegaard's Presence in Contemporary American Life*. Metuchen, 1970. A collection of essays by American authors that attempts to trace Kierkegaard's influence on a number of diverse areas (e.g., anthropology, logic, psychoanalysis, theology, etc.). Though interesting in themselves, these essays do not, by any means, exhaust the degree or extent of the influence of Kierkegaard on American life.

Löwith, Karl. *Kierkegaard und Nietzsche; oder philosophische und theologische Überwindung des Nihilismus*. Frankfurt, 1933. A very brief essay on Nietzsche's and Kierkegaard's attempts to overcome nihilism.

Lowrie, W. *A Short Life of Kierkegaard*. Princeton, 1942. A very sympathetic biography of Kierkegaard that contains persuasive insights into the psychological and spiritual history of Kierkegaard.

———. *Kierkegaard*. Oxford, 1938. Covers more or less the same areas as the shorter work, but is far more detailed. Includes a synopsis of Kierkegaard's writings, as well as a glossary of basic terms. An indispensable biographical study.

Mackey, Louis. *Kierkegaard: A Kind of Poet*. Philadelphia, 1971. A beautifully written, scholarly, carefully wrought essay that persuasively argues for the consistent, pervasive poetic intentions of Kierkegaard. Includes a brilliant interpretation of the aesthetic sphere of existence, and good accounts of Kierkegaard's philosophy and his version of Christianity. This is clearly the best study of Kierkegaard's "poetic program" currently available.

Malantschuk, G. *Kierkegaard's Thought*. Edited and translated by

H. V. and E. H. Hong. Princeton, 1971. A detailed scholarly presentation of the central features of Kierkegaard's reflections that persuasively delineates the dialectical structure of Kierkegaard's philosophical and religious writings. It is especially valuable for its treatment
of Danish thinkers who influenced Kierkegaard and for its accurate
accounts of the content and themes of his major works.

Martin, H. V. *Kierkegaard the Melancholy Dane*. New York 1950.
A sympathetic portrait of Kierkegaard's personality that also touches
upon a few aspects of his thought. Kierkegaard is portrayed as the
harbinger of a new reformation in the theology of Christianity.

Mesnard, Pierre. *Le vrai visage de Kierkegaard*. Paris, 1948. A
competent scholarly study that includes brief biographical information, a discussion of "the philosophy" of the stages of life, a sound
interpretation of irony, and a very good account of the relationship
between the aesthetic and the religious in Kierkegaard's thought. Also
includes a useful bibliography of French and German studies on
Kierkegaard published during the first half of the century.

Price, George. *The Narrow Pass*. London, 1963. A sprightly expo-
sition and commentary on Kierkegaard's existentialism that is especially valuable for its treatment of the concept of the self. The discussions of the ethical stage of life are reasonably accurate but too
brief to cover the notion of authentic existence. In general, this lively
and readable essay is informative and shows a fine grasp of Kierkegaard's philosophical anthropology.

Rohde, Peter. *Søren Kierkegaard: An Introduction to His Life and
Philosophy*. London. 1963. More an introduction to Kierkegaard's life
than to his thought, this study focuses upon Kierkegaard's relationships with his father and with Regine Olsen. In addition, it includes
a good account of Kierkegaard's earliest publications and his conflicts with prominent figures in the Copenhagen of his day.

Shestov, Lev. *Kierkegaard and the Existential Philosophy*. Translated by E. Hewitt. Athens, Ohio, 1969. An enthusiastic, highly impressionistic, study of Kierkegaard that, unfortunately, set the pace
for seeing Kierkegaard as an exclusively irrationalist thinker. Time
has not been kind to this evocative series of essays, which reveals a
shallow understanding of Kierkegaard's writings and is, in general,
quite unreliable.

Shumëli, Adi. *Kierkegaard and Consciousness*. Translated by N.
Handelman. Princeton, 1971. A very interesting and well-conceived
study of the various modes of consciousness described by Kierkegaard.
It takes Kierkegaard's philosophical concerns seriously and is espe-

cially useful for its interpretation of immanence and transcendence in the various stages of consciousness and for its discussions of the use and meaning of "indirect communication."

Swenson, David. *Something About Kierkegaard.* Minneapolis, 1945. A collection of articles by one of the major translators of Kierkegaard that includes discussions of the dialectic of existence and the aesthetic, ethical, and religious stages of life.

Symposion Kierkegaardianum. Copenhagen, 1955. A collection of multilingual essays, most of which are of very high quality. Of especial interest are those by Diem, Fabro, Holmer, Lønning, Malantshuk, Sløk and Niels Thulstrup.

Thomas, J. H. *Subjectivity and Paradox.* Oxford, 1957. An interesting and useful study that focuses upon religious subjectivity, the existence of God, and the paradox of Christian faith. It combines appreciations with some attempts to come to grips with Kierkegaard's thought from within. Although this essay does not in other respects do justice to the "philosophical" (ethical) form of subjectivity, it is a reliable interpretation of Kierkegaard's thought.

Thompson, Josiah. *The Lonely Labyrinth: Kierkegaard's Pseudonymous Works.* Carbondale, 1967. Sets forth an imaginative theme, later to be pursued in Thompson's biographical study of Kierkegaard, that Kierkegaard's pseudonymous authorship represents a striving for health and stability or an attempt to overcome variously designated pathologies of consciousness. Interesting as a speculative psychological portrait of Kierkegaard the man.

———. *Kierkegaard: A Collection of Critical Essays.* New York, 1972. An excellent set of interpretive discussions of such topics as the meaning of inwardness, Kierkegaard's use of irony, the pseudonymous authorship, the existential ethics, and analyses of Kierkegaard's philosophy of religion. Includes a fairly extensive bibliography.

———. *Kierkegaard: A Biographical Essay.* New York, 1973. A very fine biographical study that is informed with a scholarly grasp of Kierkegaard's writings and is especially valuable for its attempts to probe Kierkegaard's thought through interpretations of the pseudonymous writings as "self-referential." The essay shows a good understanding of Kierkegaard's literary self-consciousness.

Thomte, Reidar. *Kierkegaard's Philosophy of Religion.* Princeton, 1948. A competent, detailed discussion of specific issues and arguments in Kierkegaard's religious thought.

Wahl, Jean. *Etudes kierkegaardiennes.* 2 vols. Paris, 1949. Provides a very good account of previous research on Kierkegaard's

thought and is especially valuable for the illuminating treatment of
Kierkegaard's relationship to twentieth-century existential philosoph-
ers. Remains one of the best interpretive and expository works on
Kierkegaard in French.

Walker, Jeremy. *To Will One Thing: Reflections on Kierkegaard's
'Purity of Heart'*. Montreal and London, 1972. A short, lively essay
that offers an incisive analysis of Kierkegaard's *Purity of Heart*.
Although the author veers away from Kierkegaard's thought and does
not seek support for his arguments from Kierkegaard's other writings,
the essay is intrinsically valuable and insightful. It contains very good
discussions of ethical punishment, the concept of "the Good," and the
conception of "the ethical."

Wilde, F. E. *Kierkegaards Verständnis der Existenz*. Copenhagen,
1969. A very scholarly treatment of Kierkegaard's existence that
displays a thorough familiarity with original sources. Although a very
careful study of the central idea in Kierkegaard's existentialism, it
seems to miss the full significance of authentic existence as a way of
being and acting. Includes an extensive bibliography of German and
Danish studies of Kierkegaard.

Wyschogrod, M. *Kierkegaard and Heidegger: The Ontology of
Existence*. New York, 1954. A very good, philosophically illuminating
study of the relationship between Kierkegaard's existentialism and
Heidegger's existential phenomenology of human existence. This
essay remains a stimulating interpretation of existentialism in general
and Kierkegaard in particular.

III. Articles About Kierkegaard

Adorno, T. W. "On Kierkegaard's Doctrine of Love." *Studies in
Philosophy and Social Science*, VIII (1940), 413–29.

Ahlstrom, Sidney E. "The Continental Influence on American Christian Thought Since World War I." *Church History*, XXVII (1958),
256–72.

Allen, E. L. "Introduction to Kierkegaard." *Durham University
Journal*, XXXVI (1943), 9–14.

———. "Kierkegaard and Karl Marx." *Theology*, XL (1940), 117–21.

———. "Pascal and Kierkegaard." *London Quarterly and Holborn Review*, CLXII (1939) 150–64.

Allison, Henry E. "Christianity and Nonsense." *Review of Metaphysics*, XX (1967), 432–60.

———. "Kierkegaard's Dialectic of Religious Consciousness." *Union
Seminary Quarterly Review*, XX (1965), 225–33.

Anderson, Betty C. "The Melville-Kierkegaard Syndrome." *Rendezvous*, III (1968), 41–53.

Anderson, Raymond E. "Kierkegaard's Theory of Communication." *Speech Monographs*, XXX, 1–14.

Angoff, Charles. "Letters and the Arts." *Living Age*, CCCLVII (1940), 89.

Ansbro, John J. "Kierkegaard's Gospel of Suffering." *Philosophical Studies*, XVI (1967), 182–92.

Auden, W. H. "A Preface to Kierkegaard." *New Republic*, 110 (1944), 683–84.

———. "Knight of Doleful Countenance." *The New Yorker*, XLIV (1968), 141–42, 144–46, 151–54, 157–58.

Babbage, S. Barton. "Søren Kierkegaard." *Evangelical Quarterly* (1943), 56–72.

Barrett, Cyril. "Søren Kierkegaard: An Exception." *Studies* (Dublin), XLV (1956), 77–83.

Barth, Karl. "Kierkegaard and the Theologians." Translated by H. M. Rumscheidt. *Canadian Journal of Theology*, XIII (1967), 64–65.

———. "Thank You and a Bow: Kierkegaard's Reveille." Translated by H. M. Rumscheidt. *Canadian Journal of Theology*, XI (1965), 3–7.

Bedell, George C. "Kierkegaard's Conception of Time." *Journal of the American Academy of Religion*, XXXVII (1969), 266–69.

Bernstein, Richard J. "Consciousness, Existence, and Action: Kierkegaard and Sartre," in *Praxis and Action: Contemporary Philosophies of Human Activity*. Philadelphia: The University of Pennsylvania Press, 1971, 84–164.

Billeskov-Jansen, F. J. "The Universality of Kierkegaard." *American-Scandinavian Review*, LI, 145–49.

Bixler, J. X. "On Being Absurd!" *The Massachusetts Review*, X (1969), 407–12.

Blackham, H. J. "The Comparison of Herzen with Kierkegaard; A Comment." *Slavic Review*, XXV (1966), 215–17.

Blanshard, Brand. "Kierkegaard on Faith." *The Personalist*, XLIX (1968), 5–23.

Bogen, James. "Kierkegaard and the 'teleological suspension of the ethical'." *Inquiry*, V (1962), 305–17.

———. "Remark on the Kierkegaard-Hegel Controversy." *Synthese*, XIII (1961), 372–89.

Bolman, Frederick de W., Jr. "Kierkegaard in Limbo." *Journal of Philosophy* XLI (1944), 711–21.

————. "Reply to Mrs. Hess." *Journal of Philosophy,* LXII (1945), 219–20.

Bowen, James K. " 'Crazy Arab' and Kierkegaard's 'Melancholy Fantastic'." *Research Studies, XXXVII,* 60–64.

Brandt, F. "Ce Qu'il y a de Réalité dans les Oeuvres de Søren Kierkegaard." *Revue Philosophique,* 126 (1938), 257–77.

Bretall, R. W. "Kierkegaard: A Critical Survey." *The Examiner,* 11 (1939).

Brookfield, C. M. "What was Kierkegaard's Task? A Frontier to Be Explored." *Union Seminary Quarterly Review,* XVIII, 23–35.

Broudy, H. S. "Kierkegaard's Doctrine of Indirect Communication." *Journal of Philsophy,* LVIII (1961), 225–33.

Buch, Jorgen, "Kierkegaard Anniversary." *Hibbert Journal,* LXII (1963), 24–26.

————. "A Kierkegaard Museum." *American Book Collector,* XII (1961), 5–7.

Callan, Edward, "Auden and Kierkegaard: The Artistic Framework of For the Time Being." *Christian Scholar,* XLVIII (1965), 211–23.

————. "Auden's New Year Letter: A New Style of Architecture." *Renascence,* XVI (1963), 13–19.

Campbell, R. "Lessing's Problem and Kierkegaard's Answer." *Scottish Journal of Theology,* XIX (1966), 35–54.

Cardinal, Clive H. "Rilke and Kierkegaard: Some Relationships Between Poet and Theologian." *Bulletin of the Rocky Mountain Modern Language Association,* XXIII (1969), 34–39.

Cattani, G. "Bergson, Kierkegaard and Mysticism." Translated by A. Dru). *Dublin Review,* 192 (1933), 70–78.

Celestin, George. "Kierkegaard and Christian Renewal." *Dominicana,* XLIX (1964), 149–57.

Channing-Pearce, M. "Repetition: a Kierkegaard Study." *Hibbert Journal,* 41 (1943), 361–64.

Chari, C. T. K. "On the Dialectic of Swami Vivekenanda and Søren Kierkegaard: an 'Existential' Approach to Indian Philosophy." *Revue Internationale de Philosophie,* X, no. 37 (1956), 315–31.

————. "Søren Kierkegaard and Swami Vivekenanda: A Study in Religious Dialectics." *Vedanda Kesari,* XXXIX (1952), 107–10.

Charlesworth, James H. "Kierkegaard and Optical Linguistics," in *Kierkegaardiana,* VII. Copenhagen: Munsgaard, 1966, 231–34.

Anonymous. "Choose, Leap, and Be Free." *Times Literary Supplement,* XLV (1946), 109–11.

Christensen, M. G. "Gruntvig and Kierkegaard." *Lutheran Quarterly,* II (1950), 441–46.

Clive, Geoffrey, "Demonic in Mozart." *Music and Letters,* XXXVII (1956), 1–13.

———. "Seven Types of Offense." *Lutheran Quarterly,* X (1958), 11–25.

———. "The Sickness unto Death in the Underworld: A Study of Nihilism." *Harvard Theological Review,* LI (1958), 133–67.

Closs, August. "Goethe and Kierkegaard." *Modern Language Quarterly,* X (1949), 264–80.

Cochrane, A. C. "On the Anniversaries of Mozart, Kierkegaard, and Barth." *Scottish Journal of Theology,* IX (1956), 251–63.

Cole, J. D. "Kierkegaard's Doctrine of the Atonement." *Religion in Life,* XXXIII (1964), 592–601.

Cole, J. Preston, "The Existential Reality of God: A Kierkegaardian Study," *Christian Scholar,* XLVIII (1965), 224–35.

———. "The Function of Choice in Human Existence." *Journal of Religion,* XLV (1965), 196–210.

Collins, J. "Faith and Reflection in Kierkegaard." *Journal of Religion,* XXXVII (1957), 10–19.

Comstock, W. R. "Aspects of Aesthetic Existence: Kierkegaard and Santayana." *International Philosophical Quarterly,* VI (1966), 189–213.

Cook, E. J. Raymond. "Kierkegaard's Literary Art." *The Listener,* LXXII (1964), 713–14.

Copleston, Frederick C. "Existence and Religion." *Dublin Review,* CCXX (1947), 50–63.

Crites, Stephen, "The Author and the Authorship: Recent Kierkegaard Literature." *Journal of the American Academy of Religion,* XXXVIII (1970), 37–54.

———. "Pseudonymous Authorship as Art and as Act," in Josiah Thompson, ed., *Kierkegaard: A Collection of Critical Essays.* Garden City, N. Y.: Doubleday & Company, Inc., 1972, 189–236.

Croxall, T. H. "The Death of Kierkegaard." *The Church Quarterly Review,* CLVII (1956), 271–86.

———. "A Strange but Stimulating Essay on Music." *Musical Times,* XC (1949), 46–48.

Cumming, R. "Existence and Communication." *Ethics,* LXV (1955), 79–101.

Dallen, James. "Existentialism and the Catholic Thinker." *Catholic World,* CC (1965), 294–99.

Dauenhauer, B. P. "On Kierkegaard's Alleged Nihilism." *The Southern Journal of Philosophy,* XII (1974), 153–63.

Davison, R. M. "Herzen and Kierkegaard." *Slavic Review,* XXV (1966), 191–221.

———. "Reply." *Slavic Review,* XXV (1966), 218–21.

Demant, V. A. "S. K.: Knight of Faith." *Nineteenth Century,* 127 (1940), 70–77.

Denison, D. "Kierkegaard's Sociology with Notes on Its Relevance to the Church." *Religion in Life,* XXVII (1958), 257–65.

De Rosa, Peter. "Some Reflections on Kierkegaard and Christian Love." *The Clergy Review* (London), XLIV (1959), 616–22.

Dewey, Bradley R. "The Erotic-Demonic in Kierkegaard's 'Diary of the Seducer'." *Scandinavia,* X (1971), 1–24.

———. "Kierkegaard and the New Testament." *Harvard Theological Review,* LX (1967), 391–409.

Diamond, Malcolm L. "Faith and Its Tensions: A Criticism of Religious Existentialism." *Judaism,* XIII (1964), 317–27.

———. "Kierkegaard and Apologetics." *Journal of Religion,* IV 1964), 122–32.

Dietrichson, Paul. "Kierkegaard's Concept of Self." *Inquiry,* VIII (1965), 1–32.

Dodd, E. M. "Kierkegaard and Schweitzer." *London Quarterly Review,* 170 (1945), 148–55.

Dru, Alexander. "Kierkegaard: A Great Christian Thinker." *Listener,* LIV (1955), 841–42.

———. "Reply with Rejoinder." *Dublin Review,* CCXXI (1948), 183–88.

Duncan, Elmer H. "Kierkegaard's Teleological Suspension of the Ethical: A Study of Exception-Cases." *Southern Journal of Philosophy,* I (1963), 9–18.

———. "Kierkegaard's Uses of Paradox-Yet Once More." *Journal of Existentialism,* VII (1967), 319–28.

Dupré, Louis K. "The Constitution of the Self in Kierkegaard's Philosophy." *International Philosophical Quarterly,* III (1963), 506–26.

Durfee, Harold A. "The Second Stage of Kierkegaardian Scholarship in America." *International Philosophical Quarterly,* III (1963), 121–39.

Durkan, J. "Kierkegaard and Aristotle: a Parallel." *Dublin Review,* 213 (1943), 136–48.

Earle, William. "Hegel and Some Contemporary Philosophies." *Philosophy and Phenomenological Research,* XX (1960), 352–64.

———. "The Paradox and Death of God: Kierkegaard and Nietzsche," in C. W. Christian and Glenn R. Wittig, eds., *Radical Theology: Phase Two*. Philadelphia: J. B. Lippincott Company (1967), 27–42.

————. "Phenomenology and Existentialism." *Journal of Philosophy*, LVII (1960), 75–84.

Edwards, Brian F. M. "Kafka and Kierkegaard: A Reassessment." *German Life and Letters*, XX (1967), 218–25.

Edwards, C. N. "Guilt in the Thought of Søren Kierkegaard." *Encounter*, XXVII (1966), 141–57.

Eller, Vernard. "Existentialism and the Brethren." *Brethren Life and Thought*, V (1960), 31–38.

————. "Fact, Faith, and Foolishness: Kierkegaard and the New Quest." *Journal of Religion*, XLVII (1968), 54–68.

————. "Kierkegaard Knew the Brethren! Sort of." *Brethren Life and Thought*, VIII (1963), 57–60.

Elrod, J. W. "The Self in Kierkegaard's Pseudonyms." *International Journal for Philosophy of Religion*, IV (1973), 218–240.

Evans, Robert O. "Existentialism in Greene's 'The Quiet American'." *Modern Fiction Studies*, III (1957), 241–248.

Fabro, Cornelio. "The Problem of Desperation and Christian Spirituality in Kierkegaard." *Kierkegaardiana*, IV. Copenhagen: Søren Kierkegaard Selskabet (1962), 62–69.

————. "The 'Subjectivity of Truth' and the Interpretation of Kierkegaard." *Kierkegaard-Studiet*, I, (1964), 35–43.

————. "Why did Kierkegaard Break Up with Regina?" *Orbis Litterarum*, XXII, 387–92.

Fairhurst, Stanley J. "Søren Kierkegaard [a Bibliography]." *Modern Schoolman*, XXI (1953), 19–22.

Farber, Marjorie. "Subjectivity in Modern Fiction." *Kenyon Review*, VII (1945), 645–52.

Fasel, Oscar A. "Observations on Unamuno and Kierkegaard." *Hispania*, XXXVIII (1955), 443–50.

Fenger, Henning. "Kierkegaard—A Literary Approach." *Scandinavica*, III (1964), 1–16.

Ferm, Deane W. "Two Conflicting Trends in Protestant Theological Thinking." *Religion in Life*, XXV (1956), 582–94.

Fitzpatrick, M., Jr. "Current Kierkegaard Study: Whence-Whither?" *Journal of Religion*, L (1970), 79–90.

Fleisner, E. M. "Legacy of Kierkegaard." *New Republic*, CXXXIII (1955), 16–18. Reply: CXXXIV (1956), 22–23. Rejoinder: CXXXIV (1956), 23.

Ford, Richard S. "Existentialism: Philosophy or Theology?" *Religion in Life*, XXVIII (1959,) 433–42.

Forshey, Gerald. "Pharoah, Kierkegaard, and Black Power." *Christian Advocate*, XII (May 30, 1968), 7–8.

"Four Articles on Kierkegaard" [Anonymous]. *Anglican Theological Review*, XXXVIII (1956), 1–41.

Freehof, Solomon B. "Aspects of Existentialism." *Carnegie Magazine*, XXII (1949), 292–94.

Friedrich, Gerhard. "Reply to Llewellyn Jones." *Christian Century*, LXIX (1952), 674–75.

Fromm, H. "Emerson and Kierkegaard: The Problem of Historical Christianity." *Massachusetts Review*, IX (1968), 741–52.

Gallagher, Michael P. "Wittgenstein's Admiration for Kierkegaard." *Month*, XXIX (1968), 43–49.

Gallagher, T. "Søren Kierkegaard," in Frederick Patka, ed., *Existentialist Thinkers and Thought*. New York: Philosophical Library (1962), 75–92.

Gardiner, Patrick. "Kierkegaard's Two Ways." *British Academy Proceedings*, LIV (1968), 207–29.

Garelick, Herbert, "The Irrationality and Supra-rationality of Kierkegaard's Paradox." *Southern Journal of Philosophy*, II (1964), 75–86.

Geismar, E. "Søren Kierkegaard." *American Scandinavian Review*, 17 (1929), 591–599.

Genet, J., "Letter from Paris." *The New Yorker*, XL (1964), 170.

Gerber, R. J. "Kierkegaard, Reason, and Faith." *Thought*, XLIV (1969), 29–52.

Gill, Jerry H. "Kant, Kierkegaard and Religious Knowledge." *Philosophy and Phenomenological Research*, XXVIII (1967–68), 188–204.

Gimblett, Charles. "SK: A Strange Saint." *London Quarterly and Holborn Review*, CLXXX (1955), 280–82.

Glicksberg, C. I. "Aesthetics of Nihilism." *University of Kansas City Review*, XXVII (1960), 127–30.

"Gloomy Dane: The Sesquicentennial of Kierkegaard's Birth." [Anonymous]. *Tablet*, CCXVII (1963), 482.

Goulet, Denis A. "Kierkegaard, Aquinas, and the Dilemma of Abraham." *Thought*, XXXII (1957), 165–88.

Graef, H. C. "Prophets of Gloom." *Catholic World*, CLXXXIII (1956), 202–6.

Green, Allan. "Søren Kierkegaard in Berlin." *Finsk Tidskrift*, VI (1957), 261–68.

Grene, Marjorie. "Kierkegaard: The Philosophy." *Kenyon Review,* IX (1947), 48–69.

Griffith, G. O. "Kierkegaard on Faith." *Hibbert Journal,* 42 (1943), 58–63.

Griffith, Richard M. "Repetitions: Constantine (S.) Constantius." *Journal of Existential Psychiatry,* II (1962), 437–38.

Grimsley, Ronald. "Hugo, Kierkegaard, and the Character of Nero." *Revue de Littérature Comparée,* XXXII, 230–36.

———. "Kierkegaard and Descartes." *Journal of the History of Philosophy,* IV (1966), 31–41.

———. "Kierkegaard and Leibniz." *Journal of the History of Ideas,* XXVI (1965), 383–96.

———. "Kierkegaard and Scribe." *Revue de Littérature Comparée,* XXXVIII (1964), 512–30.

———. "Kierkegaard, Vigny and 'the Poet.'" *Revue de Littérature Comparée* (1970), 52–80.

———. "Modern Conception of the Demonic." *Church Quarterly Review,* CLVII (1957), 185–94.

———. "Romantic Melancholy in Chateaubriand and Kierkegaard." *Comparative Literature,* VIII (1956), 227–44.

———. "Rousseau and Kierkegaard." *Cambridge Journal,* VII (1954), 615–26.

———. "Some Implications of the Use of Irony in Voltaire and Kierkegaard," in Froncois Jost, ed., *Actes du IVe Congrès de l'Association Internationale de Littérature Comparée, Fribourg, 1964 (I-II).* The Hague/Paris, 1966, 1,018–24.

Guterman, N. "Kierkegaard and his Faith." *Partisan Review,* (1943).

Halevi, Jacob L. "Kierkegaard and the Midrash." *Judaism,* IV, 23–28.

———. "Kierkegaard's Teleological Suspension of the Ethical: Is it Jewish?" *Judaism,* VIII (1959), 292–302.

Hamburger, Michael. "Under the Volcano: The Last Years: Journals 1853–55." *Spectator* (1965), 174–75.

Hamilton, Kenneth M. "Created Soul-Eternal Spirit: A Continuing Theological Thorn." *Scottish Journal of Theology,* XIX (1966), 23–34.

———. "Kierkegaard on Sin," *Scottish Journal of Theology,* XVII (1964), 289–302.

———. "Man: Anxious or Guilty? A Second Look at Kierkegaard's *The Concept of Dread.*" *Christian Scholar,* XLVI (1963), 293–99.

Hamilton, William. "Daring to be the Enemy of God: Some Reflections on the Life and Death of Mozart's Don Giovanni." *Christian Scholar,* XLVI (1963), 40–54.

Hanzo, Thomas. "Elliot and Kierkegaard: 'The Meaning of Happening' in *The Cocktail Party.*" *Modern Drama,* III, 52–59.

Hare, Peter H. "Is There an Existential Theory of Truth?" *Journal of Existentialism,* VII (1967), 417–24.

Haroutunian, Joseph. "Protest to the Lord." *Theology Today,* XII (1955), 295–96.

Hartman, Robert S. "The Self in Kierkegaard." *Journal of Existential Psychiatry,* II (1962), 409–36.

Hartt, J. N. "Christian Freedom Reconsidered: The Case of Kierkegaard." *Harvard Theological Review,* LX (1964), 133–44.

Heinecken, M. J. "Kierkegaard as Christian." *Journal of Religion,* XXXVII (1959), 20–30.

Held, M. "Historical Kierkegaard: Faith of Gnosis." *Journal of Religion,* XXXVII (1949), 260–66.

Hems, John M. "Abraham and Brand." *Philosophy,* XXXIX (1964), 137–44.

Hendry, George S. "The Gospel in the Age of Anxiety." *Theology Today,* XII (1955), 283–89.

Herbert, Robert. "Two of Kierkegaard's Uses of 'Paradox.' " *Philosophical Review,* LXX (1961), 41–56.

Hess, M. S. "Browning: an English Kierkegaard." *Christian Century,* LXXIX (1962), 569–71.

———. "Browning and Kierkegaard as Heirs of Luther." *Christian Century,* LXXX (1963), 799–801.

———. "The Dilemma in Kierkegaard's 'Either/Or'." *Journal of Philosophy,* XLII (1945), 216–19.

———. "Kierkegaard and Isaac Penington." *Catholic World,* 162 (1946), 434–37.

———. "Kierkegaard and Socrates." *Christian Century,* LXXXII (1965), 736–38.

———. "Three Christians in Literature: "Browning, Kierkegaard, Heine." *Christianity Today,* VIII (1964), 13–15.

———. "What Luther Meant by Faith Alone." *Catholic World,* CXCIX (1964), 96–101.

Hill, Brian V. "Søren Kierkegaard and Educational Theory." *Educational Theory,* XVI (1966), 344–53.

Hill. E. F. F. "Kierkegaard: The Man and His Thought." *World Review* (1948), 58–62.

Holmer, Paul. "James Collins and Kierkegaard." *Meddelelser fra Søren Kierkegaard Selskabet,* IV (1954), 1–8.

———. "Kierkegaard and Ethical Theory." *Ethics* LXIII, (1953).

———. "Kierkegaard and Logic." *Kierkegaardiana,* II (1957), 25–42.

———. "Kierkegaard and the Sermon." *Journal of Religion,* XXXVII (1957), 1–9.

———. "Kierkegaard, a Religious Author." *American Scandinavian Review,* 33 (1945), 147–52.

———. "Kierkegaard and Theology." *Union Seminary Quarterly Review,* XII (1957), 23–31.

Holmes, Roger W. "The Problems of Philosophy in the Twentieth Century." *Antioch Review,* XXII (1962), 287–96.

Hong, Howard. "The Kierkegaard Papers." *TriQuarterly,* No. 16 (1969), 100–23.

Hook, S. "Two Types of Existentialist Religion and Ethics." *Partisan Review,* XXVI (1959), 58–63.

Horgby, Ingvar. "Immediacy-Subjectivity-Revelation." *Inquiry,* VIII (1965), 84–117.

Horn, Robert L. "On Understanding Kierkegaard Understanding . . . ." *Union Seminary Quarterly Review,* XXI (1966), 341–45.

Hubben, William. "Kierkegaard and the Friends." *Friends Intelligencer* (1953), 230–34.

Hyman, Frieda Clark. "Kierkegaard and the Hebraic Mind." *Journal of Ecumenical Studies,* IV (1967), 554–56.

Irving, John A. "Thoughts on Existentialism." *Queen's Quarterly,* LVII (1950), 298–303.

James, Ingli. "The Autonomy of the Work of Art: Modern Criticism and the Christian Tradition." *Sewanee Review,* LXX (1962), 296–318.

Jansen, F. J. B. Universality of Kierkegaard." *American Scandinavian Review,* LI (1963), 145–49.

Jorgensen, Carl. "The Ethics of Søren Kierkegaard." *Atti XII Congr. intern. Filos.,* 243–50.

Johannesson, E. O. "Isak Dinesen, Søren Kierkegaard, and the Present Age." *Books Abroad,* XXXVI (1962), 20–24.

Johnson, Howard. "The Deity in Time: An Introduction to Kierkegaard." *Theology Today,* I (1945), 517–36.

———. "Review of Gemenskapsproblemet hos Søren Kierkegaard (P. Wagndal)." *Review of Religion,* XXI (1956), 77–79.

Johnson, William A. "The Anthropology of Søren Kierkegaard." *Hartford Quarterly,* IV (1964), 43–52.

Jones, W. Glyn. "Søren Kierkegaard and Paul Martin Møller." *Modern Language Review,* LX (1954), 73–82.

"Kierkegaard and the Bible" [Anonymous]. *Theology Today.* X (1953), 247–48.

"Kierkegaard in France" [Anonymous]. *Times Literary Supplement,* XXXIV (1935), 324.

Killinger, John. "Existentialism and Human Freedom." *English Journal,* L (1961), 303–13.

King, Joe M. "Kierkegaard as an Existentialist." *Forman Studies,* XV, 35–44.

King. W. L. "Negation as a Religious Category." *Journal of Religion,* XXXVII (1957), 109.

Klemke, E. D. "Insights to Ethical Theory from Kierkegaard." *Philosophical Quarterly* (St. Andrews), X, No. 41, 322–30.

———. "Logicality vs. Alogicality in the Christian Faith." *Journal of Religion,* XXXVIII (1958), 107–15.

———. "Some Misinterpretations of Kierkegaard." *Hibbert Journal,* LVII (1958–59), 359–70.

Koenker, Ernest B. "Søren Kierkegaard on Luther," in Jaroslav Pelikan, ed., *Interpreters of Luther: Essays in Honor of Wilhelm Pauck.* Philadelphia: Fortress Press, 1968, 231–52.

Kraft, Julius. "The Philosophy of Existence." *Philosophy and Phenomenological Research,* I (1941), 339–58.

Kraushaar, O. F. "Kierkegaard in English." *Journal of Philosophy,* 39 (1942), 561–83, 589–607.

Kreyche, G. "A Glance at Existentialism." *Ave,* CII (1965), 10–13.

Kritzek, J. "Philosophers of Anxiety." *Commonweal,* LXIII (1956), 219–44.

———. "Kierkegaard or Hegel?" *Revue Internationale de Philosophie,* (1952), 1–18.

———. "Kierkegaard's Understanding of Hegel." *Union Seminary Quarterly Review,* XXI (1966), 233–44.

Kurtz, P. W. "Kierkegaard, Existentialism, and the Contemporary Scene." *Antioch Review,* XXI (1961–62), 71–89.

Lal, Basant Kumar, "Kierkegaard's Approach to Ethics." *The Philosophical Quarterly* (Amalner, India), XXXVIII (1965–66), 181–190.

Lampert, E. "Herzen or Kierkegaard." *Slavic Review,* XXV (1966), 210–14.

Langan, T. "The Original Existentialist Revolt: Søren Kierkegaard," in Etienne Gilson, ed., *Recent Philosophy: Hegel to the Present.* New York: Random House, 1966, 69–78 (notes 684–86).

Larsen, Robert E. "Kierkegaard's Absolute Paradox." *Journal of Religion*, XLII, 34–43.

Lawson, Lewis A. "Cass Kinsolving: Kierkegaardian Man of Despair." *Wisconsin Studies in Contemporary Literature*, III (1962), 54–66.

———. "Kierkegaard and the Modern American Novel," in Jean Jacquot, ed., *Le théâtre moderne, 11: Depuis la deuxième guerre mondiale*, (Paris: Editions du Centre Nationale de la Recherche Scientifique, 1967), 113–25.

———. "Walker Percy's Indirect Communication." *Texas Studies in Literature and Language*, XI (1969), 867–900.

Lee, R. F. "Emerson Through Kierkegaard: Toward a Definition of Emerson's Theory of Communication." *A Journal of English Literary History*, XXIV (1957), 229–48.

Lefevre, Perry. "Hong Translation of Kierkegaard's Papirer." *Journal of Religion*, L (1970), 69–78.

———. "Snare of Truth." *Pastoral Psychology, XIX* (1968), 33–34.

Lessing, Arthur. "Hegel and Existentialism: On Unhappiness." *Personalist*, XLIX (1968), 67–77.

Levi, A. A. "A Hundred Years After Kierkegaard." *Kenyon Review*, XVIII (1956), 169–81.

———. "Socrates in the Nineteenth Century." *Journal of the History of Ideas*, XVII (1956), 104–06.

Livingston, G. H. "Kierkgeaard and Jeremiah." *Asbury Seminarium*, XI (1957), 46–61.

Lowrie, Walter. "Existence as Understood by Kierkegaard and/or Sartre." *Sewanee Review*, LVIII (1950), 379–401.

———. "Qualified Retraction and an Unqualified Apology." *Theology Today*, XVI (1959), 267.

Lund, Margaret. "The Single Ones [Kierkegaard and Nietzsche]. *Personalist*, XLI (1960), 15–24.

Lund, Mary Graham, "The Existentialism of Ibsen." *Personalist, XLI* (1960), 310–17.

Lønning, Per. "The Dilemma of 'Grace Alone.' " *Dialog*, VI (1967), 108–14.

Löwith, Karl, "Nature, History, and Existentialism." *Social Research*, XIX (1952), 79–94.

———. "On the Historical Understanding of Kierkegaard." *Review of Religion*, IX (1943), 227–241.

Macfadden, R. "Nuclear Dilemma, with a Nod to Kierkegaard." *Theology Today*, XVII (1961), 508–18.

MacIntyre, Alasdair. "Søren Aabye Kierkegaard," in Paul Edwards, ed., *The Encyclopedia of Philosophy*, IV. New York: The Macmillan Co. (1967), 336–40.

Mackey, Louis. "The Analysis of the Good in Kierkegaard's 'Purity of Heart,' " in Irwin C. Lieb, ed., *Experience, Existence, and the Good: Essays in Honor of Paul Weiss*. Carbondale: Southern Illinois University Press (1961), 260–74.

———. "Kierkegaard and the Problem of Existential Philosophy." *Review of Metaphysics*, IX (1956), 404–19, 569–88.

———. "Kierkegaard's Lyric of Faith: A Look at Fear and Trembling." *Rice Institute Pamphlets*, XLVII (1960), 30–47.

———. "Loss of the World in Kierkegaard's Ethics." *Review of Metaphysics*, LX (1962), 602–20.

———. "Philosophy and Poetry in Kierkegaard." *Review of Metaphysics*, XXIII (1969), 316–32.

———. "The Poetry of Inwardness," in George A. Schrader, ed. *Existential Philosophers: Kierkegaard to Merleau-Ponty*. New York: McGraw-Hill (1967), 45–107.

———. "Some Versions of the Aesthetic: Kierkegaard's Either/Or." *Rice University Studies*, L (1964), 39–54.

———. "The View from Pisgah: A Reading of Fear and Trembling," in Josiah Thompson, ed., *Kierkegaard: A Collection of Critical Essays*. Garden City, New York: Doubleday & Company, Inc. (1972), 407–42.

Madden, M. C. "Kierkegaard on Self-Acceptance." *Review and Expositor*, XLVIII (1951), 302–09.

Magel, Charles R. "Kierkegaard's Logically Contradictory Christianity." *Graduate Review of Philosophy*, II (1960).

Mairet, Philip. "Delayed Action." *New Statesman*, LXXII (1966), 234–35.

Malmquist, C. P. "A Comparison of Orthodox and Existential Psychoanalytic Concepts of Anxiety." *Journal of the Nervous and Mental Diseases*, CXXXU (1960), 371–82.

Manasee, E. M. "Conversion and Liberation: A Comparison of Augustine and Kierkegaard." *Review of Religion*, 17 (1943), 361–83.

Manger, Philip. "Kierkegaard in Max Frisch's Novel Stiller." *German Life and Letters*, XX (1967), 119–31.

Mantripp, J. C. "Søren Kierkegaard." *London Quarterly Review*, 164 (1939), 237–43.

Marcel, Gabriel. "Some Reflections on Existentialism." *Philosophy Today* VIII (1964), 248–57.

McInerny, Ralph. "The Ambiguity of Existential Metaphysics." *Laval Théologique et Philosophique,* XII (1956), 120–24.

———. "Connection Seen in Ethics of Kierkegaard and Aquinas." *Christian Messenger,* LXXXII (1964,) 4.

———. "Kierkegaard and Speculative Thought." *New Scholasticism, Modern Schoolman,* XXXIII (1956), 219–39.

———. "Ethics and Persuasion: Kierkegaard's Existential Dialectic." XL (1966), 23–25.

———. "The Teleological Suspension of the Ethical." *Thomist,* XX (1957), 295–310.

McKeon, R. "The Philosophy of Kierkegaard." *New York Times Book Review,* (1945), 1.

McKinnon, Alastair. "Barth's Relation to Kierkegaard: Some Further Light." *Canadian Journal of Theology,* XIII (1967), 31–41.

———. "Believing the Paradox: A Contradiction in Kierkegaard?" *Harvard Theological Review,* LXI (1968), 633–36.

———. "Kierkegaard and his Pseudonyms: A Preliminary Report." *Kierkegaardiana,* VII. Copenhagen: Munksgaard (1966), 64–76.

———. "Kierkegaard: 'Paradox' and Irrationalism." *Journal of Philosophy,* LXII (1965), 651–52.

———. "Kierkegaard: 'Paradox' and Irrationalism." *Journal of Existentialism,* VII (1967), 401–16.

———. "Kierkegaard's Irrationalism Revisited." *International Philosophical Quarterly,* IX (1969), 165–76.

———. "Kierkegaard's Pseudonyms: A New Hierarchy." *American Philosophical Quarterly,* VI (1969), 116–26.

McKinnon, A., and Roger Webster. "A Method of 'Author' Identification." *Computer Studies in the Humanities and Verbal Behavior,* II (1969), 19–23.

McMinn, J. B. "Value and Subjectivity in Kierkegaard." *Review and Expositor,* LIII (1956), 477–88.

McPherson, T. "Second Great Commandment: Religion and Morality." *Congregational Quarterly* (London), XXXV (1957), 212–22.

"Meant for Mankind: Kierkegaard and Christianity as the Regulating Weight." *Times Literary Supplement,* LXVIII (1969), 281–83.

Merlan, P. "Toward the Understanding of Kierkegaard." *Journal of Religion,* 23 (1943), 77–90.

Mesnard, Pierre. "The Character of Kierkegaard's Philosophy." *Philosophy Today,* I (1957), 84–89.

Michaelson, C. "Kierkegaard's Theology of Faith." *Religion in Life,* XXXII (1963), 225–37.

Minear, Paul S. "Kierkegaard Centennial." *Theology Today,* XII (1955), 244–46.

———. "Thanksgiving as a Synthesis of the Temporal and the Eternal." *Anglican Theological Review,* XXXVIII, 4–14.

Mitchell, Charles. "The Lord of the Flies and the Escape from Freedom." *Arizona Quarterly,* XXII (1966), 27–40.

Moore, S. "Religion as the True Humanism-Reflections on Kierkegaard's Social Philosophy." *Journal of the American Academy of Religion* (1969), 15.

Moore, W. G. "Kierkegaard and His Century." *Hibbert Journal,* 36 (1938), 568–82.

Mourant, John A. "The Limitations of Religious Existentialism." *International Philosophical Quarterly,* I (1961), 437–52.

Muggeridge, Malcolm. "Books." *Esquire,* LXX (1968), 30.

Murphy, Arthur E. "On Kierkegaard's Claim that 'Truth is Subjectivity,' " in his book, *Reason and the Common Good: Selected Essays.* Englewood Cliffs, N. J.: Prentice-Hall (1963), 173–79.

Murphy, J. L. "Faith and Reason in the Teaching of Kierkegaard." *American Ecclesiastical Review,* 145 (1961), 233–65.

Naess, Arne. "Kierkegaard and Values of Education." *Journal of Value Inquiry,* II (1968), 196–200.

Nagley, Winfield E. "Kierkegaard on Liberation." *Ethics,* LXX (1959), 47–58.

———. "Kierkegaard's Irony in the 'Diapsalmata'." In *Kierkegaardiana, VI.* Copenhagen: Munksgaard (1966), 51–75.

Nakamura, Kohei. "On the Relation of Human Being and Science by Kierkegaard." *Kierkegaard-Studiet,* I (1964), 69–73.

Neumann, Harry. "Kierkegaard and Socrates on the Dignity of Man.' *Personalist,* XLIII (1967), 453–60.

Nicholson, G. E. "A Dramatic Approach to Christianity." *Christendom,* IX (1944), 462–75.

Noxon, James. "Kierkegaard's Stages and A Burnt-Out Case." *Review of English Literature,* III (1962), 90–101.

Noyce, Gaylord B. "Wounded by Christ's Sword." *Interpretation,* VIII (1954), 433–43.

O'Donnell, William G. "Kierkegaard: The Literary Manner." *Kenyon Review,* IX (1947), 35–47.

"The 'Offense' of the God-Man: Kierkegaard's Way of Faith." *Times Literary Supplement,* XXXVI (1937), 229–30.

Ofstad, Harald. "Morality, Choice, and Inwardness." *Inquiry,* VIII (1965), 33–72.

Otani, Hidehito. "The Concept of a Christian in Kierkegaard." *Inquiry*, VIII (1965), 74–83.

Otani, Masaru. "The Past and Present State of Kierkegaard Studies in Japan." *Orbis Litterarum*, XVIII (1963), 54–59.

———. "Self-manifestation of Freedom in 'Anxiety' by Kierkegaard." *Orbis Litterarum*, XXII, 393–98.

Owen, P. O. "Existentialism and Ascetical Theology." *Church Quarterly Review*, CLX (1959), 226–31.

Pait, James A. "Kirekegaard and the Problem of Choice." *Emory University Quarterly*, II (1946), 237–45.

Palmer, Donald D. "Unamuno's Don Quixote and Kierkegaard's Abraham." *Revista de Estudios Hispanicos*, III (1969), 295–312.

Paul, W. W. "Faith and Reason in Kierkegaard and Modern Existentialism." *Review of Religion*, XX (1956), 149–63.

Percy, Walker. "The Message in the Bottle." *Thought*, XXXIV (1959), 405–33.

Perkins, Robert L. "Kierkegaard's Epistemological Preferences." *International Journal for Philosophy of Religion*, IV (1973), 197–217.

———. "Persistent Criticisms: Misinterpretations of Soren Kierkegaard's Ethical Thoughts," in *Memorias des XIII Congreso Internacional di Filosofia*, VII (Mexico, 1964), 377–88.

———. "Søren Kierkegaard's Library." *American Book Collector*, XII (1961), 9–16.

———. "Two Nineteenth Century Interpretations of Socrates: Hegel and Kierkegaard." *Kierkegaard-Studiet* IV (1967), 1–6.

Perry, E. "Was Kierkegaard a Biblical Existentialist?" *Journal of Religion*, XXXVI (1956), 17–23.

Petras, John W. "God, Man and Society, the Perspectives of Buber and Kierkegaard." *Journal of Religious Thought*, XXIII (1966–67), 119–28.

Pittenger, W. Norman. "Søren Kierkegaard." *Anglican Theological Review* (Evanston), XXXVIII (1954), 1–3

Pondrom, Cyrena Norman. "Two Demonic Figures: Kierkegaard's Merman and Dostoevsky's Underground Man." *Orbis Litterarum*, XXIII (1968), 161–77.

Poole, Roger C. "Hegel, Kierkegaard and Sartre." *New Blackfriar's*, XLVII (1966), 532–41.

Pope, R. M. "Impression of Kierkegaard." *London Quarterly Review*, 166 (1941), 17–24.

Popkin, R. H. "Kierkegaard and Scepticism." Algemeen Nederlands tijdschrift voor Wijsbegeerte en psychologie, LI (1958–59), 123–41.

———. "Theological and Religious Scepticism." *Christian Scholar,* XXXIX (1956), 150–58.

Prenter, R. "The Concept of Freedom in Sartre Against a Kierkegaardian Background," translated by H. Kaasa. *Dialog,* VII (1968), 132–37.

Ramsey, P. "*Existenz* and the Existence of God: A Study of Kierkegaard and Hegel." *Journal of Religion,* XXVIII (1948), 157–76.

Reck, Donald W. "The Christianity of Søren Kierkegaard." *Canadian Journal of Theology,* XII (1966), 85–97.

Reichmann, Ernani. "Kierkegaard in Brazil," in *Kierkegaardiana,* V (Copenhagen: Munksgaard, 1964), 78–79.

Reinhardt, K. F. "Cleavage of Minds: Kierkegaard and Hegel." *Commonweal,* 24 (1936), 523–24.

Reinhold, H. "S. K., Great Christian of the 19th Century." *Commonweal,* 35 (1942), 608–11.

Replogle, Justin. "Auden's Religious Leap." *Wisconsin Studies in Contemporary Literature,* VII (1966), 47–75.

Rhodes, Donald W. "The Christianity of Søren Kierkegaard." *Canadian Journal of Theology,* XII (1966), 85–97.

Riviere, W. T. "Introducing Kierkegaard." *Christian Century,* 56 (1939), 1164–66.

Roberts, David Everett. "A Review of Kierkegaard's Writings." *Review of Religion,* VII (1943), 300–17.

Roberts, J. D. "Kierkegaard on Truth and Subjectivity." *Journal of Religious Thought,* XVIII (1961), 41–56.

Roubiezck, Paul. "Søren Kierkegaard." *The Times* [London] (April 27, 1968), 10.

de Rougement, Denis. "Kierkegaard and Hamlet: Two Danish Princes." *The Anchor Review,* I (1955), 109–27.

Ruoff, J. E. "Kierkegaard and Shakespeare." *Comparative Literature,* XX (1968), 343–54.

Ruotolo, L. "Keats and Kierkegaard: The Tragedy of Two Worlds." *Renascence,* XVI (1964), 175–90.

Schmitt, R. "Kierkegaard's Ethics and Its Teleological Suspension." *Journal of Philosophy,* LVIII (1961), 701–02.

———. "The Paradox in Kierkegaard's Religiousness A." *Inquiry,* VIII (1965), 118–35.

Schrader, George A. "Kant and Kierkegaard on Duty and Inclination." *Journal of Philosophy,* LXV (1968), 688–701.

———. "Norman Mailer and the Despair of Defiance." *Yale Review,* LI (1961), 267–80.

Schrag, Calvin. "Kirekegaard's Existential Reflections on Time." *Personalist*, XLII (1961), 149–64.

———. "Note on Kierkegaard's Teleological Suspension of the Ethical." *Ethics*, LXX, No. 1 (1959–60), 66–68.

Schrag, Oswald O. "Existential Ethics and Axiology." *Southern Journal of Philosophy*, I (1963), 39–47.

Schutz, A. "Mozart and the Philosophers." *Social Research*, XXIII (1956), 219–42.

Scudder, J. R., Jr. "Kierkegaard and the Responsible Enjoyment of Children." *Educational Forum*, XXX (1966), 497–503.

Sechi, Vanina. "Art, Language, Creativity and Kierkegaard." *Humanitas*, V (1969–70), 81–97.

Seidel, George J. "Monasticism as a Ploy in Kierkegaard's Theology." *American Benedictine Review*, XX (1969), 281–305.

Sen, Krishna. "Kierkegaard and St. Thomas." *Philosophical Quarterly* (Amalner, India) (1956–57), 69–74.

Sharper, P. J. "Review of Journey Through Dread by A. Ussher." *Commonweal*, LXIII (1955), 96–98.

Sjursen, Harold P. "Method and Perspective When Reading Kierkegaard," in *Kierkegaardiana*, VIII. Copenhagen: Munksgaard (1971), 199–211.

Skinner, J. E. "Philosophical Megalomania." *Theology and Life*, IX (1966), 146–59.

Slatte, H. A. "Kierkegaard's Introduction to American Methodists." *Drew Gateway*, XXX (1960), 161–67.

Smith, J. W. "Religion A/ Religion B: A Kierkegaard Study." *Scottish Journal of Theology*, XV (1962), 245–65.

Smith, Joyce Carol Oates, "The Existential Comedy of Conrad's Youth." *Renascence*, XVI (1963), 22–28.

———. "Ritual and Violence in Flannery O'Connor." *Thought*, XLI (1966), 545–60.

Smith, Ronald Gregor. "Hamann and Kierkegaard," in *Kierkegaardiana*, V. Copenhagen: Munksgaard (1964), 52–67.

———. "Hamman Renaissance; Excerpt from Introduction to J. G. Hamann." *Christian Century*, LXXVII (1960), 768–69.

Sokel, W. H. "Kleist's Marquise of O, Kierkegaard's Abraham, and Musil's Tonko: Three Stages of the Absurd or the Touchstone of Faith." *Wisconsin Studies in Contemporary Literature*, VIII (1967), 505–16.

Sontag, Frederick. "Kierkegaard and the Search for a Self." *Journal of Existentialism*, VII (1967), 443–57.

"Søren Kierkegaard." *The American Book Collector,* XIII (1963), 6–8.

"Søren Kierkegaard: The Attack upon Christendom." *Together* (1967), 58.

"Søren Kierkegaard: Danish Moralist and Author." *Review of Reviews,* IX 1894), 236.

"Søren Kierkegaard: Prophet with Honor." *Christian Century,* LXXX (1963), 943.

Spiegelberg, Herbert. "Husserl's Phenomenology and Existentialism." *Journal of Philosophy,* LVII (1960), 62–74.

Spinka, Matthew. "Søren Kierkegaard and the Existential Theology," in his book, *Christian Thought: From Erasmus to Berdyaev.* Englewood Cliffs, N. J.: Prentice-Hall (1962), 146–55.

Sponheim, Paul. "Christian Coherence and Human Wholeness," in Bernard E. Meland, ed., *The Future of Empirical Theology.* Chicago: The University of Chicago Press (1969), 195–220.

——. "Kierkegaard and the Suffering of the Christian Man." *Dialog,* III (1964), 199–206.

Stack, George, J. "Aristotle and Kierkegaard's Concept of Choice." *The Modern Schoolman,* XLVI (1968–69), 11–23.

——. "Aristotle and Kierkegaard's Existential Ethics." *Journal of the History of Philosophy,* (1974), 1–19.

——. "The Basis of Kierkegaard's Concept of Existential Possibility." *New Scholasticism,* (1972), 139–72.

——. "Concern in Kierkegaard and Heidegger." *Philosophy Today,* XII (1969), 26–35.

——. "Kierkegaard and the Logical Possibility of God." *Sophia,* (1968), 14–19.

——. "Kierkegaard and the Phenomenology of Repetition." *Journal of Existentialism,* VII (1966–67), 111–28.

——. "Kierkegaard and Romantic Aestheticism." *Philosophy Today,* (1970), 57–74.

——. "Kierkegaard: the Self and Ethical Existence." *Ethics,* (1973), 108–125.

——. "Kierkegaard's Analysis of Choice: the Aristotelian Model." *The Personalist,* (1971), 643–61.

——. "Kierkegaard's Ironic Stage of Existence." *Laval Théologique et Philosphique,* XXV (1969), 193–207.

——. "The Meaning of 'Subjectivity is Truth.' " *Midwestern Journal of Philosophy* (1975), 26–40.

Stanley, Rupert, "Søren Kierkegaard." *New-Church Magazine* (1947), 23–27.

Starkloff, C. "The Election: Choice of Faith." *Review for Religious,* XXIC (1965), 444–54.

Steer, D. "Kierkegaard in English." *Journal of Religion,* 24 (1944), 271–78.

Steinberg, Milton. "Kierkegaard and Judaism." *Menorah Journal,* XXXVII (1949), 163–80.

Strickland, Ben. "Kierkegaard and Counseling for Individuality." *Personnel and Guidance Journal,* XLIV (1966), 470–74.

Sulzbach, Marian Fuerth. "Time, Eschatology, and the Human Problem." *Theology Today,* VII (1950), 321–30.

Swenson, David F. "Søren Kierkegaard." *Scandinavian Studies and Notes,* VI (1920–21), 1–41.

Tavard, George H. "Christianity and the Philosophy of Existence." *Theological Studies,* XVIII (1957), 1–16.

"That Blessed Word, Existential." *Christian Century,* LXXII (1955), 1390–92.

Thielicke, H. "Nihilism and Anxiety," *Theology Today,* XII (1955), 342–45.

Thomas, J. H. "The Relevance of Kierkegaard to the Demythologizing Controversy." *Scottish Journal of Theology,* X (1957), 329–52.

Thompson, Josiah. "The Master of Irony," in Josiah Thompson, ed., *Kierkegaard: A Collection of Critical Essays.* Garden City, New York: Doubleday & Company, Inc., 1972), 105–67.

———. "Søren Kierkegaard and his Sister-in-Law Henriette Kierkegaard." *Fund og Forskning,* XII (1965), 101–20.

Thomte, Reidar. "Kierkegaard in American Religious Thought." *Lutheran World,* II (1955), 137–46.

———. "New Reflections on the Great Dane." *Discourse,* VI (1963), 144–55.

Tillich, P. "Kierkegaard in English." *American Scandinavian Review,* 30 (1942), 254–57.

Tracy, David. "Kierkegaard's Concept of the Act of Faith: Its Structure and Significance." *Dunwoodie Review,* (1963), 194–215.

———. "Kierkegaard's Concept of the Act of Faith: Its Structure and Significance."*Dunwoodie Review,* IV (1964), 133–76.

Updike, John. "The Fork." *The New Yorker* (1966), 115–34.

Wadia, A. R. "Søren Kierkegaard." Aryan Path, XXXV (1964), 446–50.

Wahl, Jean. "Hegel et Kierkegaard." *Revue Philosophique,* 112 (1931), 321–80.

———. "Existentialism: A Preface." *New Republic, CXIII* (1945), 442–44.

Walker, Jeremy. "The Idea of Reward in Morality," in *Kierke-gaardiana,* VIII. Copenhagen: Munksgaard (1971), 30–52.

———. "Kierkegaard's Concept of Truthfulness." *Inquiry,* XII (1969), 209–24.

Webber, R. H. "Kierkegaard and the Elaboration of Unamuno's Niebla." *Hispanic Review,* XXXII (1954), 118–34.

Weiss, P. "Existenz and Hegel." *Philosophy and Phenomenological Research,* VIII (1947), 206–16.

Weiss, Robert O. "The Levelling Process as a Function of the Masses in the View of Kierkegaard and Ortega y Gasset." *Kentucky Foreign Language Quarterly,* VII, 27–36.

Whittemore, Robert C. "Pro Hegel, Contra Kierkegaard." *Journal of Religious Thought,* XIII (1956), 131–44.

Widenman, Robert, "Kierkegaard's Terminology and English," in *Kierkegaardiana,* VII. Copenhagen: Munksgaard (1966), 113–30.

———. "Some Aspects of Time in Aristotle and Kierkegaard," in *Kierke-gaardiana,* VIII. Copenhagen: Munksgaard (1971), 7–22.

Wiegend, William. "Salinger and Kierkegaard," *Minnesota Review,* V (1965), 137–56.

Wilburn, Ralph G. "The Philosophy of Existence and the Faith-Relation." *Religion in Life,* XXX (1961), 497–517.

Wild, John. "Existentialism: A New View of Man." *University of Toronto Quarterly,* XXVII (1956), 79–95.

———. "Kierkegaard and Classical Philosophy." *Philosophical Review,* 49, 536–51.

———. "Kierkegaard and Contemporary Existentialist Philosophy." *Anglican Theological Review,* XXXVIII (1956), 15–32.

Will, Frederic. "A Confrontation of Kierkegaard and Keats." *Personalist,* XLIII (1962), 338–51 .

Wilshire, Bruce W. "Kierkegaard's Theory of Knowledge and New Directions in Psychology and Psychoanalysis." *Review of Existential Psychology and Psychiatry,* III (1963), 249–61.

Wolf, H. C. "Kierkegaard and the Quest of the Historical Jesus," *Lutheran Quarterly,* XVI (1964), 249–61.

Woodbridge, Hensley Charles. "A Bibliography of Dissertations Concerning Kierkegaard Written in the U. S., Canada, and Great Britain." *American Book Collector,* XII (1961), 21–22.

———. "Søren Kierkegaard: A Bibliography of His Words in English Translation." *American Book Collector*, XII (1961), 17–20.

Wrighton, B. "Thoughts on Kierkegaard." *Arena*, I (1933), 317.

Yanitelli, Victor, "Types of Existentialism." *Thought*, XXIV (1954), 495–508.

Zeigler, Leslie. "Personal Existence: A Study of Buber and Kierkegaard." *Journal of Religion*, XL (1960), 80–94.

Zuurdeeg, Willem F. "Some Aspects of Kierkegaard's Language Philosophy." *Atti XII Congr. Inter. Filos.*, 493–99.

Zweig, P. "Genius for Unsavoriness." *The Nation* (1968), 283–84.

Index